International Legal Aspects of Aerial Terrorism

Ius, Lex et Res Publica
Studies in Law, Philosophy and Political Cultures

Edited by Barbara Janusz-Pohl and Anna Jaroń

Volume 22

PETER LANG

Mateusz Osiecki

International Legal Aspects of Aerial Terrorism

Methods of Law Enforcement in Aviation

PETER LANG

Bibliographic Information published by the Deutsche Nationalbibliothek
The Deutsche Nationalbibliothek lists this publication
in the Deutsche Nationalbibliografie; detailed bibliographic
data is available online at http://dnb.d-nb.de.

Library of Congress Cataloging-in-Publication Data
A CIP catalog record for this book has been applied for at the
Library of Congress.

This publication was financially supported by the Lazarski University based in Warsaw.

Cover illustration: Courtesy of Benjamin Ben Chaim.

ISSN 2191-3250
ISBN 978-3-631-87539-1 (Print)
E-ISBN 978-3-631-88697-7 (E-Book)
E-ISBN 978-3-631-88711-0 (EPUB)
DOI 10.3726/b20056

Peter Lang – Berlin · Bern · Bruxelles · New York ·
Oxford · Warszawa · Wien

www.peterlang.com

Acknowledgement

I dedicate this book to all those who offered me their valuable assistance and accompanied me in the effort of drafting it. Firstly, I would like to express my deepest gratitude towards the members of Department of International Law and International Relations of the University of Łódź, in particular, prof. Joanna Połatyńska for her infinite patience in reading all drafts of this book and her professional advice on its content. Furthermore, I would like to thank a true legend of the Department, prof. Piotr Daranowski, who has accepted me as a member of the Department and has always given his blessing to all my research ideas. Also, I would like to appreciate all members of the Department who were kind enough to assist me in making this piece of writing a highly professional one. Moreover, I express my gratitude towards the members of Jean Monnet Chair of European Constitutional Law, especially dr Izabela Skomerska, who can be considered a true mother of my academic achievements. I would not have obtained a single grant or attended a conference, but for her invaluable help. Additionally, I would like to thank the reviewers of my dissertation – prof. Karolina Wierczyńska and prof. Anna Konert – the Dean of Faculty of Law and Administration at Lazarski University in Warsaw, who is my lifetime academic mentor.

I sincerely thank the true co-authors of my educational successes – my dear parents, Agata and Wojciech Osieccy, who have never ceased to believe in me and were first to encourage me to make bold decisions. Additionally, a person who deserves my great thanks is my grandma Jadwiga Marczyk, who has always had confidence in my academic achievement that she has always took as read the fact that I had passed an exam or received a grant. I also address very special thanks to my beloved partner Maria Przymusiała, who has consistently supported me in my scholarly career with her warm heart and inspiring words, even in moments of crisis.

Words of gratitude are also directed to my close friends, on whom I could have invariable counted and who served me with motivating words: Aleksandra Bogusz, Małgorzata Piera, Kordian Kręcisz, Maciej Soroczyński and Michał Borten.

Finally, I would like to pay tribute to my late grandparents – Marian Ryszard Marczyk and Krystyna & Jerzy Osieccy who, which I strongly believe, would be very proud to see me finishing this book.

Mateusz Osiecki
Łódź, October 2019

With guns you can kill terrorists, with education you can kill terrorism.

Malala Yousafzai

Table of contents

Introductory note

Terrorism is a phenomenon considered by many experts in international relations, political science and law, as well as by numerous regular citizens, as one of the most daunting challenges that humanity needs to face in the twenty-first century. States of the world, as well as international organisations have engaged such a great deal of resources to fight against terrorists, that the current situation in this matter can now be even considered a "global war on terror". Thousands of people killed, dozens of cities across the world attacked and countless attempts to spread panic among the public have made the global superpowers aware of the terrorists' real capabilities. Although terrorism itself is a problem that has been a nuisance to the mankind since centuries, the world turned attention to it and commenced to treat it seriously just a few decades ago.

Today, global terrorist networks try to target many sectors of economic and political life, but one particular is especially vulnerable to attacks, namely civil aviation. Grim events from 11 September 2001 marked an opening of a new chapter in history – a chapter in which the international community got to understand that traditional forms of fight against aerial terrorism do not suffice and more ambitious solutions need to be implemented, also on the legal level, to win this "global war on terror".

But one may inquire if this "global war", at least in relation to civil aviation, is conducted in a satisfactory way. The safety of airlines' passengers or generally people travelling by air is strongly dependent on decisions of governments and international organisations that work on improving aviation security. However, there is no single reason for protecting civil aircraft and airports from terrorist attacks. Civil aviation itself is currently a fundamental component of the world economy and even international relations. Air transport connects people inhabiting different corners of the world and brings them together, therefore allowing to maintain a peaceful and friendly coexistence of nations. It also plays a crucial role in establishing and sustaining business contacts and exchange of employees between companies across continents. Thus, its role as a basis for global economic and social development should not be underestimated. Terrorism has a potential to crush that order – some of the most spectacular attacks carried out against civil aviation did paralyse or slow down the growth in the discussed sector of transport. If improper actions from the side of the international community are taken, in a long-term perspective civil aviation might be under serious threat.

Taking into account all the above-mentioned factors, there is a need to conduct research thereon.

Although the title of the monograph suggests that its scope might be immense; in fact, the author concentrates on answering the question related to what was said in the previous paragraph, that is: whether juridical solutions undertaken by states of the world that swore to protect their citizens from internal and external hazards (such as international terrorism) are adequate to effectively counter the problem of aerial terrorism. In other words, the question is whether the international community has undertaken appropriate measures to protect civil aviation from terrorism.

In order to answer these questions, it is necessary to thoroughly analyse the legal aspects of aerial terrorism, mostly concerning international public law. Thus, such an analysis is provided on the subsequent pages of the following monograph. The criteria for providing a clear answer shall be formulated on the basis of the undermentioned research theses: states (or the international community in general) react accurately to the threats posed by aerial terrorism; state actors work prospectively in their fight against air terrorists; actions of a juridical nature are uniform to the most possible extent on the international level; legal mechanisms provided by states who are in combat against terrorism are meaningful in practice.

In order to pin down terrorism as a concept, a brief history of the phenomenon is presented in the first chapter which discusses its early roots traced to Antiquity. Subsequently, a complex study on defining terrorism, with an emphasis of its crucial elements, is carried out. Some primary aspects of the fight against terrorism are also examined, including the evolution of the approach to use force in case of a terrorist attack, and the role of state terrorism. In the first chapter, various kinds of terrorist attacks that might be carried out against civil aviation are presented in detail, including types of offences that were unknown to the international community several years ago, but have become a real threat recently. The final pages of the first chapter are dedicated to an emerging issue in aviation security, namely the role of unmanned aircraft in aerial terrorism. The studies which touch upon these issues contribute to topicality of research provided by the present author. In terms of the methodology used in the chapter, formal-dogmatic method is the dominant one. The historical method plays a supplementary role, especially for the opening part of the chapter.

The second chapter of the monograph constitutes the core part of this book and is oriented at a detailed examination of legal instruments related to combat against aerial terrorism originating in three international organisations: International Civil Aviation Organisation, United Nations and European Union. It goes without saying that there are several other organisations which give the fight against terrorism a high priority (e.g. NATO, Arab League, etc.). However, the three enumerated institutions have had the greatest influence on developing a pragmatic approach to terrorism in civil aviation and, therefore, their actions deserve a closer scrutiny. The analysis provided in the second chapter has a critical character – comments are given on both positive and negative aspects of legislative acts adopted by the above-mentioned organisations in order to suggest what improvements can be introduced to the already existing measures and expose what flaws still exist in the system. As methodology used in research for the purposes of that chapter entailed mostly analyses of legal acts, a formal-dogmatic method along with the comparative method had a key role.

The final chapter is devoted to a case study which investigates in detail four selected attacks on civil aviation from the recent past. The selection of these events is by no means incidental – each of them features a particular issue related to fight against international aerial terrorism and their analysis shall help to understand how the mechanisms of eliminating terrorism function in practice. Each case study is divided into several sections, the opening one always describes the facts known about the event and outlines the course of investigation, while the subsequent sections focus on the terrorist factor and crucial legal aspects. A more practical nature of the chapter required usage of empirical method.

The closing part summarises the results of research and formulates the answer to key questions mentioned above.

The monograph itself constitutes an important voice in the discussion on the current legal measures adopted worldwide in response to terrorist attacks that have been haunting civil aircraft and their passengers. Although publications dedicated to this area of research have been widely released, very few of them focus on assessing how the mechanisms of protecting civil aviation function in the present times of rapid development of new technologies, research on unmanned aircraft systems, or cutting-edge solutions concerning cybersecurity. The relevance of the topic together with the fact that terrorism as a domain constantly evolves and research conducted thereon is still absolutely essential were a core motive for taking up this subject matter and writing this book

As in the area of aviation law there is indeed a very strong alliance between academic researchers and representatives of political and governmental institutions, the author hopes the present work could contribute to the continuous improvement of legal measures adopted for the safety of citizens and air passengers.

Glossary of abbreviations

AAIU	Air Accident Investigation Unit
AQI	Al-Qaeda in Iraq
API	advance passenger information
APU	auxiliary power unit
ATC	air traffic control
BCN	biological, chemical or nuclear (weapons)
BEA	The Bureau of Enquiry and Analysis for Civil Aviation Safety (French: *Bureau d'Enquêtes et d'Analyses pour la Sécurité de l'Aviation Civile*)
BFU	Federal Bureau of Aircraft Accident Investigation (German: *Bundesstelle für Flugunfalluntersuchung)*
CAF	Cuban Air Force
CFSP	Common Foreign and Security Policy of the European Union
CIS	Commonwealth of Independent States
CJEU	Court of Justice of the European Union
CTC	United Nations Security Council Counter-Terrorism Committee
DPR	Donetsk People's Republic
ECHR	European Convention of Human Rights
ECOSOC	Economic and Social Council of the United Nations
ECtHR	European Court of Human Rights
EOKA	National Organisation of Cypriot Fighters (Greek: *Εθνική Οργάνωσις Κυπρίων Αγωνιστών*; *Ethniki Organosis Kyprion Agoniston*)
ETA	Land and Freedom Organisation (Basque: *Euskadi te Askatasuna*)
EU	European Union
FARC	Revolutionary Armed Forces of Colombia (Spanish: *Fuerzas Armadas Revolucionarias de Colombia*)
FBI	Federal Bureau of Investigation
GO	governmental organisation (or international organisation)
GIA	Armed Islamic Group (French: *Groupe Islamique Armé*)
GIGN	National Gendarmerie Intervention Group (French: *Groupe d'Intervention de la Gendarmerie Nationale*)
IAEA	International Atomic Energy Agency
ICAO	International Civil Aviation Organisation
ICCPR	International Covenant on Civil and Political Rights

ICJ	International Court of Justice
IED	improvised explosive device
IFSO	in-flight security officer
ILC	International Law Commission
ILS	Instrumental Landing System
IHL	International Humanitarian Law
IRA	Irish Republican Army
ISI	Islamic State of Iraq
ISIS	Islamic State of Iraq and Al-Sham
JIT	Joint Investigation Team (crash of Malaysia Airlines 17)
MAK	Interstate Aviation Committee (Russian: *Межгосударственный авиационный комитет)*
LAGs	liquids, aerosols and gels
LPR	Luhansk People's Republic
NATO	North Atlantic Treaty Organisation
NSS	National Security Strategy (United States, 2002)
OVV	Dutch Safety Board (Dutch: *Onderzoeksraad Voor Veiligheid*)
PFLP	Popular Front for the Liberation of Palestine
PICAO	Provisional International Civil Aviation Organisation
PNR	passenger name record
PIU	passenger information unit
SAARC	South Asian Association for Regional Cooperation
TEU	Treaty on the European Union
TFEU	Treaty on the Functioning of the European Union
UAV	unmanned aerial vehicle
UN	United Nations
UNCLOS	United Nations Convention on the Law of the Seas
UNGA	United Nations General Assembly
UNOCT	United Nations Office of Counter-Terrorism
UNODC	United Nations Office on Drugs and Crime
UNSC	United Nations Security Council
USCFR	Code of Federal Regulations (United States)
WTC	World Trade Center

Chapter 1. Terrorism as a legal phenomenon

1.1. Evolution of terrorist movements

1.1.1. The dawn of terrorism

Providing precise time frames of the beginnings of terrorism is complicated, mostly because of the fact that the term "terrorism" itself has been evolving through ages and its meaning is different today than some decades ago. However, nearly all movements that were classified by experts in the field under the notion of terrorism had a common goal residing in spreading fear within society by the use of violence usually against civilians.

Many authors agree in their publications that the term "terrorism" can be used when describing practices tracing back to as long time ago as Antiquity. One of the groups whose methods were based on terror was Zealots – a Jewish guerrilla formation of a religious character that was combatting against Roman occupiers of Palestinian lands in 66-70 A.D. Their principal political activity was murdering Roman citizens and those members of Jewish community that were collaborating with governing authorities.[1]

Another group that is often associated with terrorist activities were assassins (*Heyssessini*), a Muslim sect formed by Hasn-i Sabbah in the eleventh century to counter the Seljuq Turks regime imposed upon the Islamic people in the conquered lands. The Order of Assassins' members were usually terrorising the unconverted population and performing numerous killings, mainly among crusaders and political figures.[2] Their last activities were recorded at the end of the thirteenth century.[3]

---

1 A. Oehmichen, Terrorism and Anti-Terror Legislation: The Terrorised Legislator?A Comparison of Counter-Terror Legislation and Its Implications on Human Rights in the Legal Systems of the United Kingdom, Spain, Germany and France (Intersentia: Antwerp-Oxford-Portland, 2009), p. 51.

2 A. Oechmichen, Terrorism and Anti-Terror Legislation, p. 52.

3 From the name of the order - "Assassins" genetically comes the word "assassination" and its equivalents in many European languages. See T. Aleksandrowicz, Terroryzm międzynarodowy (Wydawnictwa Akademickie i Profesjonalne: Warsaw, 2008), p. 15.

1.1.2. Terrorism throughout centuries

The word "terrorism" itself was used in the political context for the first time in the late eighteenth century, when *Regime de la Terreur* (fr. Reign of Terror) was established in France as a result of the Revolution that transformed the country from the monarchy into the republic.[4] Under the leadership of Maximilian de Robespierre, the Jacobin Club aimed to eliminate all forms of disobedience to the Republic and any attempts to restore *ancient regime* and introduced a brutal system of repression.[5] Under the Reign of Terror, around 20,000 people were beheaded with a guillotine.[6] The events taking place in France are widely believed to have been the first case in history when state authorities used organised terrorism to achieve their political goals.[7]

The second half of the nineteenth century and the beginning of the twentieth century were marked by the rebirth of terrorism, thus many authors label that period as "The Golden Age of Terrorism"[8], when many anarchist movements were on rise.[9] One of the most notable of them was the organisation called *Народная Воля* (*Narodnaya Volya*, en. "Will of the People"), which operated in the nineteenth century in Czarist Russia. The group was concerned with the growing poverty and, as a result of the aggravating situation of the proletariat, conducted several attacks on political figures, eventually assassinating Tsar Alexander II.[10]

---

4 C. Townshend, Terroryzm (Wydawnictwo Uniwersytetu Łódzkiego: Lodz, 2017), p. 60.

5 M. Sczaniecki, Powszechna historia państwa i prawa (LexisNexis: Warsaw, 2009), p. 333.

6 T. R. Mockaitis, The "New" Terrorism: Myths and Reality (Stanford Security Studies: Stanford, 2008), p. 20.

7 T. Aleksandrowicz, Terroryzm międzynarodowy (Wydawnictwa Akademickie i Profesjonalne: Warsaw, 2008) p. 15.

8 A. Oehmichen, Terrorism and Anti-Terror Legislation, p. 58.

9 E. McWhinney, Aerial Piracy and International Terrorism (Martinus Nijhoff Publishers: Dordrecht 1987), p. 127. Most of those movements were founded on a Marxist philosophy concentrating on "class conflict" between those who possess capital and those who are oppressed by them. A state, or generally any kind of supreme legal authority, was viewed by socio-anarchists as a source of oppression and political leaders as people ignoring the idea of social justice. In that case, terrorism served as a tool that would change a society through revolution – by eliminating the state oppressing the proletariat and supporting class of Bourgeois, in order to build a completely new society. See T. R. Mockaitis, The "New" Terrorism, p. 21.

10 A. Oehmichen, Terrorism and Anti-Terror Legislation, pp. 60-61.

A similar situation, with anarchist movements targeting state leaders, occurred in different parts of the globe at that time. The Austro-Hungarian Empress Elizabeth was murdered in 1898 and two years later, the American president, William McKinley was shot by socialist activist Leon Czolgosz.[11] The wave of terrorism at the turn of the centuries reached a culmination on 28 June 1914 in Sarajevo where Gavrilo Princip assassinated the archduke Franz-Ferdinand, a legal successor to the Austro-Hungarian throne. This particular event is marked in the history as the direct trigger for World War I.[12]

The post-war era totally changed the political mindset of the most powerful States. The former colonial empires initiated the process of decolonisation, allowing the peoples of dependent overseas territories to determine their political status by themselves. However, the global anti-colonial tendencies fuelled movements of a nationalist nature. In contrast to revolutionist groups, nationalists were struggling to obtain independence and form a proper sovereign state which could eventually be self-governed.

It would pose a genuine challenge to enumerate all nationalist groups of a terrorist nature active in the twentieth century. Some of the most notorious included the Irish Republican Army (or "IRA"; a paramilitary terrorist group having fought for the reunification of Ireland and its transformation into a republic)[13], Basque Homeland and Liberty (or "ETA"; oriented at gaining independence of the Basque region in the northern Spain, at that time under the regime of general Francisco Franco)[14], and National Organisation of Cypriot Fighters (or "EOKA"; an armed group which aimed at establishing an independent State of Cyprus).[15]

---

11 T. R. Mockaitis, The "New" Terrorism, p. 22.

12 T. R. Mockaitis, The "New" Terrorism, p. 22. Many authors point out that this „anarchist terrorism" eventually did not contribute to a global revolution, as in states of oppressive regimes, being their primary targets, public opinion did not serve any important role in the society and therefore their efforts would have just remained unnoticed. See more: C. Townshend, Terroryzm, p. 83.

13 The IRA: 1919 to 1968. http://alphahistory.com/northernireland/ira-1919-1968/ (9 March 2021).

14 W. Anderson, The ETA. Spain Basque's Terrorists (The Rosen Publishing: New York, 2003), p. 4.

15 D. French, Fighting EOKA: The British Counter-Insurgency Campaign on Cyprus, 1955-1959 (Oxford University Press: Oxford, 2015), p. 194.

1.1.3. Fundamentalism: The fiercest face of terrorism

The historical analysis on the evolution of terrorism provided above depicts that, with time, the principal terrorist underpinnings have been changing. The scope of their activities has varied from relatively small religious groups combatting an unwanted regime, through anarchist movements of socialist tendencies to ultra-nationalist brutal forces. Then again, in the second half of the twentieth century, a new threat emerged, namely fundamentalist terrorism, which is associated with particular groups including Al-Qaeda and ISIS, characterised by brutality and vileness.

a) Al-Qaeda

Al-Qaeda (meaning "base" or "foundation" in Arabic) is an infamous terrorist organisation notorious for the attack on the World Trade Centre on 11 September 2001. A key person deemed to be the leader of the group was Osama bin Laden.

Bin Laden was born in 1957 in Saudi Arabia as the 17th son of a rich Yemeni construction entrepreneur. He underwent self-radicalisation during his university education when he was studying management at King Abdulaziz University in Jeddah, where he met Abdullah Azzam, who shared with bin Laden the idea of devoting his life to Islam. Highly influenced by Azzam's teachings, bin Laden moved to Afghanistan in the 1980s in order to fight against the Soviet Union's forces that had invaded the country.[16]

Although the military operations in Afghanistan were about to come to an end in 1988, the idea of extensive combat against the enemies of *umma* (the entire Islamic community) was developing among the followers of Abdullah Azzam. They agreed upon the necessity of continuing jihad ("sacred war against enemies to protect *umma*") even after the retreat of the Soviet forces from Afghanistan.

Al-Qaeda was officially established on 18 August 1988 by Osama bin Laden and many other radical Islam activists.[17] The founding document of the organisation consisted of several provisions on its key objectives (continuation of jihad in other regions, mainly Southeast Asia) and, above all, recruitment of new soldiers who would join global jihad and fight against infidels. The novices were

16 M. Zimny, Terroryzm samobójczy (Difin: Warsaw, 2017), pp. 23-24.

17 Some authors claim that the real foundation of Al-Qaeda is dated 17 May, 1988. See L. Wright, Wyniosłe wieże. Al-Kaida i atak na Amerykę (Wydawnictwo Czarne: Wołowiec 2018), p. 179-180.

supposed to meet a number of conditions upon their recruitment. First and foremost, they had to be able to serve long-term, be obedient to the supreme leader and show personal culture. Moreover, a recommendation from a trusted person and strict observance of the organisation's rules were needed.[18]

Al-Qaeda was growing in power systematically and bin Laden himself, in order to gain larger interest in jihad's case, returned to his homeland. But due to his negative attitude toward Saudi Royal Family, he was soon expelled and deprived of Saudi citizenship. After a longer stay in Sudan, bin Laden finally moved to Afghanistan in 1996. At that time, the mission of Al-Qaeda crystallised as a fight against the United States, Israel and the western world in general as well as all Arab States supporting them.[19]

Currently, Al-Qaeda is a global terrorist network having its local divisions in many countries (notable cells are located, among others, in Somalia, Iraq, and Northern Africa).[20] Due to intensive soldiers' training, large external financing (by states, private companies and private benefactors) and access to advanced weapons, the organisation was capable of performing many deadly terrorist actions. Among their acts of terror the most notable were the following ones (from a list prepared by A. Wejkszner): on 7 August 1998, a bombing attack occurred in Nairobi, Kenya and Dar-es-Salaam, Tanzania in which 224 people were killed and about 4000 wounded; on 11 September 2001, two jets flew into World Trade Center twin towers in New York, USA, resulting in nearly 3000 casualties and 6000 wounded; on 23 July 2005, a suicide attack in Sharm-el-Sheikh, Egypt resulted in the deaths of 88 people; on 7 January 2015, a shooting in Paris, France erupted, causing 12 people to die and a further 12 to become wounded.[21]

Although Osama bin Laden was killed in the operation "Neptune's Spear" performed by the American armed forces in 2011 and Al-Qaeda was significantly weakened, the organisation continues its violent policy of jihad and is being pursued by many states.

---

18 A. Wejkszner, Globalna sieć Al-Kaidy. Nowe Państwo Islamskie? (Difin: Warsaw, 2017), p. 28.

19 See more: M. Zimny, Terroryzm samobójczy, p. 29.

20 See more: K. Rękawek, D. Cristiani, "Al Qaeda at 25: No Point in Fighting Them Since They Themselves are Fighting Each Other?", The Polish Institute of International Affairs Policy Paper, Vol. 26 (74) 2013.

21 A. Wejkszner, Globalna sieć Al-Kaidy, pp. 265-266.
The author described in detail some most notable terrorist attacks organised by Al-Qaeda. See A. Wejkszner, Globalna sieć Al-Kaidy, pp. 265-295.

b) ISIS

The twenty-first century saw the rise of a new terrorist group that, in a relatively short time, gained immense power and the ability to control vast territories. This organisation is known as ISIS, which is an acronym for Islamic State of Iraq and al-Sham.

The origins of this group relate to Abu Musab Al-Zarqawi, a Jordanian nationalist who in the 1980s had attempted to overthrow the government of his homeland, but eventually failed. In 1989, he moved to Afghanistan to counter the Soviet forces invading the country. Having arrived after the hostilities ceased, Al-Zarqawi quickly returned to Jordan aiming to repeat his attempt of coup, but to no avail.[22]

After that, Al-Zarqawi moved to Iraq where he commenced his radical proceedings as an aftermath of the US-led invasion on the Iraqi. He established an organisation named *al Tawhid wa al Jihad* ("Monotheism and Jihad") that mounted several terrorist attacks on the key locations of the territory of occupied Iraq.[23] In 2004, he joined a local Al-Qaeda division called "Al-Qaeda in Iraq" (or "AQI")[24] and pledged his allegiance to Osama bin Laden. The partnership was a perfect settlement for both parties as Al-Zarqawi gained a source of funding and a possibility to recruit soldiers to fight against the US troops and bin Laden, in return, secured an opportunity to expand his influence in Iraq.[25],

Al-Zarqawi's campaign did not last too long as he was killed by American troops in 2006 during an air strike.[26] The leadership was then taken over by

---

22 A. S. Hashim, "The Islamic State: from Al-Qaeda affiliate to caliphate", Middle East Policy Council
Journal, Winter 2014, Vol. XXI (4), p. 1. (9 March 2021) http://www.mepc.org/islamic-state-al-qaeda-affiliate-caliphate.

23 R. Barrett, The Islamic State (The Soufan Group: New York, 2014), p. 11.
The author enumerates here three major attacks: on Jordanian Embassy in Baghdad, the United Nations headquarters in Baghdad and the Imam Ali Mosque in Najaf.

24 Known also under a longer name of Tanzim Al Qaeda fi Bilad al-Rafidayn ("Al Qaeda Organization in the Country of the Two Rivers").

25 Further examined by: M. Osiecki, "ISIS vs. the World – the Combat from the Perspective of International Law", in: Світ очима молодих. Orbis terrarum oculis iuvenibus (Прикарпатський національний університет імені Василя Стефаника: Ivano-Frankivsk, 2016), p. 107.

26 R. Rabil, "The ISIS chronicles: A History", The National Interest, 17 July 2014. (9 March 2021)
http://nationalinterest.org/feature/the-isis-chronicles-history-10895.

Abu Hamza al-Muhajir, and "The Islamic State of Iraq" (or "ISI") was formed by merging AQI with some other groups that shared similar beliefs. Abu Omar al-Baghdadi became the head of this organisation.[27] Not a long time later both al-Muhajir and al-Baghadadi were killed in 2010 and the leadership was transferred to Abu Bakr al-Baghdadi.[28]

ISI was constantly growing in power and in 2014 became fully self-sustainable and ultimately lost the support of Al-Qaeda, which resulted in ISI's separation and transformation into an independent terrorist group. Before its detachment, it took the name of "Islamic State of Iraq and al-Sham" (or "ISIS").[29] Its strong position and substantial support from rebel forces opposing the regime of Syrian president Bashar al-Assad allowed ISIS to quickly gain large parts of Syrian territory and some parts of western Iraqi territory were captured as well. On 29 June 2014, Abu Bakr officially declared the restoration of Caliphate on the conquered lands with a capital in Mosul, Iraq and pronounced himself a new Caliph Ibrahim.[30]

Currently, under Abu Bakr's leadership, ISIS functions as a group of vile fanatics. This terrorist organisation, due to an effective exercise of control over the conquered territories, executes many competences of a state, including collection of taxes, issuance of legal judgements or enforcement of *Shar'ia* law.[31] However, it does not resemble a state in the western world's understanding of this

---

27 R. Barrett, The Islamic State, pp. 11-12.

28 R. Rabil, "The ISIS chronicles".

29 Al-Sham is the Levant in Arabic language – a land comprising of a territory expanding from southern Turkey southwards to Israel and the Gaza strip on the eastern coast of the Mediterranean Sea. Hence "ISIS" is sometimes referred to as "ISIL" (where "L" stands for "the Levant"). It is worth noting that according to some experts, decoding the abbreviation "ISIS" into "Islamic State of Iraq and Syria" is wrong, as al-Sham/the Levant today consists of lands of the entire Syria, a southern part of Turkey, Jordan, Israel, the Palestinian territories, Lebanon and just a fragment of northern and western Iraq. Therefore, the Islamic State of Iraq and Levant would, in total, encompass both the entirety of al-Sham and the rest of Iraq (not normally covered by al-Sham). See J. E. Dyer, "Newly declared caliphate: Why it's 'ISIS' (not ISIL) – 'Iraq and al-Sham' (not Syria)", Liberty Unyielding, 30 June 2014. (9 March 2021) https://libertyunyielding.com/2014/06/30/newly-declared-caliphate-isis-isil-iraq-al-sham-syria/

30 R. Barrett, The Islamic State, p. 13.

31 ISIS managed to build structures of authority functioning similarly to a normal state organ. See more:
J. Neriah, "The Structure of the Islamic State (ISIS)", Jerusalem Center for Public Affairs, 8 September 2014. (9 March 2021) http://jcpa.org/structure-of-the-islamic-state/.

term as the form of rule is nothing but an oppressive regime. The civilians inhabiting the ISIS' territories are usually executed in an extremely inhuman way, for instance by beheading, or crucifixion and frequently have their limbs chopped off. It is a common practice to forcefully separate parents from their children who are often raped or sold to human traffickers.[32]

The risk to global peace and security posed by ISIS has resulted in the formation of the Global Coalition against Daesh ("Daesh" is another name for "ISIS") in September 2014, which consists of several dozen states and international organisations under the leadership of the United States. Its main objective is to jointly counter ISIS on all fronts, prevent the trafficking of weapons, launch rescue missions, etc.[33]

Needless to say, recently many more terrorist organisations that actively fight against governments and the international community as a whole have been formed. It is beyond the scope of this publication to enumerate and describe all of them, even though the monograph is dedicated entirely to the topic of international terrorism. In next the chapters, however, much attention will still be devoted to these groups in the course of analysis of particular cases of terrorist activity.

1.2. "Terrorism:" Definition and scope of the term

1.2.1. Difficulties in defining

Defining terrorism itself is a truly daunting task. The existence of numerous, various definitions provided by experts of multiple disciplines including law, sociology and political science in caused by a growing interest in this phenomenon among the society. Discord between states in relation to catalogue of acts that can be recognised as terrorist only amplifies the problem.[34]

Another difficulty resides in the fact that understanding of terrorism evolves with time and is dependent on current global political conditions (growing power of a particular terrorist group might cause states to relativise terrorism

32 J. D. van der Vyver, "The ISIS Crisis and the Development of International Humanitarian Law", Emory International Law Review. 2016, Vol. 30 (4), p. 535

33 The mission, goals and structure of Global Coalition are described on the website: http://theglobalcoalition.org/en/home/.

34 M. Lech, Ochrona prawna społeczności międzynarodowej wobec zagrożenia terroryzmem (Wydawnictwo Uniwersytetu Gdanskiego: Gdansk, 2014), p. 41.

only to their methods).[35] If taking into account, for example, the period of the 1960s and 1970s, when attacks on civil aircraft were a frequent practice, we would observe that mainly the powerful and influential states engaged in the Cold War, whereas countries of the Third World were rather struggling to resolve their internal problems, for instance: famine or the spread of diseases.[36]

However, no one may accuse scholars, state officials or international organisations of being passive in the matter of explaining what terrorism means. Many recognised experts have formed their definitions of terrorism, vital for studying the subject that are inspiring for both States that adopt anti-terrorist laws and GOs whose actions focus on combatting terrorism. Considering such a vast array of definitions of terrorism, enumerating and analysing all of them is a most difficult task. Hence, from this point on, only the most relevant definitions will be discussed.

1.2.2. Cross-section of definitions

The word "terrorism" itself has Latin origins and is derived from the verb *terrere* ("cause to tremble").[37] Setting aside the etymology of the word, numerous attempts to accurately define the term have been made by international organisations, political institutions and representatives of legal doctrines. As for GOs, they usually describe how to understand terrorism in treaties drafted as part of their legislation. However, the approach to the term varies depending on the scope of the treaty and the character of the organisation. Most of the relevant multilateral agreements do not even define terrorism *expressis verbis*, but rather regulate the question of measures that should be taken to eradicate it in the most vulnerable areas of life, including civil aviation, nuclear energy, maritime navigation, hostage-taking, and so on. The United Nations Office of Counter-Terrorism (or "UNOCT") itself posted on its website a list of 19 treaties dealing with prevention of terrorist acts developed under the auspices of the United

---

35 During the times of Cold War for instance, treating someone as a terrorist was strongly linked to a place, where an act occurred. Soviet literature was focused on assigning the centre of terrorist activities to Washington, whereas American authors mostly called Kremlin as terrorists' headquarters. See more: T. Aleksandrowicz, Terroryzm międzynarodowy, p. 18.

36 McWhinney, Aerial Piracy, p. 112.

37 R. Abeyratne, "Beijing Convention of 2010 on the suppression of unlawful acts relating to international civil aviation—an interpretative study", Journal of Transportation Security, 4/2011, p. 133.

Nations or International Atomic Energy Agency (or "IAEA"). For example, the International Convention Against the Taking of Hostages, which took place in New York on 17 December 1979, in its provisions stipulates that "it is urgently necessary to develop international co-operation between states in devising and adopting effective measures for the prevention, prosecution and punishment of all acts of taking hostages as manifestations of international terrorism."[38] In turn, the International Convention for the Suppression of the Financing of Terrorism, hosted in New York on 9 December 1999, expresses that "the financing of terrorism is a matter of grave concern to the international community as a whole"[39]; moreover, it mentions "terrorism" several times in the preamble, without giving an actual definition.

On the other hand, some international organisations of a regional range have adopted agreements that often take quite a broad approach to terrorism. Namely, they do not provide exact definitions of terrorism, but instead feature a catalogue of acts that are recognised as terrorist. A clear example here is the SAARC Regional Convention on Suppression of Terrorism, held at Kathmandu on the 11 April 1987, stipulating in Article 1 that offences within the scope of particular international treaties shall be regarded as terroristic. Similarly, the Convention on the Prevention of Terrorism, which took place in Warsaw on 16 May 2005 led by the Council of Europe, introduced the guidelines for understanding the term "terrorist offense" in Article 1, which is described as "any of the offences within the scope of and as defined in one of the treaties listed in the Appendix [to the Convention]".[40] The said Appendix enumerates the same treaties as the ones itemised in the SAARC Convention and supplements the list by adding six more.[41]

However, some other regional agreements concluded between allied states feature more vague definitions. Two particular documents might be treated here as an example, namely the Treaty on Cooperation among the State Members of the Commonwealth of Independent States in Combating Terrorism, drafted in

38 International Convention Against the Taking of Hostages done in New York, 17 December 1979, United Nations Treaty Series, Vol. 1316, Reg. 21931, Preamble.

39 International Convention for the Suppression of the Financing of Terrorism, done in New York, 9 December 1999, United Nations Treaty Series, Vol. 2178, Reg. 38349, Preamble.

40 Council of Europe Convention on the Prevention of Terrorism done at Warsaw, 16 May 2005, art. 1, Council of Europe Treaty Series, No. 196.

41 Full list of the Conventions can be accessed on the website: https://rm.coe.int/CoERMPublicCommonSearchServices/DisplayDCTMContent?documentId=090000168008371b (9 March 2021).

Minsk on 4 June 1999 (hereafter referred to as the "CIS Terrorism Treaty") and the Arab Convention for the Suppression of Terrorism held in Cairo on the 22 April 1994 (hereafter referred to as the "Arab Convention").

The CIS Terrorism Treaty is among those legal instruments that provide a wide definition of terrorism in a glossary of terms in Article 1:

> [A]n illegal act punishable under criminal law committed for the purpose of undermining public safety, influencing decision-making by the authorities or terrorizing the population, and taking the form of:
> Violence or the threat of violence against [...] persons;
> Destroying (damaging) or threatening to destroy (damage) property [...] so as to endanger people's lives;
> Causing substantial harm to property or the occurrence of other consequences dangerous to society;
> Threatening the life of a statesman or public figure for the purpose of putting an end to his State or other public activity or in revenge for such activity;
> Attacking a representative of a foreign State or an internationally protected staff member of an international organization, as well as the business premises or vehicles of internationally protected persons;
> Other acts classified as terrorist under the national legislation of the Parties or under universally recognized international legal instruments aimed at combating terrorism.[42]

Similarly, the text of the Arab Convention gives a detailed definition in its Article 1(2):

> [Terrorism is] [A]ny act or threat of violence, whatever its motives or purposes, that occurs in the advancement of an individual or collective criminal agenda and seeking to sow panic among people, causing fear by harming them, or placing their lives, liberty or security in danger, or seeking to cause damage to the environment or to public or private installations or property or to occupying or seizing them, or seeking to jeopardize national resources."[43]

In the next paragraph, the Convention makes references to some international treaties and stipulates that a "terrorist offence" is to be understood in the same way as the crimes expressed therein (in similarity to the SAARC Convention and the Council of Europe Convention).

Finally, many legal doctrine representatives elaborated their proper definitions of terrorism, highlighting some of its particular traits. It is worth to mention one

---

42 Treaty on Cooperation among the States Members of the Commonwealth of Independent States in Combating Terrorism, done at Minsk on 4 June 1999, art. 1

43 Arab Convention for the Suppression of Terrorism done at Cairo on 22 April 1994, art. 1(2).

of the oldest definitions invented by Polish researcher R. Lemkin who, in 1935, described terrorism as "isolated acts of violence susceptible of creating destructive influence on the moral condition of masses directed against public order."[44] Although formed nearly one hundred years ago, this short definition encapsulates some elements present in the more contemporary descriptions of the term "terrorism" that were analysed above; for instance, the use of violence, affecting a large number of people, or choosing public institutions as a target. Therefore, Lemkin's definition remains significant and accurate to this day; however, the reality of the fight against terrorism these days requires taking on a more progressive approach than at the beginning of the previous century. Thus, A. Jakab proposed a definition more reflective of that reality: "Terrorism is [...] an armed attack (or the threat thereof) on political or religious grounds in order to destabilise a political system or to awaken fear in the population."[45]

The study presented above shows that the understanding of the term "terrorism" strongly varies depending on several factors including the authorship of the definition or even the geographical region. Such a wide scope of definitions results in disputes on how to precisely assess what we put under the notion of terrorism and that issue is of utmost importance due to multiple reasons.

First of all, terrorism, at the time of today's globalisation, has become a worldwide problem. Therefore, unanimity of states is needed to fight it effectively. If the differences in the major operating definitions are relatively small and functionality maintained, states do not need to engage in disputes concerning delineating the meaning of terrorism as a theoretical concept, but can just take concrete measures to eliminate it.

Moreover, through ages, certain groups that have been fighting against governments were considered by many as revolutionists, or dubbed as freedom fighters, not as terrorists, which was caused by their goals having been viewed as fair when they concerned freeing people from oppression, even if it required the killing of innocents.[46]

---

44 A. Bieńczyk-Missala, S. Dębski, ed. Rafał Lemkin: A Hero of Humankind (The Polish Institute of International Affairs: Warsaw, 2010), p. 71 (author's personal translation of the quote from French language).

45 A. Jakab, "Breaching constitutional law on moral grounds in the fight against terrorism: Implied presuppositions and proposed solutions in the discourse on 'the Rule of Law vs. Terrorism'", International Journal of Constitutional Law, Vol. 1 (9) 2011, p. 65.

46 A. Oehmichen, Terrorism and Anti-Terror Legislation, p. 75.
P. Van Krieken, citing A. Schmid points out that in defining terrorism, one should not refer to relativism, i. e. recognise that one person's "terrorist" is another man's

Anti-terrorist solutions taken by states are usually related to the "clash of human rights".[47] Freedom of speech, the right to privacy, or private property are vulnerable to be restricted in the conditions of the fight against terrorism, as each person has a right to be protected from terrorism and terrorist acts.[48] A clear and precise definition would reduce the risk of conflicts between citizens and states regarding the extent of anti-terrorist measures taken by states which at some point can limit fundamental rights and freedoms.[49] In any case, it should be kept in mind that indeed States are authorised to limit human rights if justified reason exist, but first and foremost principles of necessity and proportionality should be observed, as C. Fijnaut points out [see more: sub-chapter 1.4.2.].[50]

Last, but not least, word the terrorism has become a popular one, especially among broadcast companies and press, to describe any kind of attack with use of violence on a large scale, regardless of its nature. Forming a legal definition would help to correctly distinguish terrorist attacks from other attempts.[51]

1.2.3. Characteristics of terrorism

Taking into account all the principal traits present in the most relevant definitions of terrorism, it is possible to extract their key elements and build one universal definition that would be as follows: terrorism is any unlawful act of intentional use of violence (or threat thereof) aimed at realising particular ideological or political goals and spreading fear among society that affects such entities

---

"freedom fighter". See more: P. Van Krieken, Terrorism and the International Legal Order:With Special Reference to the UN, the EU and Cross-Border Aspects (T. M. C. Asser Press: The Hague, 2002), p. 15.

47 V.-J. Proulx does not share the opinion that anti-terrorist law would stay in opposition to human rights. He postulates that both legal systems of norms work „complementarily". See V.-J. Proulx, Transnational Terrorism and State Accountability. A New Theory of Prevention (Hart Publishing: Oxford-Portland, 2012), p. 16.

48 That postulate was confirmed by the UNGA in its Resolution 58/174 from 22 December 2003 (Article 11).

49 Such a problem cannot be underestimated as in the past, States tended to infringe human rights seriously when having taken anti-terrorist solutions. See M. Marcinko, ONZ wobec terroryzmu międzynarodowego (Fundacja Instytut Studiów Strategicznych: Kraków, 2008), p. 217.

50 C. Fijnaut, J. Wouters, F. Naert, Legal instruments in the Fight against International Terrorism. A Transatlantic Dialogue (Martinus Nijhoff Publishers: Leiden/Boston, 2004), p. 226.

51 T. Aleksandrowicz, Terroryzm międzynarodowy, pp. 13-14.

as states or international organisations. Having formed that definition, it is now possible to analyse each of the characteristics separately in the following order:

1. Intentional use of violence or threat thereof,
2. Acts conducted against the law,
3. Realising particular ideological or political goals,
4. Aiming at spreading fear or threat among society,
5. Affecting entities such as states or international organisations.[52]

It might be difficult to visualise a terrorist act without any kind of violence applied. An important question to be asked here concerns the objects towards which the aggression in used. It is unquestionable that a victim would be a human being and it is repeated in many international conventions (see above).[53] Although terrorist attacks are predominantly directed at large groups of people, there are also cases of attacks on smaller groups, or even a single person. These actions should also be encompassed under the notion of a terrorist attack, as long as a certain degree of violence is present and some particular motives influence perpetrator's action, especially if such attacks are repeated in certain period of time.[54] On the other hand, terrorists seem to reach desired results of spreading fear when the attacks on a larger scale, taking the ones from 11 September as an

52 See more: T. Aleksandrowicz, Terroryzm międzynarodowy, p. 20.

53 P. Van Krieken in reference to UNGA's Sixth Committee agenda items, expressly dealing with „international terrorism which endangers or taken innocent human lives or jeopardizes fundamental freedoms" points out that the General Assembly by using that formulation differentiates terrorism that takes innocent human lives or jeopardizes fundamental freedoms from other kinds thereof that, in author's opinion do not deserve attention. That way of reasoning is not totally appropriate, as the United Nations, condemning since decades all forms of terrorist acts certainly only had a will to emphasises that an immanent trait of terrorism is endangering human lives and jeopardizing fundamental freedoms, and so it should be put into agenda with a priority. But that does not essentially mean that each single act of terrorism deprives people of lives and in consequence falls out of concern and discussion. See P. Van Krieken, Terrorism and the International Legal Order, p. 113.

54 See more: K. Wilsher, "France in shock again after Isis murder of priest in Normandy", The Guardian, 26 July 2016. (9 March 2021) https://www.theguardian.com/world/2016/jul/26/france-shock-second-isis-attack-12-days. The attack featured in the article was committed by members of ISIS on a priest in Normandy, France. Despite the fact, that one person (the priest) was killed in the assault, the then president of France, François Hollande, declared it as a terrorist attack.

example, are conducted, as they gain significant media interest attracting the entire world's attention.

Nevertheless, it seems evident that acts of violence which are targeted at properties (either public or private) may also fall under the scope of terrorism. Offenders often conduct attacks in the areas or places, where an extensive damage to property may occur (for instance: airports, metro stations, hotels, etc.). A question of how to treat an attack that does not endanger human life or their physical integrity, but only damages property may arise. The need for a strong protection against terrorism requires a wide interpretation of its definition. The use of force of a particular strength against property (provided that all other conditions listed above are fulfilled) would make it possible to classify it as terrorist. Therefore, if an attacker intentionally destroys an object of culture or blows up an abandoned railway station, with the absence of any victims, he would be pursued not as an ordinary criminal, but as a terrorist.

Similarly, an act seriously damaging the environment would also have a trait of terrorism. One can easily imagine a situation in which a terrorist group contaminates water or pollutes the air and such an activity has a significant impact on the environment and, as a result, on people. Some international treaties, like the Arab Convention or the CIS Terrorist Treaty *expressis verbis* incorporate damaging the environment into the catalogue of terrorist offences.

It is uncertain if abuse of animal rights might be regarded as a terrorist behaviour. Very few representatives of doctrine, if any, ever mention violence against animals as a trait of terrorism. What is more, none of the international treaties includes abuse of animal rights in their definition of terrorism. However, violence against animals should not be completely disregarded as not having a potentially terrorist character. It is possible that if as a result of an attack, a remaining population of a given species that somehow constitutes a symbol of a particular country (e.g. the giant panda in China, or the Siberian tiger in Russia) becomes extinct, one might consider it a terrorist assault that targeted a part of a given country's local ecosystem or even cultural heritage. The problem of animal terrorism in general certainly needs to be discussed further, but it is beyond the scope of this publication to talk about it here.

The aforementioned considerations encompass rather physical form of violence. However, no one should turn a blind eye to psychological form of terrorism, which may be a serious threat when used. Thus, using a threat itself might also be an act of terrorism. Organised terrorist groups often threaten the citizens before committing the actual offence, which is enough to already affect people or even the international community. Moreover, some international conventions and legal systems regard a threat of violence as a crime. It is positive that an act might be classified as terrorist if it is intentional – a requirement of intent is present in most legal documents criminalizing terrorist offences. However, since many experts regard also cyberattacks a form of terrorism, such an activity, although lacking the element of physical violence, would also be qualified as terrorist.

One more issue, related to the abovementioned ones, is the question whether a terrorist act can be directed only against civilians, or may also be present in warfare and target military personnel. The subject is to some extent controversial and provokes wide a discussion among researchers.[55]

Acts conducted against the law

Due to the fact that, in principle, each sovereign state regulates its criminal law system independently (which does not exclude a possibility to partially delegate such right to a supranational body; e.g. the EU), a statement that an act should be unlawful to be regarded as terrorist may sound imprecise. Although certain acts are regarded as criminal offences in nearly all states of the world (for instance: murder), there exist some kinds of acts the classification of which as criminal or not varies depending on a state. Nevertheless, due to the international community's policy of treating international terrorism as a common threat, most criminal codes (or their equivalents) in force do penalise offences which can be considered common terrorist methods. Moreover, multiple penal acts classify terrorist offences as a separate category, introducing a dichotomous division between terrorist and non-terrorist crimes. That, in consequence, justifies application of higher penalties for committing the former ones.[56] Such solutions function *inter alia* in the French Penal Code, art. 421-1 and subs., the Polish Penal Code, art. 115 §20, the Belgian Penal Code art. 137 §§1-3, and Title 18 of the U.S. Code §2331.

Realising particular ideological or political goals

The motives behind terrorism fall into three main categories; namely religious, political or ideological, as the attacks committed by terrorist offenders usually

---

55 A. H. Barrientosa, P. P. Longoria, "Understanding the Interrelationship Between Global Terrorist Attacks and the Citizen's Wellbeing: The Complexity of Terrorism", Sociology Study, Vol. 6(5) 2016, p. 284.

56 M. Osiecki, „Zamachy na port lotniczy w Brukseli – prawo międzynarodowe i europejskie wobec zdarzenia", Internetowy Kwartalnik Monopolowy i Regulacyjny, Vol 2(6) 2016, p. 65.

have such background. Although most criminal codes of particular States do not stipulate *expressis verbis* that an act inspired by political motives constitutes a "terrorist offence", that trait seems to be inseparably related thereto. Terrorism functions as a tool which is supposed to help offenders realise certain goals. Nowadays, such goals may even constitute main ambitions of some terrorist organisations. For instance, Boko Haram, a jihadist group based in Nigeria, recognised as a terrorist organisation by several states, including the United States, struggles to impose a political system of the caliphate within its country.[57] Another example, already described in one of the previous sub-chapters, ISIS, an Islamic extremist organisation responsible for planning and conducting multiple attacks, mostly on the territory of Europe, is inspired by a precise political and ideological ambition to create a caliphate all over the Arabic world which would be ruled by a single person – the caliph.[58] A vast number of similar examples could be enumerated and all of them have a common trait – the offences committed by the members of such radical groups are marked by some specific motives of religious, ideological or political nature. Thus, one could ask why then legislative documents remain silent in relation thereto. If one studies the French Penal Code for example, the article 421-1 and subsequent recognise as terrorist only crimes "committed intentionally with relation to collective or individual attempt having an aim of disrupting considerably public order by a terror or threat."[59] Similarly, the Polish Penal Code in its art. 115 §20 stipulates that a

> [C]rime of a terrorist character is an unlawful act punishable by an imprisonment penalty which upper limit is minimum of 5 years, committed in aim of: 1) serious threat to many persons, 2) forcing an organ of public power of the Republic of Poland or another state or an organ of international organisation to undertake or refrain from particular activities, 3) evoking serious disruptions in system or economy of the Republic of Poland, another state or an international organisation – as well as a threat to commit such an act.[60]

---

57 D. M. Adeniji, Nigeria: Boko Haram and National Security (Garamond Projects Ltd.: Abuja, 2015), p. 158;
M. Smith, Boko Haram: Inside Nigeria's Unholy War (I.B. Tauris: London-New York 2015), p. 12.

58 A. Lekas, ISIS: The Largest Threat to World Peace Trending Now, Emory International Law Review. 2015, Volume 30, issue 2, p. 319

59 Code pénal, Legifrance art. 421-1 [personal translation of the author from French language].

60 Ustawa z dnia 6 czerwca 1997 r. - Kodeks karny. Dz.U. 1997 Nr 88 poz. 553, art. 115 §20 [personal translation of the author from Polish language].

The lack of expressing a motive as a trait of crime is probably related to potential evidence difficulties. Proving, additionally, that a particular offence was committed for ideological reasons would be often relatively complex and could result in unnecessarily prolonging a trial. Other traits enumerated in provisions (e.g. spreading fear or acting against a state or international organisation) seem to be sufficient.

Aiming at spreading fear or threat throughout society

This particular element is strongly related to the etymology of the word terrorism. Usually, the direct targets of the perpetrators are not the only not victims and the main object of the attack is a larger public. It goes without saying that a massive scale of damage and a tremendous dead toll are often a desired effect of a terrorist attack, but the centre of gravity is located elsewhere – it resides in threatening the entire society. B. Jenkins once compared terrorism to theatre as both are designed for those, who watch, not those who are victims thereof.[61] An attack is merely a demonstration of force, which intends to affect people and threaten them and, even further, cause governments to follow certain demands [discussed below].

Affecting entities such as states or international organisations

The last element of defining terrorism refers to a certain extend to the points discussed in the previous sections. Usually the motives pushing terrorists to their ferocious activities oppose the interests of the majority of states[62], but affect them, as usually a conducted attack is a form of a request addressed to governments.[63]

---

61 Explained by: T. Aleksandrowicz, „Krótki film o ścinaniu głowy. O symbiozie między terrorystami i mediami", Wszystko co najważniejsze, 9 May 2015. (9 March 2021) https://wszystkoconajwazniejsze.pl/tomasz-aleksandrowicz-krotki-film-o-scinaniu-glowy/

62 Charles Townshend correctly affirms that states most vulnerable to terrorist strikes are those with a democratic system. Democratic states, usually adherent to values such as freedom of movement, freedom of association, multitude of potential targets and limits arising from legal system in force are "attractive" and easier to be assaulted by terrorist groups. Democracy is then a price that we pay for greater risk of terrorist attack. See C. Townshend, Terroryzm, pp. 169-170.

63 Omer Y. Elagab is one of experts that clearly exposes that countries and their inhabitants are direct targets of terrorist activities. See O. Elagab, International law Documents relating to Terrorism (Routledge: London/Sydney, 1997), p. xix.

Such a request frequently concerns imposing a change of politics of a particular State or its allies.[64] Sometimes, an attack is even conducted with aim to attract the world's attention to a particular issue.[65] Nowadays, most notorious terrorist attacks influence not only particular states or organisations, but the international community in general. It is especially visible in the wording of relevant criminal provisions – extracts from penal codes cited above include stipulations requiring an attack to cause disruption or turmoil in a state's functioning.

The last element of the definition explains why the war on terror has become a global problem. A terrorist attack, having as a final target a state, or group thereof, or an international organisation, or even the whole international community provokes a reaction from another side – assaulted states amend their law so that they make sure that no terrorist crime escapes justice, engage military actions against states cooperating with terrorists or seek support from international organisations. Today's world has become transformed into a battlefield on which states face terrorists and death spreads among innocent people.

Of course, the definition of terrorism presented here has a general character. Due to the fast development of technology and progress in society's integration, terrorists infiltrate more and more domains of life using innovative tools. In consequence, different types of terrorism, like nuclear, marine, or aerial, might be analysed from diverse perspectives and more precise definitions related to those domains might be formed.[66] As the present monograph's subject is, in principle, aerial terrorism, the majority of the subsequently described studies shall be devoted thereto.

1.3. Aspects of aerial terrorism

Through last decades, civil aeroplanes and airports were frequently selected as targets for some of the most vicious terrorist attacks in the history. The events of

64 M. N. Shaw, International Law (Cambridge University Press: Cambridge, 2014), p. 841

65 See T. Aleksandrowicz, K. Liedel, Zwalczanie terroryzmu lotniczego (Wydawnictwo Wyższej Szkoły Policji: Szczytno, 2010), p. 13. Authors, after G. Habash, evoke a „Palestinian case", claiming that before 1968, when some terrorist attacks were directed by People Front for the Liberation of Palestine, the demands of Palestinians related to lands were even unknown to international community.

66 M. Lech, Ochrona prawna społeczności międzynarodowej, p. 42 after: K. Indecki, Prawo karne wobec terroryzmu i aktu terrorystycznego (Wydawnictwo Uniwersytetu Łódzkiego: Łódź, 1998), p. 19.

11 September bombing of Air India flight 182, or El Al flight 426 hijacking have been remembered as some of the grimmest chapters of civil aviation history. If there still exists a need prove that terrorism has become a problem of the whole international community, attacks on civil aviation serve as the most distinct evidence. It, therefore, makes aerial terrorism a matter which deserves separate research. From this point onwards, the lion's share of the discussed topic shall concern aerial terrorism in particular.

1.3.1. Introductory notes

Aerial terrorism is a term seemingly understandable, but it is still challenging to find a proper definition which describes it. Neither international agreements, nor the custom provide one, as most legal acts, devoted to criminalisation of certain deeds committed against civil aviation, usually just enumerate precise offences and refer to relevant subjects including jurisdiction or extradition. However, as civil aviation has become an increasingly desirable target for international terrorist groups, more and more legislative documents talk about the acts conducted against aeroplanes or aviation infrastructure as those recognised as terrorist.

Simply speaking, aerial terrorism is a form of terrorism in which violence is directed against civil aviation.[67] Some authors, like G. Zając, expand this definition by claiming that aerial terrorism may also be perceived all unlawful acts directed against crew or passengers on board of an aircraft, that may (either hypothetically or practically) jeopardise the safety of flight, acts endangering aircraft or property on board as well as all crimes committed at airports serving civil aviation.[68] Nevertheless, such a definition is not completely accurate, as it ignores the division between acts of terrorism and other types of offences. As it was mentioned in the previous sub-chapter, if an offence is to be considered terrorist, it should fulfil certain criteria including ideological motivation or having a particular aim, etc. Thus, a simple act of violence, even if it compromises safety

---

67 Compare: K. Liedel, Zwalczanie terroryzmu lotniczego. Aspekty prawnomiędzynarodowe (Jurysta: Warsaw, 2003), p. 12, J. Walulik, „Pekińska reforma lotniczego prawa karnego – geneza, istota, rekomendacje", Ruch Prawniczy, Ekonomiczny i Socjologiczny, Vol. 3/2013, p. 36, after: Z. Galicki, Terroryzm lotniczy w świetle prawa międzynarodowego (Wydawnictwo Uniwersytetu Warszawskiego: Warsaw, 1981), p. 32.

68 G. Zając, „Prawnomiędzynarodowe regulacje dotyczące zwalczania terroryzmu w lotnictwie cywilnym", Stosunki Międzynarodowe – International Relations, Vol. 1/2 (43) 2011, p. 105.

of people on board, does not necessarily have to be terrorist. If, for example, a group of drunk or aggressive passengers violently approaches the air crew, or one of the pilots intentionally takes control of an aircraft and intentionally directs it to crash into a mountain and, in consequence, commits suicide, then certainly the safety of the aircraft is in danger, but not due to terrorist behaviour. Similarly, not all crimes that are committed at an airport serving civil aviation may be viewed as terrorist. If a person kills one of the passengers departing from an airport without any specific motive or steals a case carrying jewellery or a considerable sum of money, then they commit an offence, but it has nothing to do with terrorism. To sum up, the above definition would be more accurate if a phrase "if such acts have terrorist character"[69] was added at the end of it.

1.3.2. Why is civil aviation an "attractive target" for terrorists?

Civil aviation is generally considered to be one of the safest means of transport. In 2015, only 2.8 air accidents per million departures occurred, which represents a slight drop from 3.0 accidents per million departures a year before. In total, in 2015, 474 people died in 92 accidents.[70] What is more, 2017 was officially recognised as the safest year in post-war civil aviation history, as no single person died in a commercial jet aircraft accident.[71]

Despite those excellent safety results, many people are still afraid of dying during a flight, especially as a result of a terrorist attack and apparently this anxiety is not unreasonable.

Civil aviation constitutes a very enticing target for terrorists. Air travel bears world-wide significance, the majority of flights is international and the aircraft

---

69 Differently: A. Lele, A. Mishra, "Aerial Terrorism and the Threat from Unmanned Aerial Vehicles", Journal of Defence Studies, Vol. 3(3) 2009, p. 55. The authors state that no precise definition of aerial terrorism exists and present only a (non-exhaustive) catalogue of acts that might be recognized as such.

70 ICAO Safety Report. 2016 Edition, Montreal 2016, p. 5. (9 March 2021) https://www.icao.int/safety/Documents/ICAO_SR%202016_final_13July.pdf

71 L. Upton, "2017 was the safest year in aviation history; though caution urged on remarkable figures continuing", Transport Security World (9 March 2021) http://www.transportsecurityworld.com/2017-was-safest-year-in-aviation-history-though-caution-urged-on-remarkable-figures).
Despite global air traffic significantly dropping in 2020 amid the COVID-19 pandemic, several fatal air accidents occurred that year.

carry passengers from various countries.[72] C. Naudin identifies some noteworthy reasons why, from the perspective of an offender, an attack on civil aeroplanes may be effective: as airliners are usually made of fragile material, it is relatively easy to cause an explosion and inflict extensive damage. Moreover, civil aircraft feature flags of a particular state; thus, if an attack on a machine is conducted, it symbolically represents an attack on a particular state[73]. The view of many people suffering and seeing a big airliner crash is enough to affect the public psychologically (which is the goal of a terrorist activity; see above). Finally, the economy and social affairs are highly dependent on uninterrupted air traffic; a large-scale attack would paralyse the global trade and frustrate a big number of citizens.[74]

For all the reasons listed above, an attack usually attracts the attention of many states of the world and is widely covered in the media. This fact provides terrorists with another advantage, as even a failed attempt, unsuccessful due to the terrorists' errors or prevented by special forces, attracts the world's attention and often spreads fear among society. As it was mentioned in the previous chapter, such reaction is desired by terrorists. What is more, an aeroplane is a symbol of modernity and human technical development. Terrorist groups opposing the Western civilisation *sensu largo* manifest their condemnation of the entire western society and its policy.[75]

---

72 The attack on 11 September, although occurred on the territory of the United States, claimed the life of many people of nationalities different than American. C. Murphy gives the numbers of 67 killed Britons, 11 Germans, 10 Italians, 6 Irish, 5 Portuguese, 3 French and those only concern European countries' citizens. See C. Murphy, EU Counter-Terrorism Law. Pre-Emption and the Rule of Law (Hart Publishing: Oxford/ Portland, 2012), p. 22.

73 B. Nowak, „Akty terroryzmu w lotnictwie cywilnym a tokijsko-hasko-montrealski system międzynarodowego lotniczego prawa karnego", Studia Europejskie, 3/2003, p. 118.

According to P. Dempsey, for some nations civil aviation is a symbol of pride, global ambitions and prestige; a flag featured on an aircraft's fuselage in some way allows a state to express it publicly. See P. Dempsey, "Aviation Security: The Role of Law in the War against Terrorism", Columbia Journal of Transnational Law, Vol. 41(3) 2003, p. 651.

74 C. Naudin, Sûrete aérienne. La grande illusion (La Table Ronde: Paris, 2007), pp. 27-28

75 M. Lech, Ochrona prawna społeczności międzynarodowej, p. 51, after: B. Hołyst, Terroryzm, t.1 (LexisNexis: Warsaw, 2011), p. 59. The author admits that the target is a symbol of hatred, an enemy. Such a statement might be then used in relation to civil aviation. It is a target of terrorists because it embodies their object of hatred.

The area of civil aviation related to protection of passengers from intentional acts (therefore also terrorism) is included under the notion of security and it is usually divided into two categories: airport security and air security. The former one focuses on attempts to disrupt the functioning of airport facilities or an aircraft standing on the tarmac, whereas the latter concerns these intrusions that occur when an aircraft is airborne or generally moves on its own.

Within aviation security exists aviation safety that is devoted to protection from unintentional acts (e.g. a onboard fires, engine failure, faulty maintenance) that analogically would be divided into airport and air safety alike.[76]

1.3.3. Types of attacks

Going back to the 1960s, aerial terrorism was nearly synonymous to aircraft hijacking, as on both sides of the Atlantic, civil aeroplanes were massively captured by people willing to leave their countries either to Cuba or behind the Iron Curtain.[77] But, in the course of time, international terrorist networks have devised new means to strike. Nowadays, an attack on civil aviation in the ICAO's nomenclature is called "act of unlawful interference" and may relate to both terrorist and non-terrorist offences.

Currently, on the basis of their *modus operandi*, the following types of aerial terrorism can be distinguished: hijacking, aircraft bombing, using an aeroplane as a weapon, shooting an aircraft down, destroying the infrastructure of an airport, cyberattacks in aviation, damaging an aircraft with the use of specific types of weapons (e.g. biological, nuclear or chemical)[78] and targeting passengers directly (e.g. taking hostages).

---

76 C. Naudin, Sûrete aérienne, pp. 32-37.

77 T. Aleksandrowicz, K. Liedel, Zwalczanie terroryzmu lotniczego, pp. 11-12.

78 As no attacks featuring the two lattermost methods have been conducted so far, they rather ought to be treated as potential modus operandi of the future.
Similarly: P. Rembauville-Nicole, L'effectivité du droit de la securité aérienne, in: ed. X. Latour, La securité et la sûreté des transports aériens (L'Harmattan: Paris, 2005), pp. 34-39.
The author mentions cyberattacks and usage of nuclear, biological and chemical weapons in the context of an "evolution of attempts". A different classification was made and published by K. Jałoszyński, who diversifies acts of aerial terrorism from the perspective of the strike location:
1) on board aircraft (like hijacking, or taking hostages)
2) from air (aeroplane as a bomb)
3) on aeroplane (anti-aircraft weapons)

In history there are also examples of combined attacks, in which the offenders used several methods from the above list in one attempt (using an aeroplane as weapon is normally always preceded by its hijacking, as it was the case of 11 September or Air France flight 8969). Each of them is a complex incident and deserves some detailed explanation which will be provided in a subsequent part of the monograph.

a) Skyjacking vs. aerial piracy

Aircraft hijacking (or, in other words, skyjacking) is a type of offence which would perfectly serve as a material for, at least, a separate chapter or even an entire book to be described properly. It would not be an exaggeration to claim that skyjacking is a symbol of certain era of aviation. In fact, this particular form of offence is nearly as old as the civil aviation itself. Hijacking of aircraft occurred for the first time on 21 February 1931. Byron Rickards, having piloted Ford Tri-motor was captured by a group of local revolutionists in the town of Arequipa in south Peru. The hijackers held him captive for 10 days, until revolution ended in success. Rickards was set free under the condition of giving an airlift for one of the hijackers to the capital of Peru, Lima.[79] Since then, multiple aircraft have been illegally seized and the international community has been struggling to put an end to this practice. Aircraft piracy saw its heyday in 1960s, when American aeroplanes were massively captured and directed to Cuba. In total, only between 1948 and 1966, 47 planes were hijacked.[80] The beginning of the modern terrorism era is marked by a hijacking of an El Al Israel Airlines' jet – flight 426 en route from London Heathrow via Rome Fiumicino to Lod Airport (now known as Ben Gurion International Airport), which was captured by the members of the Popular Front for the Liberation of Palestine (or "PFLP") on 23 July 1968.[81]

---

4) on logistics infrastructure.
See T. Aleksandrowicz, K. Liedel, Zwalczanie terroryzmu lotniczego, pp. 15. After: K. Jałoszyński, Współczesny wymiar antyterroryzmu, (Trio: Warsaw, 2008), p. 178.

79 Aviation Safety Network; https://aviation-safety.net/database/record.php?id=19310221-0 (9 March 2021).

80 M. Dupont-Elleray, "Géopolitique du terrorisme aérien: de l'évolution de la menace à la diversité de la riposte", Stratégique, nr 1(85) 2005 5, p. 110;
T. Aleksandrowicz, K. Liedel, Zwalczanie terroryzmu lotniczego, pp. 11-12.

81 M. Lech, Ochrona prawna społeczności międzynarodowej, p. 85;
Aviation Safety Network, https://aviation-safety.net/database/record.php?id=19680723-0 (9 March 2021).

That was a moment of awakening of Islamic extremist groups that chose airliners as their new target. On 6 September 1970 a massive hijacking action plan was realised by PFLP members that seized four aeroplanes belonging to British Overseas Airways Corporation, Swissair, Trans World Airlines and Pan Am.[82] More than two decades later, the capital of Algeria became a crime scene for hijacking when on 24 December 1994, an Airbus A300 belonging to Air France was captured by the Armed Islamic Group whose members compelled the crew to fly to Paris and planned to crash the machine into the Eiffel Tower. After a brave rescue mission by the French National Gendarmerie, the plane was secured and all hijackers were assassinated [see more: sub-chapter 3.4.].

Fortunately, nearing the end of the twentieth century, hijackings were becoming less frequent, as sophisticated security control systems were being implemented at airports all over the globe and governments were concentrating their efforts to fight against terrorism.

Aircraft hijacking is often erroneously considered to be a synonym of aerial piracy. Although both terms are, in fact, strictly related to each other, they do not have exactly the same meaning.[83] The description of both of them is provided below.

Importantly, aerial piracy on a juridical level has closer ties with another similar offence, namely maritime piracy. Both acts have been commonly covered by the provisions of Convention on the High Seas written in Geneva on the 29 April 1958 (hereafter referred to as the "Geneva High Seas Convention"). Here, Article 15 bears particular relevance, as it includes the following wording:[84]

Piracy consists of any of the following acts:

> (1) Any illegal acts of violence, detention or any act of depredation, committed for private ends by the crew or the passengers of a private ship or a private aircraft, and directed:
> (a) On the high seas, against another ship or aircraft, or against persons or property on board such ship or aircraft;
> (b) Against a ship, aircraft, persons or property in a place outside the jurisdiction of any state;

---

82 P. Dempsey, "Aviation Security", p. 654, after:
P. Wilkinson, "Weaknesses in Airport Security Must be Fixed", The Scotsman (8 February 2000) p. 16.

83 See more: B. Nowak, "Akty terroryzmu w lotnictwie cywilnym", pp. 119-120.

84 A provision analogical in content was adopted in the United Nations Convention on the Law of the Seas, done in Montego Bay on 10 December 1982, commonly known as UNCLOS in article 101.

> (2) Any act of voluntary participation in the operation of a ship or of an aircraft with knowledge of facts making it a pirate ship or aircraft;
> (3) Any act of inciting or of intentionally facilitating an act described in subparagraph 1 or subparagraph 2 of this article.[85]

A closer look should be taken at some of the most important points quoted above. First of all, piracy, under these provisions, can only have one of three specific forms: an act of violence, detention or depredation. As S. Bazin explains, violence might be simply treated as any kind of attempt on the physical or psychological integrity of a person. What should be understood by detention is a factual exercise of power over an object that is contrary to legal norms and, finally, depredation is an illegal pillage of ownership (such as theft).[86]

Moreover, such an act shall be realised for "private ends". Although, at the beginning, this notion was understood as acts with *animus fruandi*, that is with a desire to gain a profit (e.g. by stealing an item), nowadays its interpretation is wider and includes also personal interests (like vengeance or escape). Nevertheless, it never concerns purely political goals typical of terrorist attacks.[87]

Furthermore, an attack could constitute piracy only if is performed by the passengers or crew of a private aircraft. At no point does the Geneva High Seas Convention explain how to interpret that expression, but the wording of the subsequent provision. Article 16 may be helpful as it mentions establishing the liability of the crew of a government aircraft in a case when that crew mutinies and takes control over aircraft. In consequence, any aircraft that is not used for government purposes should be seen as private.[88]

Finally, the issue of the utmost importance concerns the location of commissioning the crime. As it has been stated previously in points (a) and (b) of paragraph 1, an act of piracy may only be committed on the high seas, or in a place outside jurisdiction of any state (*terra nullius*), provided that it is directed against

85 Convention on the High Seas, done in Geneva on 29 April 1958, United Nations Treaty Series, Vol. 450, Reg. 6465, art. 15.

86 S. Bazin, Le droit pénal de l'aviation civile (Atelier National de Reproduction de Thèses: Lille, 2002) p. 109.

87 This interpretation was confirmed by the League of Nations in the draft of Geneva High Seas Convention in 1926. See S. Bazin, Le droit pénal de l'aviation civile, p. 111.

88 The expression "government aircraft" used in the Geneva High Seas Convention (and analogically in UNCLOS) does not reflect the typical expression functioning in sector treaties related to civil aviation. Chicago Convention does not refer to "government aircraft" but "state aircraft", and explains that this category consists of aircraft used in military, police or customs (article 3 (b)).

another aircraft. Here lays a crucial distinction of piracy from other kinds of offences. An aircraft might be then called pirated only if it is located in an area free from any state's jurisdiction (e.g. Antarctica or international airspace) and offenders invade it by boarding from another aircraft or ship. An imaginable and relevant situation would be the seizure of an aeroplane that was ditched on the high seas in an emergency by the crew of a pirate ship for the purpose of stealing valuable goods belonging to air passengers.

As we can conclude from the above analysis, aerial piracy, regulated by both UNCLOS and the Geneva High Seas Convention, would concern only a very limited number of attempts to invade an aircraft, committed in particular situations and always outside any state's sovereignty. It justifies classifying that offence as relevant for universal jurisdiction.[89] UNCLOS in article 105 stipulates what is the scope of actions of states interested in pursuing aerial piracy:

> [o]n the high seas, or in any other place outside the jurisdiction of any state, every state may seize a pirate ship or aircraft, or a ship or aircraft taken by piracy and under the control of pirates, and arrest the persons and seize the property on board. The courts of the state which carried out the seizure may decide upon the penalties to be imposed, and may also determine the action to be taken with regard to the ships, aircraft or property, subject to the rights of third parties acting in good faith.[90]

---

89 T. Ostropolski, a supporter of the concept that universal jurisdiction can only be based on universally (by all the states of the world) accepted customary law, and not international treaties, affirms that the Geneva High Seas Convention and UNCLOS only codified the principle of universal persecution of the crime of piracy established long before in custom. See T. Ostropolski, Zasada jurysdykcji uniwersalnej w prawie międzynarodowym (Instytut Wydawniczy EuroPrawo: Warsaw, 2008), pp. 65-68.
In turn, S. Bazin does not necessarily link universal jurisdiction to the existence of appropriate universally accepted custom, but recognizes that it can arise from international conventions on delicta iuris gentium, under the condition that they do not provide that a state party may implement any exemptions to the duty of pursuing an offender (the rule known as aut dedere aut iudicare). In other words, state judicial authorities that establish their jurisdiction over the case concerning aerial piracy must either prosecute an offender, or extradite them to another interested state. No alternative based on political, cultural or social motives is provided. See S. Bazin, Le droit pénal de l'aviation civile, pp. 47-50, 110.

90 United Nations Convention on the Law of the Seas done at Montego Bay on 10 December 1982, United Nations Treaty Series, Vol. 1833, Reg. 31363, art. 105.

As the above analysis shows aerial piracy would not be a synonym of aircraft hijacking. The latter term refers to a slightly different phenomenon that shall be described below.

Similar to aerial piracy, also aircraft hijacking is defined in legislature, encompassing international treaties, European law acts as well as domestic legal systems provisions. Thus, the question is what can be viewed as an aircraft hijacking. The most relevant definition can be found in the Protocol Supplementary to the Convention for the Suppression of Unlawful Seizure of Aircraft, held in Beijing on 10 September 2010 (hereafter referred to as the "Beijing Protocol") that came into force on 1 January 2018. That treaty, according to official ICAO reports, is designed to supplement the slightly outdated Convention for the Suppression of Unlawful Seizure of Aircraft composed in The Hague on 16 December 1970 (hereafter referred to as "The Hague Convention") and adapt it to the reality of the twenty-first century [both treaties are overviewed in detail in chapter 2]. Although the titles of both acts use the wording "unlawful seizure of aircraft", for the purpose of this monograph, this term, along with aircraft hijacking, or skyjacking shall be treated as synonymous.[91]

The Beijing Protocol defines aircraft hijacking in article II replacing article 1(1) of The Hague Convention by stipulating that "[a]ny person commits an offence if that person unlawfully and intentionally seizes or exercises control of an aircraft in service by force or threat thereof, or by coercion, or by any other form of intimidation, or by any technological means."[92] Those provisions might be recognised as a definition of skyjacking, as a similar regulation is also present in domestic penal legislation enacted by the concerned states. From the wording of

91 S. Bazin points out that during the Hague Conference during which the Hague Convention was being prepared, there were many concerns regarding the name of the offence. Aerial piracy was rejected, and discussion was mainly concentrated on either using the expression "hijacking" or "unlawful seizure of aircraft". As "hijacking" was interpreted by some experts simply as the change of an aeroplane's itinerary, it did not cover all cases of unlawful control takeover. In turn, "unlawful seizure of aircraft" seemed to be a term of larger scope, covering also hijacking and was ultimately inserted into the Convention. Anyway, both terms are generally used interchangeably, even in ICAO documents, so may be treated as synonyms. See S. Bazin, Le droit pénal de l'aviation civile, pp.119-120, after: G. Guillaume, Le terrorisme aérien, in: G. Guillaume, G. Levasseur, Terrorisme international (Pédone: Paris, 1976), p. 4.

92 Protocol Supplementary to the Convention for the Suppression of Unlawful Seizure of Aircraft done in Beijing, on 10th September 2010, ICAO Doc. 9959, art. II replacing article 1(1) of the Hague Convention.

this definition, we can conclude that to define a person as a hijacker, they have to use force of any kind (or threaten to use it) in order to take control of an aircraft and such an act must be unlawful and intentional.

Applying force is a crucial element here. A person attempting to seize an aeroplane may use tools including weapons with the goal of forcing the pilots to redirect the aircraft, but they can threaten them with the use of a bomb (even if in reality they may not carry one) or using mere words if such a threat is credible and effective as well. Simply speaking, a person should use psychical or physical methods leading to seize control of an aircraft (held normally by pilots). The subsequent element is to take over control. Such a person should then, as a result of using force, have a real possibility to steer the aircraft. However, an attacker does not necessarily need to sit at the controls or contact ATC – it is sufficient that they give orders to the crew having previously overpowered them by force and, in consequence, have influence on the fate of the flight. As stated in the wording of the provision, it is clear that to hijack an aircraft, an offender does not even need to be present on board[93], because it is stipulated that an unlawful seizure can be conducted "by any technological means". This expression refers to what is popularly known as "cyber hijacking", a method of seizing an aeroplane using technological devices. This expression was used in the Beijing Protocol not without reason, as technology nowadays develops at an unprecedented rate, it is quite possible that in the near future, terrorists will be able to hijack civil planes without even boarding an aircraft or the airport premises. Instead, they could hack the on-board systems and seize the machine remotely.

The term unlawfulness should be understood widely in that case as any action against the law in force or even the internal rules applicable to an airline operating the flight or other provisions would be concerned. A pilot struggling to take control back from a hijacker holding a control column, even when using force, should not be considered an offender because he is doing his job, that being protecting their passengers in attempt to regain control.[94]

---

93 In literature published before 2010, when the Beijing Protocol was signed, it was quite common among authors to claim that hijacking could only be committed "on board" an aircraft. That was a consequence of the formulation used in the Hague Convention that was obliging its parties to criminalise acts of unlawful aircraft seizure performed only on board. It is not too surprising, as in 1970s, when the Hague Convention was drafted, technology was much less developed than it is today and hijacking using technological means was nearly unbelievable.
See more: N. M. Poulantzas, "Convention for the Suppression of Unlawful Seizure of Aircraft", World Peace through Law Center Pamphlet Series, no. 18/1971, p. 12.

94 See Z. Galicki, Terroryzm lotniczy, p. 66.

It is clear that an act of unlawful seizure must be intentional in order to be regarded as an offence. In most legal systems, intent is understood as the will to have particular consequences of an act (direct intent) or acceptance of a natural consequence of an act that has been foreseen (conditional intent).[95]

The moment the hijacking commences is also crucial. The Protocol stipulates that the seizure or exercise of control over an aircraft must take place when it is in service. The meaning of being in service is explained in one of subsequent provisions, namely article V replacing article 3(1) of The Hague Convention. It says that "an aircraft is considered to be in service from the beginning of the pre-flight preparation of the aircraft by ground personnel or by the crew for a specific flight until twenty-four hours after any landing." As we can see, even when the ground staff prepares an aeroplane for a flight, and no single passenger in on board yet and the crew is not even present in the cockpit, an attempted seizure can be qualified as a hijacking.

Finally, it is obvious that an offence cannot be called "aircraft hijacking" when it does not concern an aircraft. What can be recognised as an aircraft is defined in Annexes to Convention on International Civil Aviation, signed in Chicago on the 7 of December 1944 (hereafter referred to as the "Chicago Convention"). Based on that definition, an aircraft is "any machine that can derive support in the atmosphere from the reactions of the air other than the reactions of the air against the earth's surface."[96] Thus, regardless of the type of machine (jet aircraft, turboprop, or even hydroplane), a person seizing it unlawfully by force would be a hijacker.

The problems caused and the sheer scale of this type of offence are of such magnitude, that among conventions devoted to aviation security, skyjacking is regulated by documents separate from those treating on other offences against aviation. A similar diversification is made by some authors; they claim that an offence of aircraft hijacking forms a category independent of other aerial terrorism acts.[97]

---

95 On Polish criminal law: A. Zoll, W. Wróbel, Polskie prawo karne. Część ogólna (Wydawnictwo Znak: Kraków, 2010), p. 204-205.

96 Annex 7 to Convention on International Civil Aviation, signed in Chicago, 7 December 1944 – Aircraft Nationality and Registration Marks, Sixth Edition 2012, art. 1. See more: M. Żylicz, Prawo lotnicze międzynarodowe, europejskie i krajowe (Wydawnictwo LexisNexis: Warsaw, 2011), p. 25

97 G. Zając, "Prawnomiędzynarodowe regulacje" p. 106. However, the provided classification of crimes is non-exhaustive. Most acts of aerial terrorism are indeed aircraft hijackings, exercised either to change the direction of aircraft, or to force external

Some authors, including E. McWhinney, categorise hijackings on the basis of the offenders' motives:

– "Political escape" is a type of skyjacking of a more historical meaning and relates mostly to those who were hijacking planes in order to flee from communist countries. Nowadays, hijacking for the purpose of escape is much less popular.
– "Lunatic fringe" is connected primarily to the hijacking of aeroplanes from the United States to Cuba in the 1960s and the 1970s. The concept of "lunatic fringe" refers to the offenders who desired to be known to a wider public due to their supposedly heroic act of hijacking planes to their homeland. Studies show that the majority of them were mentally unbalanced.
– "Sky bandits", as the name suggests, encapsulates those hijackers who expect to obtain a ransom. They are usually skilled and well-equipped professionals with a military background.
– "Privileged combatancy" is an enigmatic name which refers to hijackings that are echo of some unresolved political conflicts. Associated mostly with perpetrators originating from the Middle East countries, those offences reflect the political atmosphere on the globe. A perpetrator, by the act of hijacking, in some way participates in an ongoing conflict and manifests their dedication to a given case.[98]

McWhinney called the last types of skyjackings enumerated above an "international terrorism". That claim is accurate as in fact, most cases of hijacking motivated by a desire to fight a political enemy feature all traits of terrorism (presented in the previous sub-chapter). That explains why the international community has engaged all efforts to eliminate the problem of "privileged combatancy". In a situation when the possibility of a quick end of a given political conflict is low, states of the world and international organisations would just target most dangerous groups that pose significant danger to air passengers.

b) Aircraft bombing

Explosives have been used by aerial terrorists as one of the most common weapons. Some of the most notable air accidents were caused by an intentional bombing, but an equal number of attempts to blow up a plane failed due to either

---

entities to behave in a specific way, but there are numerous other potential and real methods of attack (see page 11).

98 E. McWhinney, Aerial Piracy, pp. 11-13.

a successful operation conducted by special forces, or mistakes committed by the perpetrators. The first officially documented act of bombing occurred on 7 May 1949 over the territory of Philippines. Douglas DC-3 belonging to a national carrier, Philippine Airlines, exploded when performing a domestic flight from Daet to Manila. The perpetrators were a woman and a man who delivered explosives to the aircraft in order to kill the woman's husband. Their attempt was more than successful, as all the passengers and the crew (13 people in total) died.[99] Since then, around 90 air incidents or accidents involving bombing took place to this date. They include some most infamous cases such as Lockerbie catastrophe, or the attempt to blow up several transatlantic flights in 2006.[100] Other notable attacks involved flights of Gulf Air (June 1985), Air India (June 1985), Korean Air (November 1987), UTA (September 1989) and Avianca (September 1989).[101]

Aircraft bombing is, like skyjacking, sanctioned by law. In spite of no proper legal definition, an accurate regulation might be found at least in the Beijing Convention that came into force on 1 July 2018. It was the fruit of long-term efforts of the international community focused on creating a universal convention which would widely sanction terrorist offences against civil aviation and assure punishment of perpetrators in all countries of the world.[102]. Article 1(c) which stipulates that a person commits an offence if one "places or causes to be placed on an aircraft in service, by any means whatsoever, a device or substance which is likely to destroy that aircraft, or to cause damage to it which renders it incapable of flight, or to cause damage to it which is likely to endanger its safety in flight."[103] Such an act must certainly be unlawful and intentional to be perceived as an offence.

Taking into account the abovementioned wording, one can conclude that no matter what type of explosives are used by perpetrators, their act would be rated as an offence. Such explosives do not even necessarily need to destroy the

---

99 Aviation Safety Network database; https://aviation-safety.net/database/record.php?id=19490507-0 (9 March 2021).

100 Aviation Safety Network database; https://aviation-safety.net/database/dblist.php?Event=SEB (9 March 2021).

101 S. Bennett, "Commercial Aircraft Bomb-Proofing Technologies: A Social Science Critique", Risk Management, Vol. 1(3) 1999, p. 51.

102 See Convention on the Suppression of Unlawful Acts Relating to International Civil Aviation, ICAO Doc. 9960, List of parties; https://www.icao.int/secretariat/legal/List%20of%20Parties/Beijing_Conv_EN.pdf (9 March 2021)

103 Convention on the Suppression of Unlawful Acts Relating to International Civil Aviation, done at Beijing, 10th September, 2010, ICAO Doc. 9960, art. 1(c).

aircraft's fuselage, but it is sufficient that it damages the machine in a way it is not flyable, or its safety is jeopardised. What is important is the moment of placement of the explosives: an explosive device or substance should be placed (or caused to be placed) on an aircraft when it is in service at any moment "from the beginning of the pre-flight preparation of the aircraft by ground personnel or by the crew for a specific flight until twenty-four hours after any landing" (Article 2(b) of the Beijing Convention). In practice, it means that no matter if a person physically carries a bomb in hand luggage, puts it into a checked bag subsequently passed to cargo hold, or even plants it somehow onto the aircraft when it still stands on the tarmac or in a hangar. In each of the enumerated cases they would be held responsible.

Some acts of terrorist bombings that occurred in the past were crucial for the improvement of the present system of airport security and changed the rules of controlling the passengers' luggage. For instance, in the aftermath of a terrorist plot to blow up some transatlantic flights in 2006 using explosive materials hidden in soft drinks, multiple states enacted laws banning liquids in carry-on luggage in containers exceeding 100 millilitres.

c) Usage of an aeroplane as a weapon

The first ever attempt to use a civil aeroplane as a weapon was committed by Algerian terrorists on 24 December 1994, when they hijacked Airbus A300 performing flight 8969 operated by Air France [see sub-chapter 3.4.] is recognised as the beginning of a new era of the fight against international terrorism. Their plan was to direct the plane over Paris and then crash it into the Eiffel Tower. The event opened the eyes of the international community for a totally new threat that soon brought a huge death toll with the events of 11 September, 2001.[104]

Although no presently enforceable international act uses the exact name of "usage of an aircraft as a weapon" *expressis verbis*, a provision that perfectly coves that type of offence is Article 1 paragraph 1(f) of Beijing Convention. It stipulates that a person commits an offence when one "uses an aircraft in service for the purpose of causing death, serious bodily injury, or serious damage to property or the environment."[105] The cited Convention introduces a quite wide regulation – an aircraft is considered to be used as a weapon when such usage is directed to cause death or injury, as well as damage to property or the natural environment.

---

104 G. Zając, "Prawnomiędzynarodowe regulacje", p. 4.

105 Convention on the Suppression of Unlawful Acts Relating to International Civil Aviation, done at Beijing, 10th September, 2010, ICAO Doc. 9960, art. 1(1)(f).

It is vital to remind here that, normally, an aeroplane becomes a weapon as a result of a preceding action. A typical situation would be to hijack such a machine and consequently direct it onto a densely populated area, where a crash would result in the death or serious injury of as many people as possible. Nevertheless, such cases are not necessarily limited only to hijacking, as the provisions do not require an unlawful takeover of control before attack for criminalising it. A perpetrator may also shoot an aircraft down over a protected area, so that upon its downfall it causes an extensive fire and further damage. Also, Article 1 paragraph 1(f) does not evoke the use of violence or threat – it means that a potential offender could as well use such an aircraft without the application of force. One can imagine a possible situation in which an airline pilot would be being a secret member of a terrorist group. This pilot would lock himself in the cockpit, then take over the controls and direct the plane to crash in a city centre.

For the purposes of the Convention, the expression in service should be interpreted the same as its equivalent in the Beijing Convention. Finally, using an aeroplane as a weapon might be regarded as a terrorist attack, only if it fulfils particular traits thereof [see previous sub-chapter].

d) Shooting down an aircraft

Aeroplanes in non-civil service, including military, police or customs service have frequently been targeted, especially in war zones. But a similar fate unfortunately met civil aircraft many times, especially recently. Interestingly enough, the entities responsible for shooting down an airplane were often states themselves, mostly when an airliner flew into their aerospace. At some point, the international community understood that such a practice jeopardises the lives of people on board a civil aircraft and commenced working on improving the situation. Such initiatives were, in particular, motivated by an accident that occurred on 1 September 1983 over the territory of the former Soviet Union. Korean Air Boeing 747 performing flight 007 from JFK Airport in New York to Seoul flew into the USRR airspace due to a navigation fault of the crew. As Soviet Union at this time was in a state of Cold War with the Western world, the presence of a South Korean jet in their airspace caused concern among state authorities. They perceived the machine as a spy aircraft and gave orders to shoot it down by a squadron of fighters. The order was executed and, in effect, Korean Air 007 plummeted into the Sea of Japan. All 269 passengers on board died.[106] Numerous discussions

106 M. Osiecki, "Zestrzelenie samolotu a zasada zwierzchnictwa powietrznego", Studia Prawno-Ekonomiczne, Vol. 101, p. 102.

concerning the safety of civil aircraft, finally, resulted in an amendment to the Chicago Convention – Article 3 *bis* obliging state parties to refrain from using weapons against a civil aircraft in-flight and to make sure that, in case of interception, the lives of people on board are not in danger.

The acts of shooting down airliners by non-state actors need to be looked at separately. Terrorists have reached for missile weapons long ago, but some bolder attacks occurred not earlier than in the twenty-first century. On 22 November 2003, an Airbus A300 belonging to European Air Transport operating in DHL's fleet very shortly after its departure from Baghdad International Airport and heading to Bahrain was hit with a surface-to-air missile used by fighters allied with Saddam Hussain. Despite some damage suffered by the jet, the pilots landed safely back in Baghdad and there were no fatalities.[107]

So far, no international convention treats an offence of shutting down an aircraft separately from other offences, but rather includes them in a common category with other offences related to damaging or destroying an aircraft. A good example is the already mentioned Beijing Convention, which stipulates in Article 1(b) that a person commits an offence when one "destroys an aircraft in service or causes damage to such an aircraft which renders it incapable of flight or which is likely to endanger its safety in flight."[108] Here, by "in flight" one should understand the period at "any time from the moment when all [...] external doors [of an aircraft] are closed following embarkation until the moment when any such door is opened for disembarkation" in accordance with Article 2(a) of the Convention. The term "in service" is interpreted in the same way as it was explained previously in this publication.

The solution presented in the provision should be well-rated, as it criminalises all kinds of attacks that may damage or destroy an aircraft, or endanger its safety, regardless of their nature. A potential terrorist, to be held accountable, would use any kind of weapon with the intent of hitting an aeroplane. Therefore, the said provision would also apply in relation to attacks with specific types of armaments.

---

107 M. Osiecki, "Shooting down civil aircraft in the light of Sovereignty in the Airspace", Sociology Study, Vol. 6(6) 2016, p. 397.

108 Convention on the Suppression of Unlawful Acts Relating to International Civil Aviation, done at Beijing, 10th September, 2010, ICAO Doc. 9960, art. 1(b).

e) Destruction of airport infrastructure

Not only were aeroplanes targeted by aerial terrorism, more and more frequently perpetrators have been performing assaults at airport areas. Such an attack gives a terrorist some advantages. First of all, airport terminals, especially departure halls, are more easily accessible than aircraft themselves. Virtually every person may enter the premises of an airport without any prior checks if no extraordinary circumstances occur (for instance, restrictions related to an epidemic). Secondly, large international airports are usually crowded with people of varied nationalities; thus, in case of an attack, media attention is at stake. The sheer fact that a paralysis in traffic caused by an attack usually disrupts the normal functioning of air traffic makes an airport an even more attractive target for terrorists, which has unfortunately been proven in the recent years.

Since the 1970s, international airports across the globe have been become crime scenes of numerous bombings. Some of the most remarkable attacks happened at Rome Fiumicino Airport in 1973[109], Paris-Orly Airport in 1983, Moscow-Domodedovo Airport in 2011 and Brussels National Airport in 2016. Several international organisations, including ICAO, the Council of Europe, or the European Union, concerned with the emerging threat, enacted new legal provisions related to juridical protection of passengers travelling through airports. Again, the most relevant regulations can be found in the Beijing Convention in Article 1 paragraph 2(a), to quote: "act of violence against a person at an airport serving international civil aviation which causes or is likely to cause serious injury or death."[110] Similarly, a person commits an offence, if one "(b) destroys or seriously damages the facilities of an airport serving international civil aviation or aircraft not in service located thereon or disrupts the services of the airport."[111] All of those acts are crimes if committed with any kind of substance, device, or weapon. From the structure of this provision one can conclude that a protection predicted thereby is extensive. First of all, only an attack conducted by an armed person (using a device, substance or weapon) might be criminalised. Therefore, one could understand that only acts of physical violence are criminalised, as no provision of the Beijing Convention rates the threat of

109 Aviation Safety Network database: https://aviation-safety.net/database/record.php?id=19731217-3(9 March 2021).

110 Convention on the Suppression of Unlawful Acts Relating to International Civil Aviation, done at Beijing, 10th September, 2010, ICAO Doc. 9960, art. 1 paragraph 2(a)

111 Convention on the Suppression of Unlawful Acts Relating to International Civil Aviation, done at Beijing, 10th September, 2010, ICAO Doc. 9960, art. 1 paragraph 2(b).

using violence as an offence. Moreover, violence should be directed against a person – merely destroying property or killing an animal, even intentionally, is exempted as an offence. Nevertheless, it is problematic to define "the airport" itself, as no convention related to civil aviation explains the term. However, both the Chicago Convention and its Annexes define the word "aerodrome" multiple times and this word might be understood synonymously with "airport".[112] The definition of "aerodrome" used, *inter alia* in Annex 14 seems to be adequate also for the term "airport" and reads as follows: "a defined area on land or water (including any buildings, installations and equipment) intended to be used either wholly or in part for the arrival, departure and surface movement of aircraft."[113] Again, the structure of the provision extensively protects the passengers, regardless of airport size, its actual ownership (private or public), or purpose (permanent or seasonal), acts of terrorism should be criminalised. Only one condition applies here: an airport should serve international civil aviation. It then automatically excludes airports licensed for serving only domestic (as opposed to international) flights.[114] The legislator here leaves some freedom for state parties in regulating the issue of responsibility for crimes committed at domestic airports, which may be regarded as a single limitation to protection of passengers against terrorism. However, as it was mentioned previously, terrorism bears strong international notionw and domestic flights are rarely targeted. In order for states or international organisations to undertake particular measures, terrorist actions gain more media coverage, when an international airport is attacked and, in effect, people of multiple nationalities die. Thus, the Beijing Convention mostly complies with the necessity of juridical protection against terrorism.

Additionally, the said provision does prohibit acts that would damage or destroy an aircraft not in service stored at an airport or those deeds that would only disrupt the airport's services. Wide protection is visible here as well, whereas the provisions of the Beijing Protocol and the Beijing Convention analysed in previous sub-chapters limit the definition of an offence to acts committed against aircraft being in service or in flight at the time of committing the offence, Article 1 paragraph 2 of the Convention, in turn, bridges the gap. It incurs responsibility of those who perform attacks on aircraft not in flight or service, but still located

112 M. Żylicz, Prawo lotnicze, p. 222. "Airports", according to the Convention should be only distinguished from "landing areas" which is stipulated in its Article 37(b).

113 Annex 14 to Convention on International Civil Aviation, signed in Chicago, 7 December 1944 – Aerodromes, Vol. 1, Fifth edition, art. 1.1.

114 See M. Żylicz, Prawo lotnicze, p. 204.

within the airport area. It typically concerns aeroplanes being maintained or repaired.

f) *Cyberattacks in aviation*

Development of information technology and easier-than-ever access to information via the Internet makes the cyberspace vulnerable to a terrorist activity.[115] Although cyberattacks like hacking are not as frequent as the more "traditional" forms of terrorism so far, the risk of such acts slowly grows and the international community has already taken some steps to prevent them. Therefore, a brief overview of the phenomenon is provided in the subsequent paragraphs.

First of all, it needs to be discussed what cyberterrorism is and how to distinguish it from the regular form of terrorism. The topic has not been researched extensively by academics yet, but some worthy publications can be cited here.

P. Reambauville-Nicolle affirms that cyberterrorism constitutes the use of cybernetic attacks or threats thereof in order to create fear, with the intent of forcing states (i.e. governments) or societies to achieve certain objectives, mostly of political, religious or ideological nature.[116]

The author further enumerates some most typical forms of cyberterrorism: clandestine seizure of control of a system, denial of service providing, destruction or stealing of sensitive data, cracking (i.e. breaking software protection) and phreaking (i.e. sabotage or taking control over a telephone network).[117]

The Federal Bureau of Investigation, as a body responsible for preventing and investigating terrorist attacks in the United States, formed its own definition as well: "the premeditated, politically motivated attack against information, computer systems, computer programs, and data which results in violence against non-combatant targets by sub-national groups or clandestine agents."[118]

If one, in turn, studies the WordNet database, we would come across a short definition of cyberterrorism that reads as follows: "an assault on electronic communication networks."[119]

Therefore, a question may be posed concerning how complete and useful these definitions are for the purposes of researching cyberterrorism in aviation.

115 Similarly: T. R. Mockaitis, The "New" Terrorism, p. 37
116 P. Rembauville-Nicolle, L'effectivité du droit, p. 37
117 P. Rembauville-Nicolle, L'effectivité du droit, p. 37.
118 R. Abeyratne, "Cyber terrorism and aviation – national and international responses", Journal of Transportation Security, Vol. 4(4) 2011, pp. 338-339
119 http://wordnetweb.princeton.edu/perl/webwn (9 March 2021).

The one published in the WordNet database provides a general view of the discussed term, but is definitely oversimplified, as it completely lacks the element of terrorism. As it has been discussed already, terrorism is a phenomenon featuring very particular traits [see the previous sub-chapter]. According to the definition in WordNet, cyberterrorism may include any kind of assault directed against electronic communication networks. Therefore, such a definition may serve as a basis for understanding the nature of cyberterrorism, but plays little role in research due to its inaccuracy.

On the contrary, the considerations of Reambauville-Nicolle depict the problem much more accurately. The definition presented by her contains most elements characteristic for terrorism *in genere* and adapts it to the cybernetic environment. It is then perfect to use this definition when conducting any research on the topic.

One cannot argue the value of the approach provided by the FBI. The definition mostly focuses on the subject of an attack (i.e. information, computer systems, computer programs, data) and offenders (i.e. sub-national or clandestine agents), with a less significant concentration on purely terrorist traits of such attacks. In consequence, that definition should be treated as having a rather working or operational purpose and being intended for FBI officers and agents, whose job is to pursue offenders and identifying targets, and is only loosely related with research. Nevertheless, the definition also has a practical nature as in fact, most offenders are clandestine agents or members of sub-national groups, mostly of terrorist character.

As we can see from the definition built by Reambauville-Nicolle, forms of cyberterrorism are numerous and can also target civil aviation. The potential attacks may include hacking entire air traffic systems, interfering with radio communications, or as it has been already mentioned, cyber hijacking. Some of the recently published reports in the United States only prove that argument.

In 2016, an experiment prepared and conducted by American authorities exposed that the menace of cyber hijackings would be a fact in the not-too-distant future. On 19 September, a Boeing 757 jet was successfully hacked and remotely diverted to land in Atlantic City, New Jersey. The official report on that was issued in November 2017 by the US Department of Homeland Security.[120] Although the whole operation was planned in advance, it served one important

120 P. Paganini, "DHS – Tests demonstrate Boeing 757 airplanes vulnerable to hacking", Security Affairs, 13 November 2017; (9 December 2020) https://securityaffairs.co/wordpress/65463/hacking/dhs-boeing-757-hacking.html

purpose: to prove that airliners are now vulnerable to skyjacking with the usage of technological methods. With the ongoing technological development and state-of-the-art devices, terrorist networks would be able to acquire access to modern weapons or instruments that would help them in attacking aeroplanes without even touching them. The whole project proved that creating a system of protection against cyberterrorism is urgent.

Although very few international conventions deal with cyberterrorism, sector treaties related to protection of civil aviation, such as the Beijing Convention and Beijing Protocol mentioned in this publication many times, contain appropriate provisions. One of the offences enumerated in the Convention (in Article 1 paragraph 1(d)) is the destruction of or damage to air navigation facilities or interference with their operation likely to endanger the safety of an aircraft in flight. Albeit the provision does not expressly refer to cyberterrorism, it is the closest possible of all the existing documents. "Air navigation facilities" should be interpreted rather widely – a definition functioning in the Convention itself might be helpful here, as Article 2(c) stipulates that "[a]ir navigation facilities include signals, data, information or systems necessary for the navigation of the aircraft."[121] Under the scope of air navigation facilities fall countless electronic devices the operation of which might be disrupted or damaged by external factors including human interference. Likewise, such activities, if they objectively result in endangering the safety of an aircraft, might be rated as a crime. R. Abeyratne expresses his distress regarding the wording of the provision suggesting that the moment of commission of such an offence is limited only to the period when an aircraft is "in flight" (from the moment when all its external doors are closed after embarkation until the moment when any door is open for disembarkation) and, consequently, such a solution automatically exonerates all acts affecting an aeroplane when passengers are still in the process of boarding the plane, including a hacking of the on-board computers in the cockpit during pre-flight checks.[122] However, this concern is rather misplaced here. The Convention, as Abeyratne noticed correctly, uses the expression "in flight" more in reference to the time when the aircraft itself is put in danger, not the moment when a destructive or damaging action is performed. It is imaginable that a particular device or

121 Convention on the Suppression of Unlawful Acts Relating to International Civil Aviation, ICAO Doc. 9960, art. 2(c).

122 See more: R. Abeyratne, "Cyber terrorism and aviation", p. 137, R. Abeyratne, "Ethiopian airlines hijacking - the international perspective", Journal of Transportation Security, 7/2014, pp. 195.

element of the navigation system could be sabotaged by a terrorist even before an aeroplane is prepared for a flight, but the interference caused affects the safety of an aircraft later on, once it is in flight. Therefore, to criminalise interfering with air navigation systems, the precise time of committing the act itself seems to be irrelevant.

The potential consequences of such a cyberattack would be catastrophic. Jamming the ILS system or creating intensive static in radio communication would make the crew break stray from the planned route, which, especially at night, might lead to flying off-course and finally crashing. It is even more dangerous as a cyberterrorist may remain anonymous and difficult to detect, which makes it challenging to pursue such a criminal.[123]

g) Usage of specific types of weapons (e.g. biological, nuclear or chemical)

The problem of airliners as potential targets of innovative types of weapons, or as means of transport used for their covert transport, has been an issue for aviation security experts for many years. The aeroplane itself is a very convenient means in the process of spreading toxic chemicals and biological substances that, in large amounts, may cause death or serious injury to a vast number of people, animals or to the natural environment. When a substance is placed on board of an airliner, it can already poison or infect the passengers, but the consequences would be even worse when displaced in an international airport, which is a gathering of thousands of people flying to various destinations all over the world, causing the toxic substances to spread even further.[124] The scale of possible transfer of biological agents by aeroplanes was clearly seen during the COVID-19 pandemic, as the virus was spread from China to other countries on all inhabited continents mainly through international air travel.

When it comes to nuclear weapons, a civil airliner can be both a tool used to spread nuclear waste or a carrier of a bomb to be detonated later.

Just like in the other cases of innovative forms of attacks, also here a legal definition, along with obligation of criminalisation is present in Beijing Convention. Three consecutive provisions, namely article 1 paragraph 1(g), (h) and (i) are dedicated to BCN weapons. They state as follows:

Any person commits an offence if that person unlawfully and intentionally:

---

123 R. Abeyratne, Ethopian airlines, p. 135.

124 P. Reambauville-Nicolle, L'effectivité du droit, pp. 38-39.

(g) releases or discharges from an aircraft in service any BCN weapon or explosive, radioactive, or similar substances in a manner that causes or is likely to cause death, serious bodily injury or serious damage to property or the environment; or
(h) uses against or on board an aircraft in service any BCN weapon or explosive, radioactive, or similar substances in a manner that causes or is likely to cause death, serious bodily injury or serious damage to property or the environment; or
(i) transports, causes to be transported, or facilitates the transport of, on board an aircraft [specific kinds of weapons, substances or devices].

It is vital to admit here that this is the first existing regulation of crimes linked to BCN in the aviation sector convention. What is more, it is quite extensive, as the provisions stipulate that any kind of release or discharge of a BCN weapon, regardless if performed from an aircraft or on board one, is considered an offence. In fact, the sole act of transporting or facilitating the transportation of such arms is criminalised.[125] The cited provision subsequently enumerates all kinds of BCN weapons that are forbidden from being carried onboard of an aircraft.

The international community's efforts to prevent the release of BCN weapons have reasonably affected the civil aviation sector. Spreading BCN weapons by air transport might become an easier and a much more effective way of terrorising the world population than the usage of conventional weapons and, therefore, should be treated by states opposing terrorism as a problem of utmost importance.

h) Targeting passengers directly

Although aerial terrorism activities are focused on attacks against an aircraft or airport structures, assaults conducted exclusively against people on board of aeroplanes, that is: the passengers or the crew, should not be omitted here. Again, relevant regulations can be found in the Beijing Convention in Article 1 paragraph 2(a) stipulates that "Any person commits an offence if that person unlawfully and intentionally performs an act of violence against a person on board an aircraft in flight if that act is likely to endanger the safety of that aircraft."

---

125 The structure of that provision is controversial, as many states are reluctant to ratify the Beijing Convention on the grounds that their airlines would be declared guilty if they transport BCN weapons or explosives taken by passengers on board while unaware of them being illegally carried on board. That statement, however, seems to be non-convincing. Under the Convention's provisions, only those acts that are committed intentionally are regarded are regarded as an offence. Therefore, carrying BCN weapons or explosives by perpetrators when the airline is unaware would not incur criminal liability.

That provision has a general scope and introduces criminalisation of any act conducted against any person present on board an of aircraft (i.e. a passenger, a crew member, a sky marshal), but only if an aircraft is in flight. Thus, when an aeroplane is not yet airborne, a perpetrator would incur responsibility, but not on the basis of the said provision. Furthermore, such an act needs to jeopardise the safety of an aircraft. Here, the possibilities for a terrorist are limited. A typical situation would be murdering of one of pilots.

As it has already been mentioned if such an offence is to be classified as "terrorist", it should fulfil certain criteria (see sub-chapter 1.1.).[126] Whenever violence and unlawfulness is applicable, others specific motives affecting a particular entity (a state or an international organisation) and the spread of fear shall be discussed. First of all, the perpetrator needs to be motivated by an ideological, political or religious reason, as mentioned before. An aggressive passenger who hits the captain approaching him in order to calm them down would not by any means be considered a terrorist. As for the next element, targeting entities such as states or international organisations one could easily imagine a situation in which an aircraft carrying important state personnel or members of government is attacked. Thus, it might definitely have a significant meaning for the policy of a given state. In other cases, assessing if a given deed is terrorist in nature is strongly dependent on circumstances. If a person is attacked by a member of a terrorist group, known for demonstrating hatred towards the Western Civilisation or particular states, then the offender would be regarded as a terrorist. Finally, the spread of fear through society is usually achieved when news about an attack is broadcast. In addition, if the wounded or killed person is famous or widely respected, the effect is amplified even further.

Terrorist attacks involving persons on board that are excluded from the scope of Article 1 paragraph 2(a) of the Beijing Convention ought to be looked at separately. A good example may be taking hostages. During an aircraft hijacking, passengers are often treated as hostages, but neither the safety of an aircraft nor machinery necessary for flight operation is endangered (when, as it was in the

---

126 The Council of Europe's Convention on the Prevention of Terrorism done at Warsaw, 16 May 2005 simplifies the approach and treats all offences featured in international treaties mentioned in the relevant Appendix (including the Montreal Convention) as "terrorist", but only for the purposes of the Council of Europe Convention applying common solutions (concerning jurisdiction, extradition etc.) for enumerated offences.

case of Air France 8969, the plane remains on the tarmac).[127] In such circumstances, the perpetrators would incur responsibility on the basis of other provisions than those present in the Convention.

The above study shows the multiplicity of aspects of aerial terrorism and how we can define them on the basis of existing international legal regulations. The catalogue of potential attempts is not by any means exhaustive as it is quite probable that in the upcoming years, due to technological development and easier access to as yet unknown weapons, terrorists will invent new forms of attacks against the civil aviation. At this point, it would be fair to affirm that those really influencing the system of combat against aerial terrorism are not states, or international organisations, but terrorists themselves. The majority of the offences described in various aviation conventions are those that have already been committed or are of a higher risk of taking place in the near future.

It seems rather grim that civil aviation and terrorism exist in a certain system. The fact that aeroplanes remain a symbol of human development and progress in technology attracts terrorist offenders who want to partake in the "war against the Western Civilisation." It is thus evident that as long as humanity continues to accept civil aviation as a means of transport and it remains to be a symbol of internationalism, the terrorist threat will not go dormant.

1.4. Use of force in response to terrorism

The creators of the Chicago Convention prioritized the peaceful development of civil aviation, which is expressed even in the document's Preamble. It underlines the necessity of civil aviation for the creation and preservation of friendship and understanding between nations. But, at the same time, it emphasizes that abuse of civil aviation may become a threat to public security. Also brought forth is the importance of cooperation between nations upon which peace of the world depends. Such statements only confirm the main principles of the United Nations, which in its Charter states its aim to "maintain international peace and security, and to that end: to take effective collective measures for the prevention and removal of threats to the peace."[128]

---

127 Air France 8969 was hijacked by a group of Algerian mujaheddins who seized the machine when it was still standing on the tarmac at Algiers Airport. Not all doors were closed following embarkation, so the plane was not considered to be "in flight".

128 Charter of the United Nations, United Nations Treaty Series, art. 1.

The evolution of global terrorism strongly influenced the approach to use force in international relations. Back in the 1990s, the United Nations General Assembly was, in its resolutions, condemning terrorist activities, but it stressed the importance of fighting against its causes, including human rights abuses, persecution of national groups, and similar issues. In the following years, the centre of gravity in those resolutions shifted into combatting terrorism and ensuring effectiveness of measures against it.[129] This tendency was based on the increasing brutality of terrorist attacks and more bold methods used by perpetrators. As a result of the 11 September attacks, the discussion focused on yet another aspect: the use of force against terrorists.

1.4.1. Classical approach to the fight against terrorism

Over the years, the fight against aerial terrorism has primarily been a domain of internal enforcement services.[130] That tendency is reflected by the structure of sector conventions dealing with acts of unlawful interference. The Tokyo, Hague, Montreal and Beijing Conventions all regulate persecution of offenders, jurisdiction of states (mainly criminal), and extradition [to be discussed in detail in the next chapter]. From a more practical point of view, the situation is identical. Hijacked aircraft were, upon landing, stormed and perpetrators were either killed or arrested. Analogically, terrorist networks responsible for bombings are pursued by intelligence agencies. Nowadays, the balance is shifting towards engagement of military forces. As a result, the rules applicable to the conflict are constantly derived from laws of war, rather than criminal law.[131] In parallel, the changing of the semantics behind the term "war on terror" from a metaphoric sense to a rather literal meaning occurs. Terrorism is often regarded as an asymmetrical conflict in which two parties are of a different nature.[132] A state is

129 M. Marcinko, ONZ, p. 53.

130 See more: T. Aleksandrowicz, "Zamach terrorystyczny w świetle prawa międzynarodowego: przestępstwo czy akt walki zbrojnej? Ius ad bellum a współczesne zagrożenia antyterrorystyczne – uwagi de lege lata i de lege ferenda", in: Prawo międzynarodowe – teraźniejszość, perspektywy, dylematy. Księga jubileuszowa Profesora Zdzisława Galickiego, eds. E. Mikos-Skuza, K. Myszona-Kostrzewa, J. Poczobut (Lex: Warsaw, 2013), p. 563.

131 E. A. Heinze, "The evolution of international law in light of the 'global War on Terror'", Review of International Studies, Vol. 37 2010, p. 1070.

132 E. A. Heinze, "The evolution of international law", p. 566, M. Lech, Ochrona prawna społeczności międzynarodowej, p. 23.

a more powerful opponent than terrorists, though terrorist organisations ones have resources enabling them to strike in disguise, omit their adversary's strong points and destroy the most vulnerable structures.[133] A good example may be aerial transport – not engaging in direct hostilities with a state, terrorists attack without a prior signal of warning an aircraft or airport premises and, at the same time, endanger the safety of passengers.

Such a solution (especially its legality) should be analysed on the basis of Article 2(4) of the UN Charter, establishing the renunciation of using force in international relations. Apart from three exemptions to the rule, no force might be employed on another state's territory. Those exemptions are the following: (a) an authorisation given by the Security Council, (b) a state acting in self-defence in response to an armed attack under Article 51 of the UN Charter, (c) a state against which force is used gives consent.[134]

1.4.2. Understanding the "use of force" in relation to terrorism

The world has been witnessing a progressive change in understanding the use of force. To present the topic in an accurate way, it is necessary to explain first how the "use of force" (expressed in Article 2(4) of the UN Charter) is related to an "armed attack," described in Article 51. J. Wouters and F. Naert notice that the usage of different terms in two separate provisions itself proves they are not of identical meaning. To achieve the level of an armed attack, the use of force must thus be of particular strength.[135] Then, a capturing or assassination of an important official or secret service agent by another state's forces on the former one's territory would hardly be regarded as an armed attack. It seems clear that engaging the military or any armed troops under a state's authority would absolutely be categorized as armed attack, even if operations are not being conducted exactly on its territory, but target another states' units; for instance, ships passing

133 T. Aleksandrowicz, "Zamach terrorystyczny", p. 566, after: M. Madej, Zagrożenia asymetryczne bezpieczeństwa państw obszaru transatlantyckiego, (PISM: Warsaw, 2007), pp. 41-47.

134 A. Szpak, Międzynarodowe prawo humanitarne (Wydawnictwo Naukowe Uniwersytetu Mikołaja Kopernika: Toruń, 2014), pp. 21-22.

135 C. Fijnaut, J. Wouters, F. Naert, Legal instruments in the Fight against International Terrorism, p. 430, after:
Y. Dinstein, War, Aggression and Self-Defence, Cambridge University Press, Cambridge 2001, pp. 173-174.

territorial waters (which was confirmed by an ICJ in *Corfu Channel* case).[136] There is a question of how such a situation can be relate to a self-defence.

Traditionally, it was perceived that an armed attack could have only been carried out by a state actor. In fact, Article 51 does not require it, but it is an exception to the rule expressed in article 2(4) of the UN Charter that deals with use of force between states.[137] A confirmation thereof can be found *inter alia* in Annex to UNGA's Resolution nr 3314 adopted on the 14 of December 1974. It says that "[a]ggression is the use of armed force by a state against the sovereignty, territorial integrity or political independence of another state, or in any other manner inconsistent with the Charter of the United Nations, […]."[138] In this provision there is no single mention of terrorism. As a result, a state that was assaulted by terrorists (so a non-state actor), even if it suffered a significant damage and lost many of its citizens, could not claim that it was "an armed attack" which automatically excluded the possibility of self-defence in such circumstances. One can easily imagine a situation in which a state A was attacked by terrorists and responded with an armed attack carried out on the territory of a state B, then state A breached international law, namely article 2(4) of the UN Charter, even if its act of retaliation was not directed against state B itself, but against a terrorist group that had previously assaulted state A and whose base was located within the territory of a state B.[139]

What is more, when invoking the right to self-defence, an attacked state should have respected certain principles. A. Cassese has formed a catalogue of the relevant ones: a forcible action has to be instant, overwhelming and leaving no choice of means and no moment for deliberation[140], use of force needs to be directed only in order to repel the aggression of another state, proportionality of

---

136 The court named the activity of People's Republic of Albania "use of force" in the judgement. Albania was protecting its territorial waters in 1946 to that extent it fired guns to some British ships passing through North Corfu Channel. See Corfu Channel case, Judgement of 9 April 1949: ICJ Reports 1949, p. 18.

137 C. Fijnaut, J. Wouters, F. Naert, Legal instruments in the Fight against International Terrorism, p. 431, after:
L. Condorelli, "Les Attentats du 11 Septembre et Leurs Suites: Où Va le Droit International?", RGDIP, Vol. 105/2001, p. 835.

138 United Nations General Assembly Resolution 3314, 14 December 1974.

139 C. Tams, "The Use of Force against Terrorists", The European Journal of International Law, Vol. 20 (2) 2009 p. 364.

140 The argument literally repeats a statement expressed in Caroline doctrine. See infra.

a retaliation needs to be preserved[141], use of force has to be terminated as soon as the hazard is ceases or when the Security Council takes appropriate measures and, last but not least, states taking part in hostilities must observe the rules of international humanitarian law.[142] That catalogue of relevant conditions, therefore, ensures that if a state struck by a terrorist attack (e.g. against civil aircraft) decides to retaliate, measures taken by the latter one are not overwhelmingly harmful to the attacker and comply with international law. A terrorist attack itself simply does not entail right of a victim state to strike back in any manner.

1.4.3. Change of perception

The viewpoint of international lawyers has drastically changed at the beginning of the twenty-first century, when the world was shocked by terrible attacks of 11 September – an event which was clearly unprecedented and fell outside the scope of international law of that time.[143] It is visible in particular in Resolutions 1368 and 1373 adopted by the UN Security Council shortly afterwards. The attack itself, as well as other similar deeds were declared to be "threat to international peace and security and the readiness was expressed to combat all forms of terrorism."[144] Therefore, the definition of an aggressor, upon the resolution has undergone a major transformation – to the scope of potential attacking entities used to entail only states and then terrorist organisations were included as well. Consequently, states have acquired a right to retaliate in case of a terrorist attack, which was impossible before.[145]

---

141 The criterion of proportionality is one of the least disputed in the concept of self-defence. As J. Wouters and F. Naert explain, self-defence should be necessary to repel the attack to which it is a response.
C. Fijnaut, J. Wouters, F. Naert, Legal instruments in the Fight against International Terrorism, p. 439, after: C. Gray, International Law and the Use of Force (Oxford University Press: Oxford, 2000), p. 106.

142 A. Cassese, "Terrorism is also Disrupting Some Crucial Legal Categories of International Law", European Journal of International Law, Vol. 12(5) 2001, p. 995.

143 C. Greenwood, "International law and the 'war against terrorism'", International Affairs, Vol. 78(2) 2002, p. 301.

144 United Nations Security Council Resolution 1368, 12th September 2001,
United Nations Security Council Resolution 1373, 28th September 2001.

145 J. Wouters and C. Naert managed to attribute the responsibility of attacks of 11th September to Taleban – the then governing regime of Afghanistan. Two options were taken into account: first one assuming that Al-Qaeda was a sort of organ acting on behalf of Taleban, an emanation thereof. In such circumstances, Al-Qaeda could have been treated as a government entity and acting in its capacity. But the research did not

A short overview of the new approach should be made here. At first, the target of retaliation needs to be stated precisely. An attacked state, apart from responding with force against a terrorist organisation itself, might also strike on the territory of a state where the terrorists have their main headquarters or bases of operation, or the state which is their haven.[146] It seems clear that for the application force, legal provisions and laws of war, relevant is only a retaliation performed on a territory of a state different than one attacked, as in internal enforcement measures it is domestic law that applies.[147]

Secondly, it is important to assess the moment of occurrence of self-defence. In a traditional interpretation of Article 51 of the Charter, a recourse to counter

---

prove that to be truthful. Another possibility was an attribution of a private conduct to a state. That would be the case if the overall control and particularly a control over a specific action was exercised. According to a report Responsibility for the Terrorist Atrocities in the United States, 11 September, 2001, prepared by the United Kingdom government, Osama bin Laden was closely allied with Taleban regime and was providing it with troops, financial support, training for military etc. In return, bin Laden had a guaranteed safe haven, permission to conduct operations and establish terrorist training camps. And although that report could be claimed as correct, it might not suffice to affirm "overall control" by Taleban over Al-Qaeda here.

R. Wolfrum and C. E. Philipp postulate another argument – a state (in this case – Afghanistan under Taleban rule) assists another state or non-state actor (Al-Qaeda) in violation of international law and that assistance is a necessary prerequisite for a violation in question. In any case, the global support for American operation against Taleban regime (Enduring Freedom) entitles to attribute Al-Qaeda's act to the state of Afghanistan. See C. Fijnaut, J. Wouters, F. Naert, pp. 456-458; R. Wolfrum, C. E. Philipp, "The Status of the Taliban: Their Obligations and Rights under International Law", Max Planck Yearbook of United Nations Law, Vol. 6 (2002), pp. 191-195.

146 T. Aleksandrowicz, "Zamach terrorystyczny", p. 571; after: J. Kranz, Wojna, pokój czy uspokajanie? współczesne dylematy użycia siły zbrojnej (Fundacja Centrum Stosunków Międzynarodowych: Warsaw, 2006), p. 38.

After attacks of 11 September, many governments have been evoking so-called unwilling or unable doctrine to somehow justify acts in self-defence against terrorist organisations on the territories of third states. Under that doctrine, state-victim may use force against non-state actor within territorial state as a retaliation for an armed attack, provided that the territorial state is unwilling or unable to prevent attacks of that non-state actor and does not give a state-victim a consent to use force in response (hence the name of the doctrine). See more: C. Martin, "Challenging and Refining the "Unwilling or Unable" Doctrine", Vanderbilt Journal of Transnational Law, Vol. 52 (387) 2019.

147 C. Tams, "The Use of Force against Terrorists", p. 362.

measures was eligible only in response to an attack which has already been realised, including terrorist attempts.[148] Currently, the doctrine is divided in the question of striking prior to actual assault, so-called "anticipatory self-defence"; however, in result of a general change of perception of self-defence's nature, the tendency is to accept such force measures, but only under certain conditions. The approach emerges from the so-called *Caroline* doctrine having its roots in 1837.[149] The doctrine is now fundamental for theories justifying anticipatory self-defence. Expert researchers, including Aleksandrowicz or Heinze, divide it into two categories: pre-emptive and preventive self-defence. Pre-emptive self-defence is undertaken when an expected attack is imminent or highly probable, and other measures cannot be exercised to deter it. Preventive self-defence is, in turn, the use of force not directed to eliminate an imminent danger but to make it impossible to take place in the future. Thus, in case of pre-emptive self-defence a state strikes when an attack is under way, whereas in preventive self-defence such a strike occurs even before a potential attack, so that it subsequently never occurs.[150] The word imminence is distinctive here and determines whether or not the use of force is eligible. William J. Haynes II, a General Counsel of the U.S. Department of Defence in office at that time drafted on 16 October 2002 a document to the Secretary of Defence explaining the idea of imminence in relation to terrorist attacks. He points out the statement of Nuremberg Tribunal that "preventive action in foreign territory" is justified in a face of an imminent attack.[151] Likewise, he refers to the text of National Security Strategy stating that

---

148 See more: C. Fijnaut, J. Wouters, F. Naert, Legal instruments in the Fight against International Terrorism, pp. 427-429.

149 During a rebellion against British rule by Canadians, an American steamer christened Caroline was destroyed by Britons, as the ship was intended to supply the rebels on a Canadian side of Niagara River. As a result of the incident, a US Secretary of State – Daniel Webster affirmed in a written communication that use of force in self-defence is genuine if the necessity of the resort to force was 'instant, overwhelming, and leaving no choice of means, and no moment for deliberation'. See more: E. A. Heinze, "The evolution of international law", p. 702, after: "Destruction of the "Caroline"", in: J. B. Moore, A Digest of International Law, 1 (Washington: Government Printing Office, 1906), pp. 409–14.

150 E. A. Heinze, "The evolution of international law", p. 1073.
T. Aleksandrowicz, "Zamach terrorystyczny", pp. 572-573.

151 W. Haynes, Info memo from 16 October 2002 for Secretary of Defense, in: *Legal Distinction Between Preemption, Preventive and Anticipatory Self-Defense*, Rumsfeld Papers. (9 March 2021) http://library.rumsfeld.com/doclib/sp/2564/2002-10-16%20from%20William%20Haynes%20re%20Legal%20Distinction%20Between%20Pre

"[…] international law recognised that nations need not suffer an attack before they can lawfully take action to defend themselves against forces that present an imminent danger of attack", at the same time reminding that according to NSS "imminent threat" must be adapted to "the capabilities and objectives of today's adversaries".[152] In another document, drafted on 2 August 2002, Haynes also explained, on the basis of the *Caroline* doctrine, what requirements should be fulfilled by such an anticipatory attack. They are the following: state recurring to use of force reasonably believes that an imminent terrorist attack shall occur, non-military remedies are inefficient, chances of significant harm would unreasonably grow if a delay of recourse is longer and proportionality of the response is preserved (which just repeats the general criterion applicable to recurrence of self-defence; see above).[153]

Then again, the element of imminence is at hand. That explains why international community, although mostly supportive of the concept of using pre-emptive self-defence, looks rather sceptically at its preventive form. Generally, there is much greater evidence of problems in regards to preventive attack, as an interested state should prove that in spite of no direct and imminent threat, an alleged aggressor's potent and policy indicate an inevitable future strike. A potential victim state should assess economic losses.[154]

The lack of imminence would then give additionally wide leeway for a state to perform a strike – hence controversies among the international community in relation to preventive self-defence. An unequivocal acceptance for such practice would push states to attack their enemies just on the basis of information provided by its intelligence service and not yet confirmed or if they conduct inconvenient or suspicious policy. On the other hand, as terrorist organisations similarly to states might be treated as aggressors, a preventive strike would weaken such a group before a subsequent attack. Usually, when a notorious organisation confessing its responsibility for multiple attacks is involved (for instance ISIS, Boko Haram or Al-Qaeda), the evidence of the aggressor's capabilities and enemy's policy is quite obvious. In general, the way of thinking among governments in regard to a possibility of a terrorist attack post 11 September does not allow for even the lowest margin of risk. That reflects the so-called "One Percent

---

emption,%20Preventive%20and%20Anticipatory%20Self-Defense.pdf#search="william haynes"

152 W. Haynes, Info memo.

153 W. Haynes, Info memo.

154 T. Aleksandrowicz, "Zamach terrorystyczny", p. 574.

Doctrine" established by Richard Chenney, Vice-President of the United States in George W. Bush office. Chenney himself said that "[i]f there's a 1% chance that Pakistani scientists are helping al-Qaeda build or develop a nuclear weapon, we have to treat it as a certainty in terms of our response. It's not about our analysis... It's about our response".[155] The conclusion is simple, the tolerable risk of a chance of terrorist attack precluding the option of preventive self-defence is close to 0%. Nevertheless, the preventive self-defence concept still arouses controversies and is far from being generally accepted.

1.4.4. "War on terror:" The perspective of civil aviation

Now, having studied most aspects of use of force in the light of "war on terror" one should assess the possibilities of a legal response to an attack targeting civil aviation.

Each aircraft, to be legally operated should have one and only one state of registry (a rule arising from Articles 17 and 18 of the Chicago Convention), which marks its nationality. Most experts agree that such an aircraft is a symbol of a state of registry and, therefore, needs to be treated quasi-territorially.[156] However, such an argument should not be interpreted too widely – the board of an aircraft is thus not a territory of a state of registry *per se*, but only an object of its effective jurisdiction.[157] Here, it generates a problematic issue. Such jurisdiction is unquestionable, when an aircraft flies over a territory of a state of registry. It arises from the fundamental rule of civil aviation, namely sovereignty in the airspace, confirmed by Article 1 of Chicago Convention. It stipulates that "[e]very state has a complete and exclusive sovereignty in the airspace over its territory."[158] Then, if an aircraft belonging to a particular state flew over its territory, an attack on it, e.g. hijacking followed by usage of the aircraft as a weapon,

---

155 C. Murphy, EU Counter-Terrorism Law, p. 11. This doctrine is also a main topic of the book titled „One Percent Doctrine" written by Pulitzer Award-winning author R. Suskind. See R. Suskind, The One Percent Doctrine. Deep Inside America's Pursuit of Its Enemies Since 9/11 (Simon & Schuster Paperbacks: New York, 2007).

156 M. Żylicz, Prawo lotnicze, p. 41, V. P. Cogliati-Bantz, Means of Transportation and Registration of Nationality: Transportation Registered by International Organizations (Routledge: London/New York, 2015), p. 27, after: B. Cheng, The Law of International Air Transport (Stevens: London, 1962), p. 110.

157 R. Bierzanek, J. Symonides, Prawo międzynarodowe publiczne (LexisNexis: Warsaw, 2005), p. 246.

158 Convention on International Civil Aviation, signed in Chicago, 7 December 1944 (hereafter "Chicago Convention"), art. 1.

would be treated as an assault on that state only. It would be problematic in case of a concurrent jurisdiction – when a state of registry is different from the one of the aircraft's current flyover. Then, jurisdiction of both states applies, in accordance with the principle of the sovereignty in the airspace, as well as nationality of an aircraft. As a result, a terrorist offence committed against an aircraft in such circumstances would be rated as an attack on both states.[159] Theoretically, in the case of conflict of jurisdiction, the one of state of flyover should prevail, but when at stake is a terrorist attack, still both would be involved, as, according to mentioned in previous sub-chapter UN resolutions, terrorism has become a threat to global security and therefore whole international community may react in collective self-defence measures. Similarly, it would be analogical in the case of an attack on airport serving civil aviation – although such a strike normally involves just one state on which territory it is located, an act treated as terrorist justifies a military response against its offenders.

The question of anticipatory self-defence is relevant in a sense that civil aviation is one of the most widely secured and monitored domains of life. Intelligence services and enforcement corps constantly gather information on potential targets and planned operations by terrorist organisations. Sometimes even accurate security control at the airport might reveal the threat; for example, explosives hidden in a luggage or guns smuggled in clothing. But even in such circumstances resorting to military actions might not be eligible. It goes without saying that detection of an attack under way would entitle a potential state-victim to react, but according to *Caroline* doctrine, an armed attack would be genuine only if the non-military measures were ineffective. In case of a prediction that a terrorist attack on civil aviation is being prepared, states usually undertake measures of enforcement, including arresting offenders or raiding their havens. In such a situation, there is no necessity to perform any military operation in order to prevent a single event if an effective pursuit is engaged.

On the other hand, aerial terrorism, just like other types of terrorism is in present times strongly related to large terrorist networks, like Al-Qaeda whose centres of operations are spread across the world. If then, under the UN Security Council resolutions, states are authorised to use the force against terrorist organisations, then military operations in the framework of anticipatory self-defence

---

159 See more: S. Schubber, Jurisdiction over Crimes on Board Aircraft (Martinus Nijhoff: The Hague, 1973), p. 53. The author does not refer to terrorist attack, but only to „crimes", as in 1973, when the book was published, discussion on state's rights in case of terrorist act was focused on criminal, and not military actions.

might be legitimate. As J. Haynes pointed out in his response to the Secretary of Defence, by decrypting the word "imminent" we should take into account the capabilities and objectives of adversaries. ISIS, Al-Qaeda or other similar organisations claimed responsibility for several attacks against civil aviation and that would be used as evidence for states interested in eliminating them. Consequently, military actions aimed at preventing further terrorist attacks conducted on the territories where such organisations operate would be perceived as lawful. For instance, currently acting Global Coalition against Daesh, formed in September 2014 leads missions in Iraq and Syria to eliminate ISIS and prevent the future attacks. As the number of allied partners therein reaches more than 70, we may see an acceptance of such a form of fight against terrorism.[160]

Another argument against a further delay potentially causing a significant harm, is strong in relation to civil aviation. Attacks involving an aircraft or airport infrastructure usually cause extensive damage and cost many people their health or even life. An effective preventive strike might save airlines' passengers and reduce the risk of losses.

Finally, the issue of proportionality shall be discussed. An attack carried out in retaliation should be proportional, or else it is disqualified from being self-defence.[161] Numerous definitions and interpretations of the term proportionality were provided, but still it has no single and unambiguous meaning which could be accepted. However, some authors, like D. Kretzmer argue that when

---

160 As for preventive self-defence, T. Aleksandrowicz, citing J. Kranz evokes criteria necessary to regard it lawful. Including therein is approval for action by Security Council or at least another international body representing interests of international community aiming at eliminating a potential threat, like NATO. In the case of fight against ISIS, a Coalition comprises of several international organisations representing the will of multiple states. Those are: European Union, Arab League, Interpol and NATO. See T. Aleksandrowicz, "Zamach terrorystyczny", p. 574-575; after: J. Kranz, Między wojną a pokojem, p. 152 and subs.

161 The literature dedicated to aerial terrorism published before 11 September, 2001 was often condemning any kind of military actions launched as a response to a terrorist attack, regardless of its magnitude. The military operation was just treated as disproportional and therefore contrary to customary international law and UN Charter provisions, which is confirmed inter alia by C. Emanuelli in Les moyens de prévention et de sanction en cas d'action illicite contre l'aviation civile internationale. The author tended to accept as proportional only sanctions affecting international trade or communication, rights of citizens and moral persons of another state, as well as capital. See C. Emanuelli, Les moyens de prévention et de sanction en cas d'action illicite contre l'aviation civile internationale (Editions A. Pedone: Paris, 1974), pp. 112-113.

assessing the proportionality, several points should be considered, including, but not limited to the nature and scale of the armed attack, the identity of those who carried it out, and the preceding relationship between the aggressors and the victim state.[162] Clearly, a counter measure does not reflect the eye for an eye concept[163], which is also sanctioned in regard to civil aviation – taking as an example a case of hijacking or shooting down an aircraft by terrorists, state of registry or holding sovereignty in the airspace has limited rights against the enemy's civil aircraft. Article 3 *bis* (a) of the Chicago Convention stipulates that "every state must refrain from resorting to the use of weapons against civil aircraft in flight and that, in case of interception, the lives of persons on board and the safety of aircraft must not be endangered."[164] Under the provision, even if aboard of civil aircraft belonging to a state sponsoring terrorism or sheltering terrorist groups, a member thereof is present, a victim state should refrain from using arms against such an aircraft. But still, the Convention prohibits the use of weapons, and not force, which gives states some leeway in reacting to an attack. If a victim state decides finally to attack a civil aircraft of its adversary, it may recourse to other form of usage of military force than weapons. That would be the case of advanced technology used to crack onboard computers, e.g. autopilot and directing an aeroplane to a demanded destination. Applying such a solution in a state of warfare would be a realistic possibility in the near future. In any case, if a state victim, applying self-defence decides to take measures against an aggressor's aircraft, then he needs to comply with point (b) of the Article 3 *bis*. It states that "every state, in the exercise of its sovereignty, is entitled to require the landing at some designated airport of a civil aircraft flying above its territory without authority or if there are reasonable grounds to conclude that it is being used for any purpose inconsistent with the aims of [the] Convention."[165]

Based on the evoked provisions, we can conclude that a state aiming at resorting to self-defence has limited rights in regards to its aggressor. The requirement of proportionality and the principles of the Chicago Convention mostly exclude the possibility of attacking a civil aircraft, even if a victim state itself lost or would lose an aircraft as a result of a terrorist attack. However, as the Chicago

---

162 D. Kretzmer, "The Inherent Right to Self-Defence and Proportionality in Jus Ad Bellum", The European Journal of International Law, Vol. 24 (1) 2013, p. 240.

163 C. Greenwood, "International law and the 'war against terrorism'", p. 314.

164 Chicago Convention, art. 3 bis (a).

165 Ibidem, art. 3 bis (b).

Convention does not regulate state aircraft (used for police, customs or military), a right to perform self-defence against them seems fully legitimate.

It should be clear that, not all offences against civil aviation are treated as terrorist; thus, if an attack has no traits of terrorism (e.g. hijacking of an aircraft by a pilot aiming to flee from his home country), then the question of aggression is irrelevant, and only jurisdiction in respect to other kinds of crimes is taken into account. In such circumstances, the question of jurisdiction is regulated by relevant provisions of sector conventions. In any case, apart from pursuing an offender, a victim state may resort to other forms or measures, including retortions against a state harbouring a perpetrator: temporary or permanent ban of flights between these states, suspension of providing facilitations vital for an aircraft, like flight information (e.g. on weather conditions), or decline of permission for technical stopovers, interdiction of a flight in the airspace of a victim state for aeroplanes registered in harbouring state.[166]

1.5. Role of state terrorism

1.5.1. Brief analysis

State terrorism is a term on which should be looked at slightly differently than the traditional form of terrorism analysed in the previous sections, mainly due to the fact that some traits by which terrorism is identified, are not relevant for state terrorism. Although the goals and methods of conduct are often nearly identical, the difference lies in the perpetrator themselves and, in consequence, the applicable law.

Some facts about the phenomenon of state terrorism have already been presented in the first sub-chapter dedicated to history of terrorism. It explained that through centuries, several governments were resorting to terror in order to impose their rule on society, taking France during Jacobin club regime, as one of the most remarkable examples. But even many years later, terror has been used as a tool by governments. In the twentieth century, the regimes of Adolph Hitler in Nazi Germany, or Joseph Stalin in the Soviet Union were strongly marked by terror, as they were all using violence and brutal methods in their internal policy.[167] The totalitarian authority

---

166 C. Emanuelli, Les moyens de prévention, p. 114.

167 T. R. Mockaitis, The "New" Terrorism, p. 4.

apparatus in those states resulted in thousands of civilian victims in mass murders.[168]

But one could ask what exactly state terrorism is and how it differs from traditional form of terrorism. Constructing a proper definition that would satisfy all states of the world and meet a general acceptance has been a daunting task. In short, according to A. Aust, this term can be used when referring to "a terrorist act committed by a state against another one or the latter's nationals [...], or widespread acts of cruelty committed by a state against its own nationals."[169] From this definition we can clearly see that a crucial (but not sole) difference between traditional, or (using more scientific terms) national, and state terrorism lies in the person of a perpetrator. As J. Lambert reasonably notices, acts of national terrorism can be committed by individuals, informal organisations or legal persons (and, therefore, calls it "bottom-up terrorism"), whereas state terrorism can be attributed only to state actors.[170]

Another element that separates both categories of terrorism is its legal status. As it has already been shown, a trait inseparably connected to national terrorism is that terrorist offences breach the law. Paradoxically, the practice of state terrorism usually performs a function of law-making itself. Terrorist states enact statues, or execute their powers thereby exercising normal state attributes. But they do take the form of mass arrests, killings, oppressive measures or intimidation of their own population or particular groups within.[171] Consequentially, in such states, the law in force becomes influenced by terrorist.

But, as it can be inferred from the definition above, a terrorist state may also take a violent action against another state, or its citizens. One could ask if such an act of violence would equally constitute use of force [discussed in the previous chapter]. An answer can be found in the argument of F. Staroushenko, a Soviet

---

168 See more on state terrorism in Soviet Union and Third Reich: A. Zalman, "Is State Terrorism Different than Terrorism?", ThoughtCo, 9 June 2017 (9 March 2021) https://www.thoughtco.com/definition-of-state-terrorism-3209371
I. Primoratz, State terrorism and Counterterrorism, Centre for Applied Philosophy and Public Ethics Working Paper 2002/3 (University of Melbourne: Melbourne, 2002), p. 7.

169 A. Aust, Handbook of International Law (Cambridge University Press: Cambridge, 2010), p. 265.

170 P. Van Krieken, Terrorism and the International Legal Order, p. 16, after: J. J. Lambert, Terrorism and Hostages in International Law (Grotius Publications Ltd.: Cambridge, 1992), pp. 178-179.

171 A. Oehmichen, Terrorism and Anti-Terror Legislation, p. 99.

jurist, presented during the International Law Association reunion in Paris in 1984. He claimed as follows:

> Theoretically, the distinguishing feature between state terrorism and aggression is that terrorism does not allow the use of armed forces but this is only a theory. State terrorism opens the way to the use of armed forces and thus poses a direct threat to the world peace. That is why it is so dangerous. Using the armed forces against another state's sovereignty, its territorial integrity and political independence – and being the first to do so – constitutes an act of aggression. Inflicting any "preventive" blows, without the Security Council sanctioning them, is also a crime. State terrorism is the shortest way to aggression, and very often it is a deliberate preparation for an act of aggression.[172]

F. Staroushenko accurately affirms that a difference between state terrorism and aggression has a rather theoretical significance. Though, we have already shown that an act of aggression implies involvement of armed forces, which stands in contrast to terrorism, a terrorist strike carried out either by a state itself, or entities under its control would provoke an attacked state to retaliate. Although this statement of F. Staroushenko was delivered long before the 11 September 2001 attacks, its importance has grown with time. Today, a terrorist attack of a certain magnitude would be considered an entitling resort to use self-defence by a victim state (as indicated in a previous sub-chapter) even if it is committed by a non-state actor. If a state is liable for that terrorist attack, then the right of self-defence is even solid. An act of self-defence may as well institute military operations, which might end in war. Thus, a claim that state terrorism is a threat to the world peace is a completely genuine one. Even more importantly, a terrorist attempt that can be attributed to a state constitutes a breach of international law.

1.5.2. Ensuring safety without infringing human rights

a) Preventing terrorism: Sources of duty

The duty to prevent acts of terrorism emanating from their territory is bestowed upon states by international law through legal instruments, judgements of judicature and Security Council resolutions. As V.-J. Proulx claims, it stems from the principle of sovereignty and is strongly related to obligation of due diligence in the field of terrorism. The author refers to the definition of due diligence after F. Dubuisson: "Due diligence constitutes a classical obligation under general international law and is construed as a corollary of sovereignty. It assumes that states shall, to the best of their ability, ensure that no activities injurious to foreign

---

172 International Law Association, Paris Reunion 1984, Report, pp. 168-169.

interests or aliens take root on territories under their jurisdiction or control."[173] This notion is quite general, as it encompasses all kinds of activities that are harmful to another state or its citizens, but also comprises terrorist acts. Simply speaking, by virtue of being a sovereign entity, a state has a duty to prevent terrorist acts that may emanate from its territories, which certainly include acts of state terrorism.

A confirmation of the aforementioned rule can be derived from *United States Diplomatic and Consular Staff in Tehran Case* (Iran vs. US). Iran, alleged by the US of infringing international law provisions, including Optional Protocols to the two Vienna Conventions of 1961 and 1963 on, respectively, Diplomatic and Consular Relations, and the 1955 Treaty of Amity, Economic Relations, and Consular Rights (between those two states) has violated its duties owned to its partner, *inter alia* by abstaining from taking any actions to put an end to the situation when American diplomatic staff were kept hostage in the American Embassy by Iranian agents.[174] Iran, exercising its jurisdiction in its territory, even openly accepted the occupation of Embassy by its nationals and confirmed seizure of its assets. It caused the Islamic Republic to be found liable for breach of international law. It is then clear that the state ignored its duties arising from due diligence rule by causing foreign nationals (in that case diplomatic personnel) to be injured on its territory.

Following attacks on 11 September, Security Council adopted many resolutions treating on prevention of terrorism by states, with particular stress on financing and giving safe haven for entities responsible for terrorism. The cornerstone document is an already evoked Resolution 1373 adopted on 18 September 2001 that consists of many relevant provisions [document shall be analysed thoroughly in sub-paragraph 2.3.2. section c)]. The following duties

---

173 V.-J. Proulx, Transnational Terrorism and State Accountability, p. 23. Earlier in his book, Proulx refers to a case Trail Smelter (United States vs. Canada). Although the judgement in the case was issued in 1941, long before the global discussion on modern terrorism crystallised, it is considered to be a landmark one in the topic. It was sentenced that activities carried out within one state's jurisdiction may not spill over and adversely affect the environment of third States. Many publicists postulate that this judgement gave a basis for provisions on prevention of terrorism, as it also covered contaminations caused by terrorist organisations. Nevertheless, that statement is controversial. See Trail Smelter Case (US vs. Canada) (1941), Reports of International Arbitral Awards, p. 1905.

174 United States Diplomatic and Consular Staff in Tehran Case, Judgement of 24 May, 1980: ICJ Reports 1980, para 90-92.

can be enumerated as the most relevant for the present study: to prevent and suppress any kind of financing of terrorist acts (Article 1(a)), to freeze all assets of persons committing or attempting to commit a terrorist act (Article 1(c)), to halt any support for entities involved in terrorist activities, including supply of weapons or providing training for recruits (Article 2(a)), to deny safe haven to those who finance, plan, support, or commit terrorist acts, or provide safe havens (Article 2(c)), to prevent movement of terrorists or terrorist groups through effective border controls (Article 2(g)).[175]

The Security Council should be praised here for the implementation of a concrete list of actions that are oriented at prevention of terrorism. The events of the last decades have shown that terrorist groups can conspire easily due to assistance offered by governments of supporting states and also receive substantial financing therefrom. In such circumstances, there can be no place for compromise – only imminent and complete suppression of all activities supporting terrorism would comply with a rule of terrorism prevention.

Joint efforts of international community delivered also a multitude of sector conventions dedicated to prevention of terrorism by states, including the Convention on the Marking of Plastic Explosives for the Purpose of Detection held in Montreal on 1 March 1991, the International Convention for the Suppression of the Financing of Terrorism taking place in New York on 10 January 2000, the International Convention for the Suppression of Acts of Nuclear Terrorism in New York on 14 September 2005, and many others. All of them comprise provisions imposing duties on state-parties to strengthen efforts to prevent terrorism [to be described more accurately in the subsequent chapter].[176]

b) Clash of rules of prevention with human rights protection

In similarity to a plethora of other principles existing in international law (or law in general), also the rule of preventing terrorism is not of an absolute character. The states do not have at hand an unlimited catalogue of measures that can be applied to repel a terrorist threat. Unsurprisingly, a system that secures the strictest limits thereto are human rights.[177]

---

175 United Nations Security Council Resolution 1373, 28 September 2001, art. 1-2.

176 A list of International Legal Instruments on Counter-Terrorism Measures can be viewed on the webpage of United Nations Office of Counter Terrorism: https://www.un.org/counterterrorism/international-legal-instruments (9 March 2021).

177 C. Fijnaut, J. Wouters, F. Naert, Legal instruments in the Fight against International Terrorism, p. 226.

A state enacting laws intended to prevent terrorism can quickly become itself a terrorist state if it does not respect human rights that it swore to protect. That problem brings up the question of the necessity of limiting freedom in order to safeguard freedom (from terrorist attacks). M. Marcinko points out that especially after the attacks from 11 September, 2001 the public opinion pressure and growing tensions in society influenced many governments to adapt provisions that, although primarily intended to prevent terrorism, in fact were repressive in regard to the political enemies and allowed stricter control of their own citizens.[178] That, in consequence, ignited an academic discussion on limits in measures aimed at repelling a terrorist threat.

As we noted earlier, states that are mostly vulnerable to terrorist attacks are those based on democratic values. Any kind of terrorist attack carried out in their territory becomes a sort of a test for its government which is supposed to check if it can keep its nationals safe without breaching the democratic principles and human rights. In that case, proportionality is the key. Human rights and measures to prevent terrorism have one thing in common: they are generally non-absolute.[179] The relation between both is accurately expressed in Universal Declaration of Human Rights, adopted by General Assembly of the UN in 1948, in its Article 29(2): "In the exercise of his rights and freedoms, everyone shall be

178 M. Marcinko, ONZ, p. 217.

179 The proportionality in limiting particular rights is evoked in nearly all legal instruments related to their protection. Charter of Fundamental Rights of the EU in its Article 52(2) stipulates that [r]ights recognised by [the] Charter which are based on the Community Treaties or the Treaty on European Union shall be exercised under the conditions and within the limits defined by those Treaties. (Charter of Fundamental Rights of the European Union (Official Journal of the European Union C 326/391, Article 18)).

In turn, European Convention on Human Rights says similarly in its Article 18: The restrictions permitted under this Convention to the said rights and freedoms shall not be applied for any purpose other than those for which they have been prescribed. (Convention for the Protection of Human Rights and Fundamental Freedoms done at Rome, 4 November 1950, Council of Europe Treaty Series, No. 005, Article 52(2)).

Another example is International Covenant on Civil and Political Rights, in whose Article 5(2) we read that [t]here shall be no restriction upon or derogation from any of the fundamental human rights recognized or existing in any state party to the present Covenant pursuant to law, conventions, regulations or custom on the pretext that the present Covenant does not recognize such rights or that it recognizes them to a lesser extent. (International Covenant on Civil and Political Rights, done at New York, 19 December 1966, United Nations Treaty Series, Vol. 999 Reg. 14668, Article 5(2)).

subject only to such limitations as are determined by law solely for the purpose of securing due recognition and respect for the rights and freedoms of others and of meeting the just requirements of morality, public order and the general welfare in a democratic society."[180]

That rule was further confirmed by the European Court of Human Rights in the *Klass vs. Germany* case whose background was the application of the provisions permitting state authorities the inspection of private e-mails and control of telephone calls in order to protect nationals against, *inter alia*, "imminent dangers" threatening the "free democratic constitutional order" and "the existence or the security" of the state. That system of surveillance was introduced in response to terrorist attacks committed by an organisation "Rote-Armee-Fraktion" (or "Red Army Faction"). The Court stressed that "[c]ontracting states [do not] enjoy an unlimited discretion to subject persons within their jurisdiction to secret surveillance. The Court, being aware of the danger such a law poses of undermining or even destroying democracy on the ground of defending it, affirms that the Contracting States may not, in the name of the struggle against espionage and terrorism, adopt whatever measures they deem appropriate."[181] Unfortunately, there is no universal prescription for all problems of balance between protection of human rights and prevention of terrorism. However, certain mechanism that would be helpful in assessing the proportionality can be derived from International Covenant on Civil and Political Rights (ICCPR) and European Convention of Human Rights (ECHR). Both instruments consist of provisions permitting contracting states to derogate from certain rights under given conditions. As for ECHR it is Article 15(1) that reads: "In time of war or other public emergency threatening the life of the nation any High Contracting Party may take measures derogating from its obligations under this Convention to the extent strictly required by the exigencies of the situation, provided that such measures are not inconsistent with other obligations under international law."

The ICCPR stipulates in turn in Article 4(1) as follows: "In time of public emergency which threatens the life of the nation and the existence of which is

180 United Nations General Assembly Resolution 217 A, 10 December 1948, Article 29(2).

181 European Court of Human Rights, Klass vs. Germany Case, 6 September 1978, Series A No. 28, para 49.

Further reading on case-law shaping the concept of state security can be found in: Council of Europe / European Court of Human Rights, National security and European case-law, 2013 (https://www.echr.coe.int/Documents/Research_report_national_security_ENG.pdf) (9 March 2021).

officially proclaimed, the state's parties to the present Covenant may take measures derogating from their obligations under the present Covenant to the extent strictly required by the exigencies of the situation, provided that such measures are not inconsistent with their other obligations under international law and do not involve discrimination solely on the ground of race, colour, sex, language, religion or social origin."

C. Michaelsen, citing S. Tierney, affirms that any state derogating from observance of human rights should satisfy two tests (related to proportionality of such derogation). The first one requires that exceptional circumstances of war or other public emergency would threaten the life of the citizens prevail over necessity to respect human rights (C. Michaelsen calls it "designation issue"). Secondly, applied measures are "strictly required by the existence of the situation (C. Michaelsen uses the term "interference issue").[182] Both issues shall be now more carefully examined.

As one can notice, none of the above provisions contains the expression "public emergency threatening the life of the nation". Helpful here in the interpretation thereof would be jurisprudence of ECtHR that took up the cause of Article 15 in several cases.[183] Michaelsen reasonably points out here, that due to the fact that both the Article 15(1) of the ECHR and Article 4(1) of the ICCPR have similar wording, the interpretative guidelines given by Commission would be perfectly applicable to both.[184]

In *Lawless vs. Ireland*, the ECtHR assumed that by "public emergency" should be understood "an exceptional situation of crisis or emergency which afflicts the

182 C. Michaelsen, "The Proportionality Principle in the Context of Anti-Terrorism Laws: An Inquiry into the Boundaries between Human Rights Law and Public Policy", in: Fresh Perspectives on the 'War on Terror', eds. M. Gani, P. Mathew (ANU E Press: Canberra, 2008), p. 112.

183 At that time, the cases reported by the Court were firstly examined on admissibility by the European Commission of Human Rights. It was a judicial tribunal established in 1954, whose main objective (besides deciding on admissibility of complaints submitted to the ECtHR) was overseeing friendly settlements and referring some cases to the Court itself. In 1998, due to reforms in the European human rights judicial system, the Commission ceased to exist and individuals can now pass their complaints to the ECtHR directly.
See https://ijrcenter.org/european-court-of-human-rights/ (9 March 2021).

184 C. Michaelsen, "The Proportionality Principle" p. 112.

whole population and constitutes a threat to the organised life of the community of which the community is composed."[185]

The issue of interference was also an object of interpretation by the ECtHR. The expression used in the Article 15(1) is the key here: "measures [...] to the extent strictly required by the exigencies of the situation". The Court in *Handyside vs. United Kingdom* found that the usage of expression "strictly required" in Article 15 signals that even higher degree of indispensability is considered in some other provisions of the ECHR (that feature phrases like "reasonableness" and "necessity") and, therefore, absolutely "strict proportionality is required.[186]

As it can be seen from the above study of derogation from human rights in applying measures of terrorism prevention, the requirements vested upon states in such process are strict and in theory do not allow to compromise too much for the sake of combat against terrorism. Those rules have even "stronger" applicability in European states, that, in case they sacrifice too much freedom of their nationals, may face litigation at the ECtHR.[187] However, as Oehmichen noticed, the post-11 September legislation adopted in many countries was, in fact, contrary to rule of law principle and in essence was restricting human rights to a large extent.[188]

Would that account for treating such states as "terrorist"? As one can remember from the definition given at the beginning of this chapter, a state might be considered terrorist if it *inter alia* commits widespread acts of cruelty against its own nationals. Undoubtedly, the practice of constant limiting of human rights (especially with ignorance of proportionality) would be rated as terrorist, if it is marked by real vileness. A mere introduction of a duty for airline passengers of providing additional data when booking a flight ticket in some period of time after a terrorist attempt would definitely not fall under the category of "a terrorist legislation". Such issues as ethnic separatism, extrajudicial sentencing, or total restriction of freedom of speech should be taken into consideration.[189]

---

185 C. Michaelsen, "The Proportionality Principle" p. 112, after: Lawless vs. Ireland Case, European Court of Human Rights, 1 July 1961, No. 3, para 28.

186 C. Michaelsen, "The Proportionality Principle" p. 113, after: Handyside vs. United Kingdom, European Court of Human Rights, 7 December 1976, para 48

187 Similarly: J. Monar, "The EU's approach post-September 11: global terrorism as a multidimensional law enforcement challenge", Cambridge Review of International Affairs, Vol. 20(2), p. 270.

188 A. Oehmichen, Terrorism and Anti-Terror Legislation, p.3.

189 A state practice declared as "terrorist" was inter alia policies against the ethnic minority of Uyghurs (consisting predominately of Muslims) in the western part of China by government authorities. See Asia-Pacific Center for Security Studies, Uyghur Muslim

1.5.3. State terrorism in civil aviation

As we illustrated in sub-chapter 1.3., there is a long catalogue of terrorist attacks on civil aviation. Unsurprisingly, all of them might also be carried out not only by terrorist groups, but also state actors. In fact, history has given many examples of attacks on civil aviation that were committed by states. Some of the most notorious include: shooting down of Korean Air 007 on its way from New York, US to Seoul, South Korea on September 1st, 1983 by Soviet fighters[190] [discussed in detail in a sub-chapter 1.3.3.(d)], shooting down of Iran Air 655 en route from Bandar Abbas, Iran to Dubai, UAE on 3 July 1988 by the American Navy.[191], bombing of Korean Air 858 performing a flight from Bangkok to Seoul-Gimpo Airport on 29 November 1987.[192]

Dozens of similar accidents can be enumerated. But a question needs to be asked if all of them have marks of state terrorism or are merely attacks without terrorist background. To answer that query, one needs to recall what are the main elements of terrorist act and match them with the definition of state terrorism, then compare to events presented above.

As it has been pointed out, there are 5 basic traits of a terrorist act: intentional use of violence or threat thereof, unlawfulness, aim of spreading fear among society, realisation of political or ideological goal and affecting a state or an international organisation. If any act distinguishes itself jointly by the presence of these elements, and is additionally attributed to a state that commits that act against another one, then without doubt it can be claimed that is is state terrorism.

Ethnic Separatism in Xinjiang, China, January 2008. Another example is (ironically) 2009 anti-terrorist law gravely restricting freedom of speech issued in Ethiopia. The act was a basis for arbitrary detentions of journalists and human rights activists in that country, which triggered the attention of the Reporters without Borders organisation. See Reporters without Borders, Anti-terrorism law among targets of Addis Ababa protest, 1 October 2013.

190 M. Osiecki, "Zestrzelenie samolotu", p. 102.

191 Aviation Safety Network database: https://aviation-safety.net/database/record.php?id=19880703-0 (19 July 2018). The Airbus A300 belonging to Iran Air was on a routine flight crossing the Strait of Hormuz having been at this time a battle place in a war between Iraq and Iran. US Navy units were also present on the waters and protecting allied ships. One of them, USS Vinceness, mistakenly identified IR665 as an enemy fighter jet and fired surface-to-air missile, ultimately destroying the aircraft. All 290 people on board were killed.

192 Aviation Safety Network database: https://aviation-safety.net/database/record.php?id=19871129-0 (9 March 2021).

In the history of civil aviation, the fine line between pure state terrorism and "a serious accident" was usually the first element: the intentional use of violence. If we take for example cases of KE 007 or IR 655 we would find out that in both of them weapons were certainly used by state authorities to shot down the targets (civil planes protected from attacks under international law), but their identity was mistakenly recognised. Of course, that does not justify the attacks, as in both events hundreds of people were killed, but we cannot treat them as state terrorism, as killing of innocent people was not an intention of states that commanded to pull the trigger (at least according to official reports). The governments that were hold accountable made unreasonable mistakes.

A contrario, we would consider a hijack, bombing, shooting down or other kinds of attacks as state terrorism, if we prove that they were carried out intentionally. Of course, that would be a problematic task, as states rarely publicly claim their responsibility. If one state wants to harm its enemy without revealing its identity, a carefully planned operation of attacking civil aircraft is far less risky option than engaging in open hostilities. Therefore, even if state employs mercenaries to sabotage the plane, plant a bomb thereon etc., it usually tries to keep their identity in secret, so that it would be harder for a victim to detect who is in fact responsible. Fortunately, there are relatively few accidents in civil aviation from the past that were clearly involving state terrorism, at least on the stage of execution of offence. States that support terrorism, usually provide clandestine financing or harbouring *post factum* that would in turn justify an armed attack carried out in its territory in retaliation [see previous sub-chapter].

1.6. Unmanned aerial vehicles: The future of terrorism (?)

1.6.1 UAV: Definition and role as a target of terrorism

Unmanned aerial vehicles (or UAVs) are by some considered to be a symbol of the future of aviation, both civil and military.[193] Already in common use are

193 In fact, the concept of unmanned flying units was being developed by the military many centuries ago. But those constructions were rather primitive, similar to today's kites. The interest in development of unmanned aerial vehicles boosted in the turn of the nineteenth and twentieth century in Europe and reached its highs during World War II. At this time, Nazi Germany was conducting works on an intelligent remotely controlled bomb called V-2 that was tested in Pas-de-Calais, France in 1943. The project was adopted by the Americans after the war for the purpose of developing their own UAV programme. See L. Hoppe, Le statut juridique des drones aéronefs non habités (Presses Universitaires d'Aix-Marseille: Aix-en-Provence), 2008, pp. 21-22.

some simple devices, like drones. However, advanced units like autonomous systems are becoming more and more popular among armies of some developed states. As for commercial aviation, the possibilities of wide usage of UAVs are rather related to the very distant future, but due to rapid progress in technological development, we should not ignore any potential opportunities that such machines would bring to the industry.[194]

Nevertheless, just like other technological gains, UAVs may also be dangerous tools in the hands of terrorists. Remote control, multi-functionality, the option of carrying arms and spy equipment make them an attractive target for terrorist groups seeking political objectives. We shall now analyse what should be understood by "UAVs" and what role might they play in aerial terrorism.

First of all, it is necessary to assess whether UAVs are relevant in the scope of "aerial terrorism". Crucially, already at the time of drafting the Chicago Convention, in the early 1940s, the international community was aware that unmanned vehicles would at some point appear in the skies. Thus, they dedicated several relevant provisions of the treaty to them. The Convention in Article 8 refers to "pilotless aircraft" and stipulates that they may fly in one state's airspace only on the basis of prior authorisation.

According to A. Lele and A. Mishra, by UAVs we may comprehend a powered, aerial vehicle that does not carry a human operator, uses aerodynamic forces to provide vehicle lift, can fly autonomously or be piloted remotely, can be expendable or recoverable, and can carry a lethal or non-lethal payload.[195] Thus, such a machine perfectly matches the definition of aircraft [see above], which is only confirmed by ICAO[196] and approved by many authors. EU also accepts that approach, which is reflected *inter alia* in Regulation (EU) 2018/1139 of the European Parliament and of the Council of 4 July 2018 on common rules in the field of civil aviation and establishing a European Union Aviation Safety Agency, and amending Regulations (EC) No 2111/2005, (EC) No 1008/2008, (EU) No 996/2010, (EU) No 376/2014 and Directives 2014/30/EU and 2014/53/EU of the European Parliament and of the Council, and repealing Regulations (EC) No

---

194 The usage of such technology is already widespread in military operations. See K. Kowalczewska, "Humanity in modern warfare, empathy and jus in bello", Security Dimensions. International & National Studies, no. 2 (12) 2014, pp. 198-199.

195 A. Lele, A. Mishra, "Aerial Terrorism and the Threat from Unmanned Aerial Vehicles", p. 61.

196 ICAO, Unmanned Aircraft Systems, ICAO Circular nr 328, para. 2.5. and 4.3 ICAO additionally provides its own, brief although precise definition of unmanned aircraft: An aircraft which is intended to operate with no pilot on board.

552/2004 and (EC) No 216/2008 of the European Parliament and of the Council and Council Regulation (EEC) No 3922/91 (hereafter referred to as "Regulation 2018/1139"). In Article 3 (a glossary) it defines "unmanned aircraft" as "any aircraft operating or designed to operate autonomously or to be piloted remotely without a pilot on board."[197]

As we can see from the above paragraph, UAVs, being aircraft in essence, might just like classical airliners become targets of aerial terrorism and in effect, sector conventions and other relevant provisions are applicable thereto. Due to the specificity of any UAV's system, they are particularly vulnerable to the following kinds of attack: hijacking, shooting down, cyberterrorism, and being used as a weapon.

1.6.2. Hijacking a UAV

UAVs constitute an attractive target of hijacking. A well-skilled hacker could take over control of a machine and use it according to his will.[198] As we showed in sub-chapter 1.3.3.(a), an American experiment conducted on a Boeing 757 proved that aircraft are vulnerable to hacking and remote controlling. Until July 2018 (the time when the Beijing Protocol came into force), virtually no protection from such offences was provided for UAVs on an international level. Only independent domestic legal systems would have then filled a gap here by criminalising the unlawful seizure of UAV via criminal codes. ICAO, concerned by that fact, also intervened in this regard, and by means of a Circular number 328 called all states for the protection of UAVs from acts of unlawful interference, including hacking, spoofing and other forms of interference or malicious hijack.[199] However, parallelly to other international organisations' unilateral acts,

---

197 Regulation (EU) 2018/1139 of the European Parliament and of the Council of 4 July 2018 on common rules in the field of civil aviation and establishing a European Union Aviation Safety Agency, and amending Regulations (EC) No 2111/2005, (EC) No 1008/2008, (EU) No 996/2010, (EU) No 376/2014 and Directives 2014/30/EU and 2014/53/EU of the European Parliament and of the Council, and repealing Regulations (EC) No 552/2004 and (EC) No 216/2008 of the European Parliament and of the Council and Council Regulation (EEC) No 3922/91 (hereafter referred to as "Regulation 2018/1139") (Official Journal of the European Union L 212/1), art. 3(30).

198 W. Wei, "You Can Hijack Nearly Any Drone Mid-flight Using This Tiny Gadget", The Hacker News, 27 October 2016. (9 March 2021) http://thehackernews.com/2016/10/how-to-hack-drone.html. The author reports about a device designed by J. Andersson able to hack drones and control them remotely.

199 ICAO, Unmanned Aircraft Systems, ICAO Circular no. 328, foreword and para. 5.36.

also the circular should have been treated as soft law and therefore non-binding for Member States of ICAO, but only creating some obligations of a political character. So, no criminalisation of hijacking an UAV in international law was present.

So, why does the Beijing Protocol drastically change the situation? As we explained many times before, it introduces the obligation of criminalisation of unlawful aircraft seizure by any technological means in Article II amending Article 1(1) of The Hague Convention. No sector treaty before protected aircraft from attacks involving technology. If then a particular unmanned aircraft is being hacked from a distance and programmed to fly differently in regard to primary itinerary, such an act would constitute an offence under the Protocol.

Separately we should analyse the situation in which an unmanned aircraft is being remotely controlled by an operator. A terrorist interested in seizing such a unit would force an operator to fly the machine in a particular way. Such a scenario is analogical to cases in which a hijacker approaches a cockpit and requests pilots to fly in a forced manner – therefore, provisions of The Hague Convention would be applicable. However, the treaty might be irrelevant still, as it establishes the criminalisation of only unlawful seizure when an aircraft is "in flight" according to the definition comprised in the Convention assuming that the flight begins when all external doors of the aircraft are closed following embarkation – as many of today used UAVs do not carry passengers or cargo, and due to being unmanned, even crew, there is no possibility of "embarkation". In consequence, unlawful seizure of an unmanned vehicle (either by technological means or force affecting the operator/controller) under The Hague Convention might not be even rated as an offence. In response then avoids risk of being controlled at the airport security zone and keeps being anonymous. However, an act of seizure by hacking *per se* is not yet regulated by enforceable law. Although The Hague Convention in its Article 1 prohibits the unlawful seizure of aircraft, the regulation is limited only to control take over by force, threat thereof, or intimidation of any form. Concerning situations in which UAV is seized by a hacker, we find more efficient solution in the Beijing Protocol, obliging to criminalise seizure occurring when aircraft is "in service" (Article V amending Article 3 paragraph 1 of The Hague Convention in relation to Article II amending Article 1 of Hague Convention).

The growing interest in the implementation of UAVs, not only in the military, constituted a strong *ratio legis* for the Beijing Protocol. As UAVs are doubtlessly rated as aircraft and due to their vulnerability to hijacking by technological means and oppression of operators, there is no pressing need of drafting a separate convention regulating the issue of hijacking UAVs, neither from representatives of the doctrine, nor from ICAO. The single problem that arises here is low number of parties to the Protocol. Although it does provide protection from hijacking UAVs on international level, until it is not ratified by most states of the world, its real significance in the matter is still quite weak.

Certainly, not all potential cases of hijacking an UAV would be presumed terrorist. Many unmanned units flyable for civil purposes are simple drones that are popular as toys or utilities. It is doubtful that such a machine, even if hijacked by a member of a terrorist group, would be viewed as a terrorist attack as we need to remember that the purpose for such an attack is spreading fear among society and feature violence. It is feasible, though, that an act of seizing an unmanned aircraft carrying, for example, dangerous goods, explosives, arms, or if conducted on the occasion of an important international event, like a UN General Assembly session, could be considered "terrorist". Nevertheless, in the latter case, such an aircraft would be considered military, and, in consequence excluded from the civil category.

1.6.3. Shooting down a UAV

Shooting down UAVs is a question of a more hypothetical character, as today no airline employs in its fleet unmanned aircraft and there are no such plans for the near future. As it was mentioned in the upper paragraph, in civil aviation widely used are rather smaller devices, of a marginal role in commercial transport. Logically, they constitute a less probable target for terrorist attacks, as a potential shooting down would cause less damage and lives than attack on airliner. But on the other hand, low-flying UAVs may become precious target for terrorist groups, due to easiness in tracking. On the level of international legislation, provisions of Beijing Convention seem to be sufficient for regulating the problem, as the definition of offence in its Article 1(b) perfectly matches the circumstances of shooting down UAV.

1.6.4. Cyber-attacks

Due to their sophisticated technology, UAVs are naturally vulnerable to cyber-attacks. Terrorist networks would opt for hacking systems of such unmanned aircraft especially if they are armed or carry military equipment. If a person breaches the internal system of the machine and takes over control, he may direct it to fire into a crowd or crash into a building causing extensive damage. A programmed unmanned aircraft vehicle might also be a valuable utility in the hands of a terrorist to assassinate heads of states, leaders of governments or other representatives of state authorities. Any kind of such act would not only violate

Article 1 paragraph 1(f) of Beijing Convention prohibiting usage of aircraft as a weapon, but also provisions of relevant criminal codes criminalising murder, causing harm etc.

The seriousness of threat that terrorist attacks involving UAVs may spread is well proved by the fact that already such incidents occurred at least several times in the past two decades. One of the most notable took place in Genoa, Italy during the G8 Summit on 21-22 July 2001. Terrorists aligned in Al-Qaeda under the command of Osama bin Laden planned to kill the then President of the United States, George W. Bush, along with other heads of states using remotely controlled vehicle carrying explosives.[200].

200 Other related accidents: In June 2002, Al Qaeda attempted to attack passenger a aircraft using a model aeroplane; in December 2002, the Palestinian Terrorist Group performed a strike on areas built up by the Israelis using small model aeroplanes charged with explosives; in March 2004 the Palestinian Extremist Group used UAVs carrying explosives to bomb Jewish settlements located in the Gaza Strip. See A. Lele, A. Mishra, "Aerial Terrorism and the Threat from Unmanned Aerial Vehicles", p. 62.

Chapter 2. Role of selected international organisations in the fight against aerial terrorism

2.1. Introduction

The growing threat from terrorist movements seen in previous and present century has shown that unilateral actions taken by states might be insufficient to effectively carry out the fight against terrorists. States of the world several times concentrated their efforts to challenge the threat on global level.

Aerial terrorism is of no exception here. Offences against civil aviation have been present on the black list of states for decades. Each single case of aircraft hijacking or bombing, attack on airport or attempt thereto was treated as a serious strike not only on an attacked state, but even on entire international community. Therefore, the balance of fight against air terrorism has been constantly shifting from individual states to international organisations, working both on a regional and a global level.

The role of some international organisations in the fight against aerial terrorism is not to be underestimated. Entities like ICAO, EU or NATO regularly include the issue in their discussion agendas and have many times drafted legal documents that would contribute to the improvement of protection of airline passengers from terrorists. This chapter is devoted to the discussion on such measures adopted by or under the auspices of selected international organisations.

2.2. The International Civil Aviation Organisation

It is difficult to analyse the legal framework of international acts devoted to the prevention of aerial terrorism without turning attention towards the International Civil Aviation Organisation. The creation of the ICAO was one of the goals of the international community, whose members participated in the drafting of the Chicago Convention. Upon its signature, the Provisional International Civil Aviation Organisation (or "PICAO") was formed and functioned until 4 April 1947, when the Convention entered into force after being ratified on the 26th.

In October of the same year, the ICAO was officially established and became a specialised agency of the UN linked to the ECOSOC.[1]

The role of the ICAO in relation to safety in the aerospace is expressed *inter alia* in Article 44 of the Chicago Convention:

- [E]nsure the safe and orderly growth of international civil aviation throughout the world [...];
- [m]eet the needs of the peoples of the world for safe, regular, efficient and economical air transport [...];
- [p]romote safety of flight in international air navigation.[2]

In order to assure the realisation of the aforementioned objectives, the ICAO has taken multiple initiatives oriented also at achieving the appropriate level of security in the skies. The organisation can be praised for having conducted countless seminars, trainings, or conferences devoted thereto, but above all, we should mention here the international conventions drafted under the auspices of the ICAO. They include the following acts: the Convention on Offences and Certain other Acts Committed on Board Aircraft, signed in Tokyo, on September 14th, 1963 (hereafter referred to as the "Tokyo Convention"); the Convention for the Suppression of the Unlawful Seizure of Aircraft signed in The Hague on 16 December 1970 (hereafter referred to as the "Hague Convention"); the Convention for the Suppression of Unlawful Acts against the Safety of Civil Aviation signed in Montreal on 23 September 1971 (hereafter referred to as the "Montreal Convention"); the Protocol for the Suppression of Unlawful Acts of Violence at Airports Serving International Civil Aviation, supplementary to the Convention for the Suppression of Unlawful Acts against the Safety of Civil Aviation signed in Montreal on 23 September 1971, signed in Montreal on 24 February 1988 (hereafter referred to as the "Montreal Protocol"); the Convention on the Suppression of Unlawful Acts Relating to the International Civil Aviation signed in Beijing on 10 September 2010 (the "Beijing Convention"); the Protocol Supplementary to the Convention for the Suppression of Unlawful Seizure of Aircraft signed in Beijing on 10 September 2010 (the "Beijing Protocol") and finally, the Protocol to Amend the Convention on Offences and Certain Other Acts Committed on Board Aircraft, signed in Montreal on 4 April 2014 (the "Montreal Protocol 2014").

1 https://www.icao.int/publications/pages/doc7300.aspx (9 March 2021).
2 Chicago Convention, art. 44.

All the aforementioned treaties form the core of the international criminal air law system, and are collectively also called the "Tokyo-Hague-Montreal-Beijing system." They shall be carefully examined in the subsequent pages of the present monograph in light of the problem of aerial terrorism.

2.2.1. Common issues

Before analysing the merits of the conventions separately, it is necessary to present several common issues.

First of all, we need to point out here that none of the treaties, neither in their titles nor their texts, use the word "terrorism", unlike in several other conventions. Tokyo-Hague-Montreal-Beijing system rather features definitions of particular offences against civil aviation [see sub-chapter 1.3.3.] and provides norms on their prosecution by contracting states.[3] It in fact means that the scope of those conventions is very wide; as we already explained, not all offences committed against civil aviation can be qualified as "terrorist", but only those that fulfil certain criteria [see sub-chapter 1.2.3.]. An aircraft hijacking, although doubtlessly an attack on civil aviation, might not be called "terrorist" if is not committed for particular purposes, does not aim to spread fear through society etc. In other words, all treaties forming the Tokyo-Hague-Montreal-Beijing system are relevant not only for aerial terrorist acts, but also other offences directed against civil aviation of non-terrorist nature (in general: criminal air law).[4]

---

3 See T. Aleksandrowicz, K. Liedel, Zwalczanie terroryzmu lotniczego, p. 29.

4 Most authors agree that the Tokyo-Hague-Montreal-Beijing system is relevant for discussion on universal jurisdiction – the concept of pursuing crimes that are directed against the whole international community, called delicta iuris gentium. According to that view, an offence and its persecution, to be qualified as delictum iuris gentium needs to be included in provisions of an international treaty. It is supported inter alia by S. Bazin, J. Walulik, or M. Żylicz. See S. Bazin, Le droit pénal de l'aviation civile, pp. 47-50, 110., J. Walulik, Pekińska reforma lotniczego prawa karnego, p. 39, M. Żylicz, Prawo lotnicze, p. 450.

Few others, like T. Ostropolski tend to attribute to universal jurisdiction only those crimes that are pursued under customary international law, whereas those that are featured in international treaties should rather be treated as existing under aut dedere aut iudicare, as it lacks the elements of "universalism" - international agreements are only binding for state-parties, and therefore usually do not form an object of interest of the entire international community. See T. Ostropolski, Zasada jurysdykcji uniwersalnej, pp. 65-68.

Secondly, the crucial part of each act deals with question of jurisdiction of states over particular offences. As P. Mendes de Leon reasonably points out, in civil aviation, having an "international character", there is a possibility of a clash of several states' competences over a particular event and therefore norms determining which state is entitled to exercise their jurisdiction are essential.[5] In the absence of such norms, it would be simply unclear which state is appropriate to establish legal proceedings when an offence against civil aviation occurs.

Based on the dominant factor in each situation, we can divide concepts of jurisdiction into the following categories:

1. classical jurisdiction competences:
(a) territorial theory: under that theory, state within whose aerospace or territory the offence was committed, has exclusive jurisdiction over it and therefore its national law will be applicable. That concept is historically the oldest one and refers directly to the principle of sovereignty in the aerospace expressed in article 1 of Chicago Convention. Certainly, according to this theory, the law of State of flyover would apply also when the offence was committed above its territorial waters.[6]
(b) nationality of aircraft theory: a state entitled to exercise its jurisdiction is the one in which the aircraft concerned is registered. Of course, that theory is taken into account only when an offence is committed on board the aircraft.[7] It is irrelevant when an airport is attacked.
(c) real interest theory[8]: crucial here is the assessment whether the fundamental interests of a particular state are infringed as a result of an offence. The expression "fundamental interests" should be interpreted narrowly and consists of public security or public order of a state-victim. But S. Bazin emphasizes here that states' interest may vary and therefore are usually assessed subjectively by them.[9]
(d) personal theory: in that case two possibilities are applicable – either a State of an offender's citizenship is relevant or the one of victim's nationality, regardless of what are the State of flyover or aircraft's registry. The theory has gained popularity in recent years, but eventually may become problematic, when victims represent many nationalities and in effect several States declare to be competent in the matter. In practice most

5 P. Mendes de Leon, Introduction to Air Law (Kluwer Law International: Alphen aan den Rijn, 2017), p. 488.
6 A. Meyer, Les infractions à bord des aéronefs. Examinées à la lumière du rapport du sous-comité du comité juridique de l'O.A.C.I., Revue Française du Droit Aérien, Vol. 4/1957, p. 306.
7 P. Mendes de Leon, Introduction to Air Law, p. 488.
8 P. Mendes de Leon uses the expression "mixed theory". See P. Medes de Leon, Introduction to Air Law, p. 488.
9 S. Bazin, Le droit pénal de l'aviation civile, 36.

commercial flights are very cosmopolitan and persons from multiple countries board their planes.

2. jurisdiction rights applicable uniquely to civil aviation (relevant only for attacks directed against aircraft, with exclusions of those targeting airport facilities)[10]:
(a) theory of the law of the state of last landing: this particular concept might seem quite logical, as the state of landing is usually the first to make contact with an offender and would immediately take them into custody and ultimately engage proceedings against him. Nevertheless, this theory might be of no use if an aircraft lands or crashes on terra mullius, like high seas or Antarctica, which, in case of terrorist attack might be probable.
(b) theory of the law of state of last departure: the most convenient from the perspective of perpetrator, as they would know, which jurisdiction would apply if they carry out an attack. If, for example they want to avoid the risk of death penalty, they would choose one of European Union countries as his point of departure, as all of them have it waived. Still, some serious disadvantages appear, like difficulties in repatriation of an offender into the place of origin if an aeroplane lands in a distant State or the one having tense relations with country of departure. And, as S. Bazin notices, usually a State of origin might not be interested in establishing its jurisdiction over events that occurred far away from it and barely affected its interests.[11]

The above-mentioned types of jurisdictions may be concurrent in particular cases or take mixed forms. However, the Tokyo-Hague-Montreal-Beijing system conventions are drafted also with the aim of assisting states in potential problems of establishing appropriate jurisdiction.

Finally, all of the presented treaties are relevant only to civil aviation and therefore are not applicable in cases of state aircraft, so those used in military, police or customs services.[12]

---

10 Those theories are different from upper ones in a way that we can only discuss about state of landing or state of departure in relation to civil aviation. Theories based on territorial, national, real or personal factors might be applicable to many other kinds of offences, including terrorist ones.

11 S. Bazin, Le droit pénal de l'aviation civile, p. 39.

12 It is of vital importance to mention that generally, the term "state aircraft" is used synonymously with "aircraft used in military, customs and police services" but a brief notice should be made on their differentiation. A basic provision dealing with the issue is Article 9 of the Chicago Convention stating that [a]ircraft used in military, customs and police services shall be deemed to be state aircraft. But the wording of this article does not indicate that only aircraft used in those services can be qualified as "state aircraft". In fact, states may use other kinds of aircraft, like aeroplanes normally used to commercial purpose, but leased for the government (which is a common practice). In other words, state aircraft is a wider category, consisting mostly of, but not uniquely, police, customs and military services aircraft. On the basis of that, we can conclude

What is necessary to mention here, each of the Tokyo-Hague-Montreal-Beijing system treaties uses some of presented above theories as a basis for its criminal jurisdiction rules. Generally, we can observe that later adopted treaties apply rules allowing wider range of States to establish their jurisdiction (which in practice might increase chances of delivering an offender before justice). Of course, a fact that certain jurisdiction theories are omitted in particular treaties does not mean that they are worthless – it should be noted that with lapse of time, States decide to modify the system of establishing jurisdiction to ensure that an offender is not left unpunished.

2.2.2. The Tokyo Convention

a) Circumstances of drafting

The Tokyo Convention was originally planned to be published as a treaty on the legal status of aircraft. The Legal Committee of ICAO, on its 9th session in Rio de Janeiro held from 25 August to 12 September 1953 formed to that end a subcommittee on the Legal Status of the Aircraft.[13] It convened several meetings in order to discuss potential content of future convention, but it was focusing mostly on civil law issues, like marriages on board aircraft, deaths, conclusion of contracts etc. But the growing number of hijackings in the late 1950s and early 1960s forced the Legal Committee to divert their focus to those matters in the convention as well. During their meeting in Rome in 1962, representatives of the United States and Venezuela addressed the problem, and the resolutions were included in the draft presented publicly on International Conference on Air Law that was held in Tokyo from 20 August to 14 September 1963.[14] After long discussions, on the last day of the conference, the participating states signed the

---

that the Tokyo-Hague-Montreal-Beijing system conventions can apply to some state aircraft, provided that they are not used in military, customs or police services. See N. M. Poulantzas, "Convention for the Suppression of Unlawful Seizure of Aircraft", p. 15, EUROCONTROL, Definition of State Aircraft, Decision of the Provisional Council session 11 on 12 July, 2001, Principle 1.

13 9th Session of the Legal Committee, Rio de Janeiro, 25 August to 12 September 1953. ICAO Doc 7450-LC/136, Vol. I, Minutes, p. XVIII, para 4(b).

14 E. McWhinney, Aerial Piracy, pp. 36-37.

Convention. But it took several years for it to enter into force. It has been in effect since 4 December 1969.[15]

b) *Scope of application*

Among all treaties forming the Tokyo-Hague-Montreal-Beijing system, the Tokyo Convention has the narrowest scope of application, which is seen through wording of its Article 1(1). It stipulates that "The convention shall apply in respect of:

> (a) offences against penal law;
> (b) acts which, whether or not they are offences, may or do jeopardise the safety of the aircraft or of persons or property therein or which jeopardise good order and discipline on board."[16] Further, stipulated is that the treaty's provisions shall only apply to acts done on board aircraft registered in any of state parties while that aircraft is in flight, or located on *terra nullius*.

We can see here that the authors of the Convention did not want to interfere with the domestic legal systems of state parties and did not define what should be regarded as an offence. However, the problem of aircraft hijacking was not completely omitted and in Article 11 (the single one present in the chapter entitled "Unlawful seizure of aircraft") a definition was given: "[unlawful commission] by force or threat thereof an act of interference, seizure, or other wrongful exercise of control of an aircraft in flight." If we compare it to the definitions functioning in the lately-adopted treaties, we can notice that the one present in the Tokyo Convention has, paradoxically, a wider scope, mostly because it qualifies an act as unlawful aircraft seizure when it happens "in flight", which, according to the Convention's Article 3(1), means "from the moment when power is applied for the purpose of take-off, until the moment when the landing run ends."[17] It effectively means that when the APU is running and passengers are still embarking the aeroplane, seizing the aircraft at that moment would be then fall within the scope of the Convention.[18] On the other hand, as the moment of being "in flight" ends with the landing run, an attempt to seize the control of aircraft afterwards,

---

15 Convention on Offences and Certain Other Acts Committed on Board Aircraft done at Tokyo, 14 September 1963, ICAO Doc 8364, list of parties; (https://www.icao.int/secretariat/legal/List%20of%20Parties/Tokyo_EN.pdf) (9 March 2021).

16 Convention on Offences and Certain Other Acts Committed on Board Aircraft done at Tokyo, 14 September 1963, ICAO Doc 8364, art. 1, para. 1.

17 Ibidem, art. 1, para. 3.

18 R. Abeyratne, Ethiopian Airlines hijacking..., p. 195.

e.g. when the plane has reached the gate and passengers are still on board, would be excluded. However, at the time when the Convention was being drafted, most hijackings occurred when aeroplanes were already airborne, so the definition might be seen as accurate for that period.

The Convention also stipulates that state parties shall take "all appropriate measures to restore control of the aircraft to its lawful commander or to preserve his control of the aircraft."[19]

c) *Jurisdiction*

The dominant jurisdiction principle under the Tokyo Convention is the nationality principle. Pursuant to its Article 3(1), a State competent to exercise jurisdiction is the one of aircraft's registration. However, exceptions to that are enumerated in Article 4, according to which, a state other than the state of registration may interfere in aircraft in flight to exercise its jurisdiction in the following cases:

> (a) the offence has effect on its territory;
> (b) the offence has been committed by or against its national or permanent resident;
> (c) the offence is against its security;
> (d) the offence consists of a breach of any rules or regulations relating to the flight or manoeuvre of aircraft in force therein;
> (e) the exercise of jurisdiction is necessary to ensure the observance of any obligation of such State under a multilateral international agreement.

In practice it means that the state where the aircraft is registered would be competent to initiate criminal proceedings against the perpetrator of the criminal act (including terrorists) or another act jeopardising the safety of an aircraft regardless of where the offence took place (aerospace of a different state, high seas etc.), but there are multiple possibilities that enable other states to establish their jurisdiction under Article 4. Point (b) itself expands the catalogue of interested States significantly. If, for example, some passengers on board are held hostage in exchange for ransom money from the government, and passengers represent different nationalities, their home countries may all decide to initiate proceedings against offenders.[20]

---

19 R. Abeyratne, Ethiopian Airlines hijacking..., art. 11, para. 1.

20 Important is to note here is that, like in other sector treaties, in the Tokyo Convention there is no priority given for a particular basis of jurisdiction. See M. Żylicz, Terroryzm lotniczy, Palestra 49/3-4 (2004), p. 127.

d) *Powers of the aircraft commander*

Article 6 of the Convention vests in the aircraft commander[21], crew members and even regular passengers' rights and duties that would ensure the safe continuation of flight or landing in case of occurrence of offence. The measures the aircraft commander may take are both of a preventative nature (taken when a person is about to commit an offence) and subsequent nature (after committing the actual offence) and may include restraining. However, on the basis of Article 5(2), they may react only to offences that occurred "at any time from the moment when all its external doors are closed following embarkation until the moment when any such door is opened for disembarkation." So, for the purposes of the powers of the aircraft commander, the definition of an "aircraft in flight" is slightly changed in comparison to the definition from Article 1(3) [see section b)]. Consequentially, when the power is applied for the purposes of take-off with the APU already running, but when the aeroplane doors remain open, the aircraft commander is not yet entitled to exercise their powers if it is apparent that a person is preparing to commit an offence. At that point, measures may only be taken by local enforcement services (e.g. the police).

There is no particular catalogue of measures, as the Convention only stipulates on purposes for aircraft commander's actions (paragraph 1 of the Article):

a) protection of the safety of aircraft, or persons or property therein;

---

21 The Tokyo Convention does not provide any definition of aircraft commander, neither do any other international air law documents. In turn, this expression is defined inter alia in the United States Code of Federal Regulations (hereafter "US CFR"). In Title 19, Chapter I, Part 122, Subpart A, Section 122.1, we read that an "aircraft commander" is any person serving on an aircraft who is in charge or has command of its operation and navigation. United States Code of Federal Regulations, Title 19, §122.1.
On an international level, Annexes to the Chicago Convention fill the gap and give the definition of "pilot-in-command", that would be assessed as synonymous to "aircraft commander". Annex 2 "Rules of the Air" stipulates that [pilot-in-command] is [t]he pilot designated by the operator, or in the case of general aviation, the owner, as being in command and charged with the safe conduct of a flight. In practice, on commercial flights, the aircraft commander status is assigned to the captain. Annex 2 to Convention on International Civil Aviation, done at Chicago, 7 December 1944 – Rules of the Air, Tenth Edition 2005, Chapter 1 .
Interestingly, for many years the powers of the aircraft commander, even those not relevant for offences on board, but for air traffic in general, were not precisely regulated by international law. See A. Knauth, The Aircraft Commander in International Law, Journal of Air Law and Commerce, Vol. 14(157) 1947.

b) maintenance of good order and discipline on board;
c) ability to deliver a person that committed or is about to commit an offence to competent authorities or to disembark that person.

What is more, provisions of the Convention only require the scope of measures be "reasonable", which entitles the aircraft commander to assess by themselves how they should react to offences or other acts on board.

Similar rights are vested in crew members and passengers. If the commander so requires, a crew member (e.g. a stewardess) may help in restraining the offender. In turn, passengers may only be requested, but never required by commander to help in restraining. What is more, crew members and passengers may take preventive measures against an offender if they have reasonable grounds to believe that it is necessary to protect the safety of aircraft, or the persons or property on board (Article 6 paragraph 2 of the Convention). That in practice means that every single person, after legally boarding any civil aircraft, *ipso iure* has the right to prevent an attack on the aircraft (including terrorist attempts) under certain conditions.

The wording of the subsequent articles indicates that the execution of power of restraint imposed on offender (or person that was about to commit an offence) should not last too long. In general, a person under restraint might be kept as such until the aircraft lands, except in three cases (enumerated in Article 7 paragraph 1): the aircraft lands in the territory of a state which is not a party to the Convention and its authorities refuse to permit disembarkation (if e.g. a person is a citizen of a state non-recognised by the landing state); or the aircraft makes a forced landing and the commander has no ability to deliver the person to the competent authorities (e.g. a plane performs a water landing in the territorial waters of a state far away from the coast); or a person under restraint agrees to be carried onward.

Under paragraph 2 of Article 7, before landing the plane, the aircraft commander should inform the authorities of the state of landing about the fact that a person on board is being restrained and provide the reasons.

Finally, Articles 8 and 9 discuss the duties of the aircraft commander regarding the disembarkation of an offender (or the person believed to have committed an offence on board the aircraft) upon landing or delivering them to the competent authorities. A mere disembarkation can only take place if the act committed by the offender was not necessarily an offence against penal law, but still jeopardised or may have jeopardised the order or discipline on board, or safety of aircraft or persons, or property on board. If an act was an offence, the commander must not merely disembark the perpetrator, but also deliver them to the authorities of the state of landing. Certainly, those powers are vested only in the aircraft commander and may not be exercised by an ordinary crew member or any of the passengers.

e) Rights and duties of states

The rights and duties of state parties to the Tokyo Convention are stated in Chapter V thereof and focus mostly on actions that states would undertake upon the landing of an aircraft with an offender on board.

Articles 12 and 13(1) impose on state parties a duty to allow the commander to disembark the offender or deliver them to the authorities. A specific solution is provided in case a person on board is suspected of having committed an act of unlawful aircraft seizure – they should be taken into custody or other relevant measures should be applied, at least until a reasonable time of initiating criminal or extradition proceedings against them. That obligation might be incurred by any of the state parties, not only the one of where the aircraft landed. Moreover, the state where the offender or aircraft hijacker was delivered should immediately launch a preliminary investigation of the offence, as well as notify the following entities about the detention of the offender or hijacker: the aircraft's state of registration, the country of origin of the detained person, any other interested state (e.g. states where the offender is being pursued by an arrest warrant).

The Tokyo Convention also protects the rights of a person taken into custody (in Article 13 paragraph 3). That person should receive immediate assistance in communication with an appropriate representative of their state of nationality.

Of note here is that on the basis of Article 14, permission for disembarkation, acceptance of deliverance or taking into custody are not automatically equal to an admission to the territory of the state party. And if an admission is not granted, or the person detained cannot or does not wish to continue their journey, then the state party may return them to the territory of the state of their nationality or permanent residence, or the one in which they began their journey.

Article 15 entitles a detained person to decide whether they wish to stay in the state of landing, or continue their journey to a particular destination. In general, the state that detains them should allow them to proceed to that destination, unless their presence there is required for the purpose of extradition or criminal proceedings (paragraph 1). With exception to laws of entry and admission, extradition and expulsion from the territory, the state detaining the person must assure them a treatment not less favourable for their protection and security than the one normally applicable to nationals of that state in similar circumstances (paragraph 2).

f) Commentary

Despite its wide scope of application and introduction of definition of unlawful seizure of aircraft (for present times slightly outdated; see sub-chapter 1.3.3.(a)), the Tokyo Convention is viewed by many experts as failing the hopes put therein. The treaty in itself does not provide sufficient juridical protection of airline passengers from attacks on civil aviation, especially terrorist ones.[22]

A strong point of the Convention is its "extension" of territorial rules to offences and other acts jeopardising safety of flight that occur on board aircraft, so that the state of the aircraft's registration may exercise its jurisdiction wherever the plane is.[23] Such a solution at least assures some kind of protection, as when an aeroplane is hijacked and the offender orders the crew to fly to a particular location, in theory, the state of registration might initiate proceedings against that person. However, another problem is exposed here – the Convention does not *expressis verbis* oblige any state to extradite the offender to the state of registration, nor it does impose a duty to prosecute them.[24] This is especially visible in cases of terrorism, where political interests are of strong magnitude. If a terrorist hijacks an aircraft and orders the flight crew to direct it to a state which secretly supports terrorism or is in a tense relationship with the state of the aircraft's registration, then they might not even be prosecuted there or extradited, but rather treated as a hero.[25] The problem with extradition here is of particular

---

22 Similarly: B. Nowak, "Akty terroryzmu w lotnictwie cywilnym", p. 121.

23 H. G. Dawson, "Civil Aviation, Hijacking and International Terrorism - An Historical and Legal Review", International Business Lawyer, Vol. 15(57) 1987, p. 59.

24 P. Dempsey indicates that this point is one the greatest weaknesses of the Convention. See P. Dempsey, "Aviation Security", p. 664.

25 During the "Golden Age of Hijacking", so in 1950s and 1960s, even Western democratic countries were refusing to extradite aircraft hijackers, usually for political reasons. In the famous case of R. Minichiello, an American citizen of Italian origin that in May 1969 (several months before the Tokyo Convention entered into force) hijacked a Trans World Airlines plane on route from Los Angeles to San Francisco and ordered the crew to fly to his home country. The plane landed safely in Italy, where Minichiello was seen as a hero – a person that managed to resist the United States, whose reputation in Europe had been declining due to unpopular foreign policy. Although the Italian government was willing to extradite Minichiello to the USA for his trial, the pressure of public opinion was so strong that he was finally prosecuted in his motherland. As aircraft hijacking was not at this time even qualified as an offence, allegations were of a rather minor nature and the sentence was not too severe. See B. I. Koerner, Niebo jest nasze. Miłość i terror w złotym wieku piractwa powietrznego (Wydawnictwo Czarne: Wołowiec, 2017), pp. 65-69.

importance – at present there exists no binding universal framework of extradition rules. Extradition is regulated mostly by bilateral agreements between states or multilateral treaties dealing with particular offences. No customary law rules have been developed for that basis.[26] As the Tokyo Convention does not provide any binding rules for extraditing offenders, states may refuse to deliver aerial terrorists for the purpose of prosecution, as its Article 13 only obliges them to keep an offender in custody for such time as it is "reasonably necessary to enable any criminal or extradition proceedings to be instituted."[27]

What is more, the Convention, originally intended to regulate the status of aircraft [see above, section a)], but then drafted for the purpose to protect civil aviation from hijacking does not even assure an expected level of that protection. Article 11, although providing a definition of unlawful aircraft seizure accurate for a 1960s reality, completely omits the question of its criminalisation. Similarly with Article 1, leaving to the states parties the right to decide via their domestic criminal law system what acts would be rated as "offences". That only strengthens the argument that a terrorist, if able to wisely choose in which states they wish to land, can keep in mind that their act is not even rated as an offence there, and as a result, avoid punishment.[28]

Taking into account all arguments presented above, we can conclude that the Tokyo Convention may not serve as a sufficient juridical tool to combat aerial terrorism. The lack of criminalisation of any act against civil aviation (including hijacking), poor jurisdiction and extradition regulation and no imposition on

---

26 See more: T. Aleksandrowicz, K. Liedel, Zwalczanie terroryzmu lotniczego, pp. 44-45.

27 Tokyo Convention, Article 13. Similarly: R. Abeyratne, Ethiopian Airlines hijacking, p. 192.

28 On that basis, it is unacceptable to call the Tokyo Convention "providing universal jurisdiction" for offences against civil aviation as inter alia A. S. Williams affirms. And that is regardless of the theory that we qualify as related to universal jurisdiction (an offence pursued on the grounds of customary law, or international treaties, see above, note 227).

Universal jurisdiction only refers to crimes which infringe the interests of all states of the world. If the Tokyo Convention does not even expressis verbis call an act of unlawful aircraft seizure "an offence", it is irrelevant to attribute it to universal jurisdiction. As for the customary law, most authors agree that acts against civil aviation have not yet been accepted by international community as custom, so again the claim that Tokyo Convention introduces universal jurisdiction does not reflect reality. See A. S. Williams, "The Interception of Civil Aircraft over the High Seas in the Global War on Terror", Air Force Law Review, Vol. 59(73) 2007, p. 23.

states the duties on prosecuting offenders makes it inappropriate for challenges related to fight against terrorism, at least on international level.

2.2.3. The Hague Convention and the Montreal Convention

a) Circumstances of drafting

Due to repetitive occurrences of attacks on civil aviation (mostly skyjackings), the UNGA in 1969 and 1970 adopted several resolutions expressing deep concern about those acts of unlawful interference and calling States to take effective measures to prevent them from happening. Moreover, it urged the ICAO to promptly draft a treaty that would introduce criminalisation of an act of aircraft hijacking and establish an obligation for state parties to prosecute those responsible.[29]

In the period of 9 February-11 March 1970, the Legal Committee of the ICAO met in Montreal to prepare the text of convention that would criminalise the act of aircraft hijacking, stipulate on judicial proceedings and extradition. The text was then approved by the ICAO Council and delivered to organisation's Member States and to the UN headquarters. In consequence, a Diplomatic Conference in The Hague was convened in December 1970 to sign the convention. Representatives of 77 States and 12 international organisations were present there. Long and hard debates were fruitful and Hague Convention was signed. It entered into force relatively quickly, on 14 October 1971.[30]

But the ICAO was aware that hijacking was not the only menace haunting the skies at that time. Bombings, sabotages and other acts of unlawful interference, having often a terrorist character were occurring more and more frequently. For that reason, during the extraordinary session of Assembly, the ICAO affirmed officially that those acts jeopardise the safety of civil aviation and fail the trust of peoples to safety air travels. The Legal Committee was then requested to draft a text of another convention devoted to acts of unlawful interference other than skyjacking.[31] The ICAO decided on organisation of another full Diplomatic Conference on which the convention would be signed. Even before, on its 13th

29 https://applications.icao.int/postalhistory/legal_instruments_related_to_aviation_security.htm (9 March 2021).

30 T. Aleksandrowicz, K. Liedel, Zwalczanie terroryzmu lotniczego, pp. 24-26.

31 T. Aleksandrowicz, K. Liedel, Zwalczanie terroryzmu lotniczego, p. 26, after: L. Łukasik, Prawnomiędzynarodowe środki zwalczania terroryzmu powietrznego, Sprawy Międzynarodowe 1973, p. 130.

Assembly in Vienna, the organisation called for speedy ratification of the treaty by its members. The conference was held from 8 to 23 September 1971 in Montreal and present were delegates from 60 States, as well as observers from one another State and 6 international organisations. Again, the conference ended with success and Montreal Convention was opened for signature. It took two years to have it entered into force. On 26 January 1973, the treaty became effective.[32]

b) Scope of application

Because both The Hague Convention and the Montreal Convention have a similar structure and system of jurisdiction, they will be analysed jointly in the present and subsequent sections.

Already in Article 1, The Hague Convention exposes a significant difference between itself and the Tokyo Convention. It stipulates as follows:

> Any person who on board an aircraft in flight:
> (a) unlawfully, by force or threat thereof, or by any other form of intimidation, seizes, or exercises control of, that aircraft, or attempts to perform any such act, or
> (b) is an accomplice of a person who performs or attempts to perform any such act commits an offence (hereafter referred to as "the offence").[33]

In contrast to its predecessor, this Convention obliges its parties to criminalise the act of hijacking, and thus imposes on a state party an obligation of including that act as an offence in its criminal law.[34] What is more, criminalisation is extended to all accomplices of the hijacker, so e.g. a person supplying them with necessary tools or weapons or overpowers crew members when the hijacker attacks the pilots. This extension concerns also accomplices not present on board aircraft in flight – a person that assisted the hijacker in acquiring weapons on the ground and never boarded the aeroplane might be then persecuted on the basis of the Convention.

---

32 https://applications.icao.int/postalhistory/legal_instruments_related_to_aviation_security.htm (9 March 2021).

33 Convention for the Suppression of Unlawful Seizure of Aircraft, done at the Hague, 16 December 1970, United Nations Treaty Series, Vol. 860, Reg. 12325, art.1.

34 N. M. Poulantzas notices that prior to Hague Convention's entry into force, there was no vaccum iuris on punishing aircraft hijackers. Relevant legal solutions were existing on the level of municipal law, but their existence was dependent on states' political interests. Creation of Hague Convention changed this by introduction of criminalisation of skyjacking on international level.
N. M. Poulantzas, "Convention for the Suppression of Unlawful Seizure of Aircraft", p. 9.

The mere attempt to hijack an aircraft is equally treated as an offence, even if it ultimately fails.

As for the Montreal Convention, the Article 1 also introduces a catalogue of acts *expressis verbis* called "offences" and criminalisation of an attempt to perform any of them. Similarly to The Hague Convention, an accomplice to the actual offender may also face prosecution. The provision stipulates as follows in paragraph 1:

> Any person commits an offence if he unlawfully and intentionally:
> (a) performs an act of violence against a person on board an aircraft in flight if that act is likely to endanger the safety of that aircraft; or
> (b) destroys an aircraft in service or causes damage to such an aircraft which renders it incapable of flight or which is likely to endanger its safety in flight; or
> (c) places or causes to be placed on an aircraft in service, by any means whatsoever, a device or substance which is likely to destroy that aircraft, or to cause damage to it which renders it incapable of flight, or to cause damage to it which is likely to endanger its safety in flight; or
> (d) destroys or damages air navigation facilities or interferes with their operation, if any such act is likely to endanger the safety of aircraft in flight; or
> (e) communicates information which he knows to be false, thereby endangering the safety of an aircraft in flight.[35]

Article 1 of Montreal Convention ends with paragraph 2 with the following wording: "Any person also commits an offence if he:

> (a) attempts to commit any of the offences mentioned in paragraph 1 of this Article; or
> (b) is an accomplice of a person who commits or attempts to commit any such offence."[36]

If we then combine the scope of acts featured in both Conventions, we would see, that most kinds of attacks on civil aviation are covered within, with the exclusion of cyberattacks, destruction of airport infrastructure and usage of aircraft as a weapon. Apart from skyjacking, the treaties also protect passengers from acts of violence directed against them (provided that they endanger safety of aircraft, e.g. attack on passengers using a weapon capable of making hole in fuselage), destruction of aircraft (e.g. shooting down), usage of substance that may damage or destroy the aircraft (e.g. chemical bomb), damage or destruction of air navigation facilities (e.g. on board computer) or communication of false information endangering safety of aircraft (e.g. sending a wrong navigation coordinates that may cause collision with

---

35 Convention for the Suppression of Unlawful Acts against the Safety of Civil Aviation, signed in Montreal, 23 September, 1971, United Nations Treaty Series, Vol. 974, Reg. 14118, art. 1.

36 Montreal Convention, art. 1.

another plane in mid-air).[37] We should notice here, that neither of the Conventions uses the word "terrorism" in its title, preamble, or content. As such, their scope of application is extensive, as they establish criminalisation of acts against civil aviation regardless of their nature (terrorist, on non-terrorist) and leave the decision on qualifying the offences as "terrorist" for state parties.

Both Conventions also oblige (The Hague Convention in Article 2, the Montreal Convention in Article 3) state parties to make offences punishable by "severe penalties". That provision has been widely criticised by many authors for not introducing a uniform system of punishment for offences against civil aviation.[38] However, we need to bear in mind that penal systems strongly vary depending on the region of the world, basing on different historical, social and cultural backgrounds.[39] In such conditions, creating a single system of penalties would be much more challenging, especially as some states accept penalties that are abolished in other states (e.g. public flagellation or capital punishment). Currently, state parties usually sentence perpetrators of offences expressed in both treaties to imprisonment, typically ranging from several years to life sentences.[40] Some of them use the death penalty, including China[41], Cuba[42], Iraq[43], Pakistan[44], United States[45] and many others.

A short overview should also be provided for the terms "aircraft in flight" (functioning in both treaties) and "aircraft in service" (present only in the

37 R. Mankiewicz affirms that except for the offence stated in Article 1(1) point a) of the Montreal Convention, all other acts enumerated in this treaty can be committed only on the ground. That argument is not totally acceptable – the destruction of aircraft, covered by point b) can be perfectly conducted on board when the machine is airborne. If a suicide terrorist carries a bomb and detonates it when an aeroplane is on its cruising altitude, he commits the offence expressed in the mentioned provision.
See R. H. Mankiewicz, "La Convention de Montréal (1971) pour la répression d'actes illicites dirigés contre la sécurité de l'aviation civile", Annuaire français de droit international, Vol. 17/1971, p. 868.

38 See E. McWhinney, Aerial Piracy, pp. 42, P. Dempsey, "Aviation Security", p. 667.

39 See more on discussion over defining "severe penalties" and criminal policy of aircraft hijacking in various states: Z. Galicki, Terroryzm lotniczy, pp. 71-77.

40 G. F. Fitzgerald, "Aviation Terrorism and the International Civil Aviation Organization", 25 Canadian Yearbook of International Law, (1987), p. 228.

41 See Criminal Law of the People's Republic of China, art. 121.

42 See Law no. 62 – Penal Code of Cuba, art. 117.

43 See Staute no. (111) 1969 – Penal Code of Iraq, §354.

44 See Act XLV of 1860 – Pakistan Penal Code, art. 402(A-C).

45 See United States Code, Title 49, § 46502.

Montreal Convention). As for the former one, both Conventions feature only one definition (unlike the Tokyo Convention, see sub-chapter 2.2.2., section d): "an aircraft is considered to be in flight at any time from the moment when all its external doors are closed following embarkation until the moment when any such door is opened for disembarkation."[46] In turn, an aircraft is considered in service "from the beginning of the preflight preparation of the aircraft by ground personnel or by the crew for a specific flight until twenty-four hours after any landing."[47] The differentiation between the periods "in flight" and "in service" is significant, as the period of being "in service" normally starts earlier and ends later than period of being "in flight" – the earliest pre-flight preparations are made even before passengers commence to embark, not to mention the moment when the last doors are closed for take-off. Briefly speaking, the protection from offences committed when an aircraft is "in service" is considerably wider than from those that occur when an aircraft is "in flight".[48]

Importantly, both Conventions apply to flights of either international or domestic character. International flights have their scheduled points of origin located in a different state than their scheduled point of destination, whereas domestic flights are those that have both points located within the same state.[49] But the difference between The Hague and the Montreal Conventions lies within the actual and intended place of landing. The Hague Convention would apply only if the actual place of landing is different than the state of the aircraft's registry, whereas the Montreal Convention also applies if an intended (not necessarily

46 Hague Convention, art. 3(1) and Montreal Convention, art. 2.

47 Montreal Convention, art. 2.

48 Z. Galicki, Terroryzm lotniczy, p. 82.

49 This interpretation is different to one presented by S. Bazin (citing here R. H. Mankiewicz), who affirms that the term "international flight" would be used to define both:
a) a flight whose point of origin and point of destination are located in two different states; and
b) a flight whose points of origin and destination are located within the same state, which is different to the state of aircraft's registry.
On the basis of that interpretation, a "domestic flight" would need to mean a flight whose points of origin and destination are both located in the territory of the state of registry, which would exclude it from the scope of application of the Hague and Montreal Conventions, although they stipulate that they apply irrespective of whether aircraft is engaged in domestic or international flight. See S. Bazin, Le droit pénal de l'aviation civile, p. 151, after: R. H. Mankiewicz, "Le détournement d'avions", Revue français de droit aérien (1971), p. 402.

actual) place of landing is different than the state of the aircraft's registry. A simple example illustrates this difference: an aircraft registered in Germany performing a scheduled flight between Frankfurt and Washington, D.C. is hijacked shortly after take-off and the offender orders the crew to fly to Berlin. If the plane ultimately lands in Berlin, The Hague Convention would not apply here and only Germany's law would be taken into consideration.[50]

In turn, on the grounds of the Montreal Convention, if a plane performs the same flight and on board one of passengers attacks others using a smuggled weapon and it is clear that the attack would endanger the safety of the flight, then the captain decides to turn back and land in Frankfurt, the provisions of the Convention would still apply to the event because the intended place of landing (Washington, D.C.) was different than the state of the aircraft's registration.

If the attack is not carried out on board the aircraft, but from outside, the Montreal Convention would apply if the state of occurrence is different than the state of registration (on the basis of Article 4 paragraph 2 point b)). If, then, an aeroplane registered in Germany flies from Frankfurt to Washington and is hit by a missile launched in German territory, the domestic law of Germany would take precedence over the provisions of the Montreal Convention. But if a missile is launched when the plane is crossing the aerospace above the high seas or the United States, the Montreal Convention would apply.

Finally, both treaties stipulate that their provisions would apply if an offender (or alleged offender)[51] is found in the territory of a state other than the state of registry. That point mostly concerns extradition of offenders that flee from the crime scene and are ultimately captured in a different State.

---

50 N. M. Poulantzas, "Convention for the Suppression of Unlawful Seizure of Aircraft", p. 16.

51 "Alleged offender" is a term not expressly defined in either of the Conventions, but functions in many other sector treaties related to international criminal law or fight against terrorism. An accurate definition thereof can be found in one of the Convention on the Prevention and Punishment of Crimes against Internationally Protected Persons, including Diplomatic Agents in its Article 1(2). It states that "[a]lleged offender" means a person as to whom there is sufficient evidence to determine prima facie that he has committed or participated in [...] crimes [...].
Convention on the Prevention and Punishment of Crimes against Internationally Protected Persons, including Diplomatic Agents, signed at New York, 14 December 1973, United Nations Treaty Series, Vol. 1035, Reg. 15410, art. 1(2).

c) *Jurisdiction*

Both The Hague and Montreal Conventions feature similar approach to question of establishing jurisdiction[52] – their authors blended several bases to widen the scope of the states concerned (The Hague Convention states this in Article 4, whereas the Montreal Convention – in Article 5, which was enriched by Montreal Protocol). In the foreground are the jurisdiction of the state of registry and the jurisdiction of the state of last landing. A particular ground of jurisdiction is also present – entitled to establish its jurisdiction would be a state of a principal place of business (or a permanent residence) of a lessee to whom the aircraft was leased on the basis of a dry-lease contract.[53] In addition to that, the Montreal Convention, due to the nature of the offences covered within, entitles a state where an offence was committed establish their jurisdiction (if this offence was not committed on board, which includes shooting down, the placement of a bomb or toxic substance etc.).

A short remark should be made on the solution present in Article 4(2) of The Hague Convention and Article 5(2) of the Montreal Convention: on the basis of those provisions, an offender (or alleged offender), if found and apprehended in the territory of one of the state parties, should be either liable for prosecution or extradited to any of the states enumerated in the previous paragraph. Some authors postulate this accounts for "universal jurisdiction", as it assures that no perpetrator would find safe haven in any of the state parties, as each of them would either extradite them, or establish its jurisdiction over the offence.[54] This statement is strengthened by the wording of the common Article 7 of the Conventions: "[t]he Contracting State in the territory of which the alleged offender

---

52 Simply put, "establishing jurisdiction" means that a particular state deals with an offender (or alleged offender) in accordance with its domestic law.
United Nations Office on Drugs and Crime, Implementation Kits for the International Counter-Terrorism Conventions – Chapter 1 . Introduction, p. 6.

53 In civil aviation, it is extremely popular among airlines or in general aeroplanes operators to obtain aircraft into their fleets via lease contracts. Usually, the contract of lease is either qualified as a "wet-lease" or "dry-lease". The former refers to an agreement under which the lessor provides for the lessee an aircraft along with the flight crew, jet fuel and some other services, whereas the latter one concerns providing only an aircraft only, without any additional services. See more: M. Żylicz, Prawo lotnicze, p. 422.

54 N. M. Poulantzas, "Convention for the Suppression of Unlawful Seizure of Aircraft", p. 20,
P. Mendes de Leon, Introduction to Air Law, p. 497
Differently: E. McWhinney, Aerial Piracy, p. 42.

is found shall, if it does not extradite him, be obliged, without exception whatsoever and whether or not the offence was committed in its territory, to submit the case to its competent authorities for the purpose of prosecution. Those authorities shall take their decision in the same manner as in the case of any ordinary offence of a serious nature under the law of that State."[55] This mechanism (commonly known as the *aut dedere aut iudicare* principle), assuring that at least state parties would not let a perpetrator be left unpunished regardless of the crime scene's location, was called by a "quasi-universal jurisdiction" (*compétence quasi-universelle*) C. Emanuelli.[56] The issue shall be discussed later in this sub-chapter.

d) Extradition

One of the most significant "sins" of the Tokyo Convention was the failure to create a framework obliging state parties to extradite hijackers. The Hague and Montreal Conventions were intended to create a remedy for that problem and effectively establish extradition rules mandatory for state parties. Does it succeed? Opinions are divided.

Article 8 of The Hague Convention and Article 8 of the Montreal Convention constitute a basis for extradition. They both state in paragraph 1 that all offences described shall be included in any extradition treaty concluded between state parties and that concerns already existing treaties, as well as those drafted in the future. That reflects what was already mentioned, namely that there is no general rule in international law obliging states to extradite perpetrators, including terrorists and that obligation is strongly dependent on existence of agreements, mostly bilateral.[57] That role is then perfectly fulfilled by both Articles 8(1).

What some authors, like P. Mendes de Leon, criticise is the wording of subsequent paragraphs. It states that "[e]xtradition shall be subject to the other conditions provided by the law of requested [s]tate,"[58] effectively meaning that no general obligation of extradition is imposed on state parties, as they may invoke their domestic legal system norms to refuse extradition.[59]

---

55 Hague Convention and Montreal Convention, common art. 7.

56 C. Emanuelli, Les moyens de prévention, p. 72.

57 P. Van Krieken, Terrorism and the International Legal Order, p. 92. It is important to indicate here that in the absence of such an agreement, extradition of an offender is usually based on the rule of reciprocity or international courtesy. See Ekstradycja, in: Encyklopedia prawa międzynarodowego.

58 Hague and Montreal Conventions, art. 8(2).

59 Z. Galicki, Terroryzm lotniczy, p. 111., P. Mendes de Leon, Introduction to Air Law, p. 497.

The right to extradite is vested not only in the state where the offence occurred, but also any of those that may establish their jurisdiction, which has been referred to above in section c). The Conventions in their Articles 8 also divide states into two categories: those that make extradition conditional upon the existence of extradition treaties, and those that do not. For the former ones, the Conventions may constitute a basis for extradition and the latter ones shall need to recognise the offences as extraditable ones.[60]

e) Other states' duties

Other duties of states stemming from the Conventions have a similar nature to those contained in the Tokyo Convention. Common provisions of Article 6 impose on a state where an offender (or alleged offender) is present the duty to take them into custody or use other measures that would assure they remain in the country, at least until criminal or extradition proceedings could be initiated. In this case, a preliminary enquiry into the facts of the event should be made and the offender must be assisted in communicating with the nearest appropriate representative of their state of nationality. Then, paragraph 4 concerns the obligation of a state party keeping the offender in its custody to inform the states entitled to establish jurisdiction about the relevant facts.

Article 9 of The Hague Convention contains a very general obligation, addressed to all state parties, of undertaking "appropriate measures" to restore or preserve control to the lawful commander (usually captain or first officer) of aircraft if it was already hijacked or is about to be hijacked. Typically, states may either attempt to negotiate with a hijacker or intercept captured aeroplane without using force but directing it to the nearest airport.

In turn, Article 10 of The Hague Convention illustrates more preventive nature of this instrument, by placing on states a duty to take all practicable measures to prevent the occurrence of offences covered within. That provision is of a very general character, as measures undertaken can be miscellaneous and may consist of: scanning of baggage for the purpose of detection of weapons, dangerous substances or drugs that be taken on board, observation and elimination of terrorist cells, deployment of sky marshals on flights etc.

Finally, both treaties introduce obligations of mutual assistance in connection with criminal proceedings brought in relation to offences (Article 10 of The Hague Convention and Article 11 of the Montreal Convention), duty to inform

60 Z. Galicki, Terroryzm lotniczy, p. 498.

the Council of ICAO about circumstances of offences and measures taken against offenders (Article 11 of The Hague Convention and Article 13 of the Montreal Convention) and provisions on dispute settlements (Article 12 of The Hague Convention and Article 14 of the Montreal Convention).

f) Commentary

It is difficult to unambiguously evaluate both The Hague and Montreal Conventions in the perspective of the fight against aerial terrorism.

What the treaties should be praised for is the first ever explicit criminalisation of attacks against civil aviation that usually have a terrorist background. Consequently, each state party has a duty to include in their domestic penal codes all offences enumerated in the Conventions. What is more, like the Tokyo Convention, the instruments do not even ascribe the terrorist character to the offences, which in fact means the protection of passengers is wider – criminalisation is absolute and concerns both acts of terrorist and non-terrorist character. Reasonable it was also that authors of the Conventions referred to the principle *aut dedere aut iudicare*, thus reducing the risk that an offender, if found on the territory of any state party would avoid punishment.[61]

On the other hand, many experts agree the norms encapsulated in the Conventions do not provide an adequate level of protection. First of all, they leave the state hosting an offender free to decide whether to extradite them or submit the case to competent authorities for the purpose of prosecution. If the second option is chosen by a state, there is virtually no guarantee that in practice any criminal proceedings shall be instituted and the offender will stand trial.[62] As a result, an offender might in fact avoid punishment, if a host state decides not to extradite them, particularly if the host state favours its own political interests – we need to keep in mind that a state requested to extradite decides on the basis of its domestic law. And if according to that law, extradition cannot be initiated if the nature of the offence is political, the requested state may paradoxically become a safe haven for a terrorist.[63] Notably, during preparations of the final draft of The Hague Convention, the concept of interdiction for states to grant asylum

61 B. Nowak, "Problemy bezpieczeństwa w międzynarodowym lotnictwie cywilnym w świetle Konwencji Haskiej z 1970 r.", Studia Europejskie, 3/2001, pp. 134-135.

62 E. McWhinney, Aerial Piracy, p. 48,
P. Mendes de Leon, Introduction to Air Law, p. 499.

63 On the lack of duty to extradite offenders, see more: M. Żylicz, Terroryzm lotniczy, pp. 127-128.

for offenders was debated, but it was ultimately rejected due to the excessive degree of interference into domestic legal systems.[64] In general, the hopes for establishing a universal system of jurisdiction against aerial terrorists in the form of The Hague and Montreal Conventions mostly failed.

The flaw rooted in both treaties is a strong dependency of their effectiveness on political priorities of the states and their factual capabilities. Some states, even if entitled to, may not be interested in commencing criminal proceedings against offenders, as it may be very costly, especially when an investigation into an air accident is involved. The trial of an offender would also trigger the attention of the public and the media which may result in tensions with the state of origin of the perpetrator, or lead to protests of groups advocating human rights, if an offender is prosecuted in a state known for the brutal treatment of prisoners or for passing death sentences. However, the political background is usually present in international issues involving criminal law.

Moreover, solutions provided in Conventions seem obsolete, if compared to capabilities of terrorists today. Their access to advanced technologies, sophisticated weapons or even unmanned aircraft requires a modern approach to fight against terrorism, different than it was in the 1960s or 1970s, when the Conventions were being drafted. If they remain a primary international instrument to suppress attacks on civil aviation, international community would lose this global war against terrorism.

Finally, both The Hague and Montreal Conventions form important elements in crystallisation of international custom, especially as they have been ratified by nearly all states of the world.[65] Such a wide acceptance of the conventions would constitute *opinio iuris* that fthe ight against attacks on civil aviation (taking mostly forms of terrorism) should be conducted and take a truly global character.

64 N. M. Poulantzas, "Convention for the Suppression of Unlawful Seizure of Aircraft", p. 26.

65 As of March 2021, 185 states are parties to the Hague Convention and 188 to the Montreal Convention.

A full list of signatories can be viewed on the official ICAO website:

https://www.icao.int/secretariat/legal/List%20of%20Parties/Hague_EN.pdf (9 March 2021)

https://www.icao.int/secretariat/legal/List%20of%20Parties/Mtl71_EN.pdf (9 March 2021)

2.2.4. The Montreal Protocol

a) *Circumstances of drafting*

Despite the decreasing number of victims of attacks on civil aviation, partially due to enforcement of The Hague and Montreal Conventions, ICAO became concerned with several terrorist attempts at international airports. Its Council decided to promptly react to this growing threat when in December 1985, simultaneous grenade and machine gun attacks were carried out at airports in Vienna and Rome. On the 26th session of ICAO on 8 October 1986, a resolution was adopted calling for draft of a new treaty on suppression of acts of violence at international airports.[66] The Montreal Protocol was then signed on 24 February 1988 and in practice only supplements Montreal Convention by adding provisions on new offences. Just a year and a half later; it entered into force: on 6 August, 1989.

b) *Enhancement of the Montreal Convention*

The Montreal Protocol's merits cover mostly provisions related to processes of ratification and signing, as only two of its Articles have a supplementary function.

Article II adds to the Montreal Convention's Article 1 a new paragraph 1 *bis* with the following wording:

> Any person commits an offence if he unlawfully and intentionally, using any device, substance or weapon:
> (a) performs an act of violence against a person at an airport serving international civil aviation which causes or is likely to cause serious injury or death; or
> (b) destroys or seriously damages the facilities of an airport serving international civil aviation or aircraft not in service located thereon or disrupts the services of the airport, if such an act endangers or is likely to endanger safety at that airport.[67]

Subsequently, Article II enhances Article 1 paragraph 2(a) by introducing the criminalisation of an attempt to commit any of the offences mentioned above. Lastly, Article III of Protocol extends the jurisdiction over offences inserted into

66 J. Huang, Aviation Safety and ICAO (Kluwer Law International: Alphen aan den Rijn, 2009), p. 139.

67 Protocol for the Suppression of Unlawful Acts of Violence at Airports Serving International Civil Aviation, supplementary to the Convention for the Suppression of Unlawful Acts against the Safety of Civil Aviation signed at Montreal on 23 September 1971, signed in Montreal on 24 February 1988 (hereafter: "Montreal Protocol"), United Nations Treaty Series, Vol. 1589, Reg. 14118, art. II.

the Montreal Convention. All other provisions, including those on extradition or duties of states, remained unamended.

Perhaps the most serious enhancement to the Montreal Convention is the extension of a possible crime scene by international airports (domestic ones are excluded from application) and their whole infrastructure (runways, hangars, control towers etc.)[68], as well as aircraft not in service located there. That theoretically allows a state in whose territory an airport was attacked to initiate proceedings against the offender as soon as the attack (using any kind of weapon, substance or device) takes place, prior to the commencement of boarding, e.g. in the departure hall or right after security checks.

c) Commentary

The role of the Montreal Protocol is not to be underestimated. It is the first-ever legal instrument with the aim of criminalising attacks at international airports and so far, the single one until today with a significant number of signatories (as of October 2018, there are 175 parties to the Montreal Protocol).[69] Upon its entry into force, the international community was equipped with juridical tools to combat with most forms of aerial terrorism (excluding use of aeroplane as a weapon and some more innovative forms thereof, like cyberattacks, or usage of BCN weapons).

Nevertheless, the will of the states of the world toward the ratification of Protocol did not reflect its real popularity. As P. Mendes de Leon underlines, no single state has ever invoked its provisions in legal proceedings concerning attacks on airports – the Protocol's signatories seem to prefer applying their domestic law instead.[70] However, until the Beijing Convention (analysed in detail in the next sub-chapter) is more widely ratified, the Montreal Protocol will remain the most valuable treaty in the fight against terrorist attacks at the airports.

---

68 United Nations Office on Drugs and Crime, Implementation Kits for the International Counter-Terrorism Conventions – Chapter 5 ..., p. 103.

69 Montreal Protocol, list of parties.; https://www.icao.int/secretariat/legal/List%20of%20Parties/VIA_EN.pdf (9 March 2021).

70 P. Mendes de Leon, Introduction to Air Law, p. 504.

2.2.5. The Beijing Convention & the Beijing Protocol

a) Circumstances of drafting

The first year of the twenty-first century left a grim mark on history of civil aviation. The cruelty of attacks on World Trade Center on 11 September, 2001 exposed to international community the capabilities of terrorists that, for the first time ever, successfully used aircraft as a weapon, and brought devastation to the bustling city of New York along with a sense of failure to the whole international community.

That tragedy, along with several other attempts that hit civil aviation in recent years convinced ICAO to again strengthen juridical measures that would keep skies safe from terrorism.[71] A pressing need for an up-to-date legal instrument that would respond to "new threats" to terrorism, little known for international community at the time when The Hague Convention, Montreal Convention and Montreal Protocol were drafted, was a motivator for the ICAO to convene another diplomatic conference. Representatives of 76 states and 4 international organisations met in Beijing on 30 August 2010 to debate on new treaties on the suppression of unlawful acts against civil aviation until 10 September 2010.[72] The fruit of the conference – the Beijing Convention and Beijing Protocol, were adopted on its last day. With Resolution No. A39-10, the ICAO Assembly urged all Member States to ratify them. Nevertheless, they did not feel considerable pressure to do so. The Protocol entered into force on 1 January 2018 following Uganda's accession[73], whereas the Convention became effective on 1 July of the same year after Turkey acceded into it.

b) Scope of application

The basic aim of the Beijing Convention and the Beijing Protocol (jointly referred to as the "Beijing instruments" in the present and following sections of this sub-chapter) is to form a new, complete legal framework on crimes against civil

71 Between 2001 and 2010, acts of unlawful interference on civil aviation reached 220 and included 60 attempted or successful hijackings, 14 acts of sabotage and 90 attacks on facilities. ICAO, Annual Report of the Council – 2010, Table 11.

72 Final Act of the International Conference on Air Law (Diplomatic Conference on Aviation Security) held under the auspices of the International Civil Aviation Organisation at Beijing from 30 August to 10 September 2010, DCAS Doc Series, No. 17, p. 2-3.

73 https://www.icao.int/Newsroom/Pages/Beijing-Protocol-to-enter-into-force-following-Ugandas-ratification.aspx (9 March 2021).

aviation. The Beijing Convention is intended to, in a certain way, replace (but not repeal) the Montreal Convention and the Montreal Protocol, as its provisions take supersede them. In turn, the Beijing Protocol is supplementary to The Hague Convention through the addition of new provisions, or replacing existing ones. As their structure is similar and they differ mostly in the scope of application, both Beijing instruments shall be analysed together in this sub-chapter.

What distinguishes Beijing instruments from previously analysed documents is their extremely large scope of application. The Convention, in its Article 1 mostly repeats what was expressed in Article 1 of the Montreal Convention. It introduces the criminalisation of certain acts committed against civil aviation, but at the same time it adds new ones into the catalogue of offences. So, under the provisions, any person commits an offence, if they unlawfully and intentionally:

> (f) uses an aircraft in service for the purpose of causing death, serious bodily injury, or serious damage to property or the environment; or
> (g) releases or discharges from an aircraft in service any BCN weapon or explosive, radioactive, or similar substances in a manner that causes or is likely to cause death, serious bodily injury or serious damage to property or the environment; or
> (h) uses against or on board an aircraft in service any BCN weapon or explosive, radioactive, or similar substances in a manner that causes or is likely to cause death, serious bodily injury or serious damage to property or the environment; or
> (i) transports, causes to be transported, or facilitates the transport of, on board an aircraft:
> (1) any explosive or radioactive material, knowing that it is intended to be used to cause, or in a threat to cause, [...], death or serious injury or damage for the purpose of intimidating a population, or compelling a government or an international organisation to do or to abstain from doing any act; or
> (2) any BCN weapon, knowing it to be a BCN weapon [...]; or
> (3) any source material, special fissionable material, or equipment or material especially designed or prepared for the processing, use or production of special fissionable material, knowing that it is intended to be used in a nuclear explosive activity or in any other nuclear activity [...]; or
> (4) any equipment, materials or software or related technology that significantly contributes to the design, manufacture or delivery of a BCN weapon without lawful authorisation and with the intention that it will be used for such purpose; [...].[74]

From the above wording, it is clear that the structure of Article 1 was strongly influenced by the attacks on WTC. It is visible especially in paragraph (f) which criminalises usage of aircraft as a weapon [see sub-chapter 1.3.3., section c].

74 Beijing Convention, art. 1.

Subsequent paragraphs touch on the release of certain types of weapons (biological, nuclear or chemical), their use on board and their unlawful transport [see sub-chapter 1.3.3., section g].

In turn, the Beijing Protocol does not extend the catalogue of offences itself, but "updates" the understanding of aircraft hijacking present in The Hague Convention. Its Article II amending Article 1 of The Hague Convention gives a very wide and most relevant definition appropriate for the reality of present times (already mentioned in sub-chapter 1.3.3., section a), which reads as follows: "[a]ny person commits an offence if that person unlawfully and intentionally seizes or exercises control of an aircraft in service by force or threat thereof, or by coercion, or by any other form of intimidation, or by any technological means."[75]

Although, in comparison to the wording of The Hague Convention, the definition has not changed drastically, but some new important elements were added: the criminalisation of cyber hijacking; the inclusion of the element of intent, besides unlawfulness for a criminal qualification; the extension of a period of commission ("in flight" is replaced by "in service"); removing the necessity of the crime having to be committed "on board" (the logical consequence of criminalisation of cyber hijacking that can be perfectly carried out from the ground); coercion as a *modus operandi* of unlawful seizure.[76]

It is worth mentioning that both Beijing instruments also oblige to criminalise making a threat to commit any of the offences or causing any person to receive such a threat (Article 1 paragraph 3 of the Convention and Article II of the Protocol supplementing The Hague Convention by Article 1 paragraph 2). The potential aim of those provisions in the instruments is probably a sort of prevention in a fight against aerial terrorism. A state party might institute criminal proceedings against potential offender already when they make a threat to commit a crime or when they cause, unlawfully and intentionally, that any person receives such a threat, if only that threat is credible. Such a solution significantly expands the protection of passengers against terrorism by eliminating the crime in its early stage, just when it is about to be committed. It also gives permission pursue

75 Beijing Protocol, art. II.

76 Coercion might be understood as both physical and psychological. The former (vis absoluta) is a situation of affection by physical strength on another person in a way it cannot be resisted. The latter one (vis compulsiva) is an affection of physical strength or by psychological means by a perpetrator on its victim's psyche in order to force them to behave in a certain way. See more: A. Zoll, W. Wróbel, Polskie prawo karne, pp. 164-167.

terrorist organisations to state authorities in case they disclose their plans to attack an aeroplane or an airport, e.g. on the television or social media.

Extension of criminalisation does not end here. The Beijing instruments (the Convention – in Article 1 paragraph 4 point (b); the Protocol in Article II supplementing The Hague Convention by Article 1 paragraph 3 point (b)) enhance the list of offences by organisation and direction to either commit any of offence mentioned above, or threat or cause another to receive a threat about commission of any of the crimes. Therefore, each person that even potentially has dominion over those that commit the offence could be held liable for that.[77]

The Beijing instruments go even further with obligation of criminalising behaviour related to terrorist activity, including assistance with evading investigation, prosecution or punishment of persons having committed any of offences against civil aviation. Doubtlessly, that solution seems quite severe and therefore both instruments permit its parties not to be bound by them (Article 24 paragraph 4 point (b) of the Convention; Article XXII point (b) of the Protocol). It is not without reason: many domestic legal systems exempt from liability for assistance in evading criminal proceedings by an offender their family members.

Another *novum* introduced into anti-terrorist legal framework by the Beijing instruments is the criminalisation of a degree of preparation to commit an offence. In the Convention, that is regulated by Article 1(5), whereas in the Protocol relevant is Article II supplementing The Hague Convention by Article 1 paragraph 4. They stipulate that crime is "agreeing with one or more other persons to commit [any kind of offence enumerated in the instruments] and contributing in any other way to the commission of one or more offences [enumerated in the instruments]"[78], by referring to both individual and collective actors ("a group", or "one or more other persons"). What is more, preparation might be considered a crime only if it is made in aim of fostering general activity or purpose of a group whose goals involve committing an offence (like aircraft hijacking, shooting it down, destroying an international airport premises etc.) or threatening to do so, or if made in a state of knowledge that such a group intends to do it. Taking into account a wording of the mentioned provision one can come into conclusion that it is targeted against all people potentially involved in terrorist organisations. A state party choosing to either be bound by Article 1(5) of the Beijing Convention or by Article 1(4) of the Beijing Protocol supplementing The Hague Convention, acquires the right to pursue persons voluntarily

77 A. Zoll, W. Wróbel, Polskie prawo karne, p. 259.

78 Beijing Convention, art. 1, Beijing Protocol, art. II

cooperating with terrorists, under the condition that they are conscious of the criminal actions of the terrorist groups or their intentions. It is vital to mention that due to the fact that preparation is in most legal systems punishable only when it is set forth *expressis verbis*, the Beijing instruments do not oblige their state parties to criminalise it in reference to aforementioned offences and in consequence leaves that to be regulated or not by the states themselves.[79]

Another "innovation" absent in previous aerial terrorism treaties is the regulation of liability of legal entities located in or organised under the law of a state party. Article 4 of the Convention and the Protocol's Article IV supplementing The Hague Convention by Article 2 *bis* provide such an option, but their wording seems controversial for some experts. Pursuant to the provision, state parties may, in accordance with their national legal principles, establish norms punishing legal entities located on their territory or registered under their laws by criminal, civil or administrative sanctions if they commit any offences against civil aviation. Certainly, such solutions are shaped to weaken or eliminate institutions financing terrorism, supporting their actions or in general entities that despite being legally registered deal with terrorist acts, or, more precisely with people responsible for their management or control. The controversy of the aforementioned regulation is reflected by some states refusing to accept it, mainly due to the possible situation when airlines are held liable for e.g. carrying hazardous materials used by terrorists to produce weapons, which the air carrier may not necessarily be aware of.[80] Nevertheless, if a state decides to enact norms constituting such sanctions, Beijing instruments stipulate (Convention in Article 4(3); Protocol in Article IV supplementing The Hague Convention by Article 2 *bis* paragraph 3) that they should be effective, proportionate and dissuasive, and may include monetary sanctions. According to preceding paragraphs, liability is incurred by an entity without prejudice to criminal liability of individuals for offences.

None of the Beijing instruments amend the provisions related to their applicability dependent on actual or intended place of take-off or landing of aircraft. However, an important amendment is implemented by the Beijing Protocol in reference to time of commission of hijacking. The treaty extends it, by using uniquely the term "in service" instead of "in flight". That change slightly improves the protection of aircraft, as criminalised should be all attempts of its seizure even

79 A. Zoll, W. Wróbel, Polskie prawo karne, p. 244
80 M. Żylicz, Prawo lotnicze, p. 99.

before passengers start to board it (the explanation of both terms - “in flight” and “in service” are presented in sub-chapter 1.3.3., sections (a) and (b)).

The final element in the context of the Beijing instruments’ application that deserves attention is evoking international humanitarian law (in Article 6 of the Convention and Article VI of the Protocol supplementing The Hague Convention by Article 3 *bis*). On one hand, both treaties recall that their provisions should not in any way affect armed activities of any party during armed conflict. On the other hand, they do not accept justification of any kind of offence against civil aviation even if it is committed in the warfare. Necessity of that solution is proven by the fact, that in the past, many attacks on civil aviation were committed in the conditions of war.[81]

Similarly to their predecessors, the Beijing instruments also oblige state parties to punish the listed offences with “severe penalties”.

c) Jurisdiction

In comparison with the Montreal Convention, the concept of jurisdiction present in Beijing instruments is much similar – bases for jurisdiction are blended and none of them prevails. However, the list of possible bases is slightly extended and now involves also personality criterion (Article 8 of the Beijing Convention and Article VII supplementing The Hague Convention by Article 4). Under the provisions of the Beijing instruments, both the state of nationality of the offender and the victim of the attack are entitled to establish their jurisdiction. In the latter case, that might in practice concern a multitude of concurrent jurisdictions – if a large aeroplane performing an international flight is attacked and on board are citizens of several states, then all of them might evoke their right to

81 A notable event is the attack on a DHL aeroplane, Airbus A300 registered OO-DLL after its departure from Baghadad Airport in Iraq on 22 November 2003 (when the War in Iraq was on). The plane was hit by a surface-to-air missile shortly after take-off, but due to the excellent navigation abilities of its pilots, it finally safely landed on the same runway it started its journey. See M. Osiecki, “Shooting down civil aircraft”, p. 397.
Another similar accident occurred on 17 July 2014 in the skies above Ukraine. Malaysia Airlines Boeing 777 performing flight 17 was en route from Amsterdam-Schiphol Airport to its home base in Kuala Lumpur, when, above the Donetsk oblast, Ukraine, it was shot by a surface-to-air missile that was probably fired by pro-Russian separatists engaged in hostilities with the Ukrainian armed forces since spring 2014. Both sides were struggling to take control over the Eastern part of the country [the case shall be described in detail in sub-chapter 3.3.]. See T. Lachowski, “Kto strzelał – kto odpowie? Kwalifikacja prawna tragedii MH17”, Studia Prawnicze KUL, Vol. 62 (2) 2015, p. 195.

establish jurisdiction, which may result in a conflict between them. In addition to that, a state in whose territory a stateless person who is an offender and has a habitual residence could also claim its jurisdiction. Therefore, a catalogue of potentially entitled states is very wide.

As for the provisions concerning detention of an offender, both Beijing instruments embody a major supplementation (the Convention – in Article 11, the Protocol – in Article X adding Article 7 *bis* to The Hague Convention). They impose on their state parties an obligation of observance of all norms related to fair treatment of a detainee, including those encapsulated in domestic law, as well as in international human rights system.

d) Extradition and duties of states

The Beijing instruments mostly repeat what was provided in The Hague and Montreal Conventions in regards to extradition. But one significant change is featured within. The Beijing Convention introduces it in Articles 13 and 14, whereas Beijing Protocol does it in Articles XII and XIII adding to Hague Convention Articles 8 *bis* and 8 *ter* respectively. Namely, it is the prohibition of regarding any of the offences as political and in consequence, declines a possibility of refusal of extradition (or mutual legal assistance in general) on the grounds of political motives.

As for the states' duties concerning mutual legal assistance, prevention of crimes and other similar issues, provisions of the Beijing instruments have nearly identical wording as The Hague and Montreal Conventions.

e) Commentary

If compared with their "predecessors" (the Tokyo, Hague and Montreal Conventions, as well as the Montreal Protocol), the Beijing instruments definitely form the most advanced treaties protecting civil aviation, best adapted for the reality of present times.

What deserves a good rating is creation of a wide catalogue of offences against civil aviation, including usage of aircraft as a weapon, or cyberattacks. That makes the Beijing instruments first of their kind to not only respond to hazards that had been already revealed (e.g. during the attacks on WTC on 11 September), but also those that potentially may happen in the future (cyber hijacking).

But what makes those Beijing treaties outstanding is great contribution to fight against terrorism (at least on juridical level). The criminalisation of making a credible threat of committing a crime obliges states to pursue terrorists already when they publicly admit that they would carry out an attack on civil aircraft or an international airport. What is more, targeted are not only individuals, but also terrorist groups whose activities are oriented at attacking civil aviation. That concept enables state parties to eliminate terrorist threat already in its stub and therefore better protect air passengers. The drafters of instruments should also be praised for having included therein criminalisation of behaviour of legal entities, that actively supply terrorists or even finance them. All of those solutions reflect a slight change of focus of the ICAO from individual offenders to organised radical terrorist networks that today pose much greater threat to safety of passengers in the skies than ever before.

Apart from enlargement of catalogue of offences against civil aviation, perhaps the most important element introduced into aviation security law by the Beijing instruments is prohibition of qualification of any of offences enumerated therein as political ones. Traditionally, the political element of an offence has been treated by states as a serious obstacle on handing over a suspect to another country.[82] Usually, requested states decline to proceed with an extradition if they are convinced that delivering the offender would harm their political interests or cause dissent. But throughout the last decades, international conventions were limiting options on refusal to extradite in relation to certain kinds of offences that are usually connected with terrorism (e.g. under Article 11 of the International Convention for the Suppression of Terrorist Bombings, all offences enumerated therein are explicitly rejected from political exemption). The Beijing instruments are the first treaties on civil aviation to involve that rejection and in consequence reduce the risk of guaranteeing an offender a safe haven in any of the states in which they are found (provided that it would be one of the state parties) and leaving them unpunished.

In spite of all those progressive inputs to the anti-terrorist legal system, the Beijing instruments do not fill the gap left by The Hague and Montreal Conventions, namely the failure to force a state to initiate criminal proceedings against a perpetrator. State parties still decide by themselves whether an alleged offender is prosecuted or extradited to the requesting state. On the other hand, imposing such an obligation on states would considerably interfere with their competences and would cause reluctance to ratify the treaties.

Since we mention the problem with ratification, that is probably the most serious issue concerning the Beijing instruments. As we have already pointed out, the treaties themselves were drafted in 2010, and ever since very few states

82 United Nations Office on Drugs and Crime, Manual on Mutual Legal Assistance and Extradition, United Nations Office, Vienna 2012, p. 49.

have signed. Both documents entered into force roughly 8 years after adoption and currently, only 25 states, have ratified, acceded or accepted the Convention, whereas the Protocol has just 2 parties more (as of October 2018). Reluctance to be bound by the instruments probably arises from their content considerably affecting the domestic legal system and does it to a much further extent than earlier treaties. However, several states, like France, have reported that the ratification of the Beijing instruments does not seriously affect domestic legislation, nor does it pose challenges for the organisation of administration or a state's budget.[83] Many states have claimed that the interpretation of Article 1(1) point (i) is especially problematic, since it introduces the criminalisation of carrying weapons for the purpose of committing a terrorist act on board an aircraft. There are concerns that airlines on board whose aircraft terrorists smuggle or wield weapons in order to carry out a terrorist attack might incur criminal liability for assisting in these activities. However, those concerns seem to be exaggerated, as Article 1 only establishes the criminalisation of unlawful and intentional acts. If an airline accepts the embarkation of a passenger against while having no evidence of them potentially carrying a weapon or other dangerous material or substance, it is highly unlikely that it would risk any criminal liability, as there is no intent to facilitate carrying them on board.

Despite all the imperfections rooted inside them, the Beijing instruments form a solid and well-suited for present times juridical tools for fight against aerial terrorism. They continue the tendency of the previously adopted treaties from the Tokyo-Hague-Montreal-Beijing system of extending the catalogue of offences and restricting the extradition procedures, so that assurance of punishing terrorists increases. The single obstacle blocking the Beijing instruments from full effectiveness – the reluctance of states to ratify them unnecessarily prolongs the time of lower protection of air passengers against acts of aerial terrorism.

---

83 In its projet de loi (draft of a bill), the Ministry of Foreign Affairs of France emphasised that the ratification of the Beijing instruments does not significantly interfere with the French penal code, as most of their materiae is already covered by its existing provisions (or other legal acts, like the Code of Transport, or the Code of Environment). Ministry for Europe and Foreign Affairs of the Republic of France, Projet de loi autorisant la ratification de la convention sur la répression des actes illicites dirigés contre l'aviation civile internationale et du protocole complémentaire à la convention pour la répression de la capture illicite d'aéronefs, pp. 5-10.

2.2.6. The Montreal Protocol of 2014

a) Circumstances of drafting

It is not only the violent terrorist attacks of high magnitude that seriously impact the security of the passengers. The international community has been observing a growing number of drug and alcohol abuse by "unruly passengers" causing flights to be disrupted and forced to land elsewhere than their originally planned destination.[84]

To effectively counter the problem, the ICAO in 2010 re-set up a Study Group on Unruly Passengers within its Legal Committee that would consider new issues related to the subject.[85] Its works convinced the Member States to organise another Diplomatic Conference on security. It was held in Montreal from 26 March to 4 April 2014 and its primary objective was to amend the aging and outdated Tokyo Convention. 100 ICAO Member States were represented, along with 9 international organisations. On the last day of the conference, the 2014 Montreal Protocol was signed by 35 states.[86] And, in accordance with its Article XVIII it entered into force on 1 January 2020, two months after being ratified by Nigeria.[87]

b) Enhancement of the Tokyo Convention

The Montreal Protocol of 2014, as explained above, was mainly intended to repel the acts of unruly passengers on board rather than terrorist attacks. However, some of its provisions are relevant for our study, so a brief analysis shall be presented.

First of all, it is visible that the Protocol does not significantly change the scope of application of the Tokyo Convention. The wording of its Article 1(1) is unamended, stating that the Convention is applicable to offences against penal law and acts that may jeopardise aircraft safety (or the safety of the persons or

---

84 Only in the period from 2007 to 2015, the number of unscheduled landings due to violent behaviour of unruly passengers reached nearly 50,000.

85 ICAO, Supplementary Report on Activities of the Organization in the First Half of 2010, ICAO Doc 9921 Supplement, p. 14.

86 https://applications.icao.int/postalhistory/legal_instruments_related_to_aviation_security.htm (9 March 2021)

87 A full list of parties can be viewed on the following website: https://www.icao.int/secretariat/legal/list%20of%20parties/montreal_prot_2014_en.pdf (9 March 2021).

property on board), or good order and discipline. However, the Protocol, via its Article II, removed from the Convention's text the ambiguous understanding of "aircraft in flight" and replaced it with a single definition, identical to the one present in the Beijing Convention, to better reflect the time when an aircraft commander's powers are applied.[88]

Another *novum* that deserves attention is entitling a "state of operator" to establish its jurisdiction over acts covered by the Convention (Article II of the Protocol amending Article 1(3) of the Convention). Usually, by state of operator, we mean the lessee of an aircraft, whose principal place of business (or place of permanent residence) is located outside the state of registry. This formulation reflects the continuous tendency for airlines to enhance their fleets by leased, rather than purchased, aircraft. More and more frequently then, the state of an aircraft's registry is different than the state of its operator. In addition to that, to the basis of Article 83 *bis* of the Chicago Convention, the latter one may, under an agreement concluded between them, have some regulatory and oversight rights transferred thereupon.[89] In such a situation, an aircraft might, apart from its registration marking, have no link to its state of registry. That only justifies granting the state of operator jurisdiction rights.

Along with the state of operator, the state of landing can also exercise their jurisdiction (under Article IV amending Article 3 of the Convention). By the state of landing, the Protocol assumes the State of the last point of departure, or the next point of intended landing of an aircraft on board which the offence is committed. Jurisdiction can be exercised only if the alleged offender is still present on board that aircraft and the safety of aircraft (or its passengers or property) is jeopardised. That construction is logical: the state of landing is the first to make contact with an unruly passenger that committed an offence on board and endangered the safety of flight. Therefore, it is usually capable of quickly initiate proceedings and detain them. Added paragraph 2 *ter* to Article 3 also requires a State of landing to assess whether an act committed on board is an offence according to its domestic law, which further increases changes for effective prosecution.[90]

---

88 J. A. Urban, "The Protocol to Amend the Convention on Offences and Certain Acts Committed on Board Aircraft: A Missed Opportunity or a Sufficient Modernization?", Indiana Law Review, Vol. 49(713) 2016, p. 719.

89 IATA, Comments on the Issue of State of Operator Jurisdiction, DCTC Doc. No. 18, para 2.

90 The argument of making the jurisdiction of a state of landing mandatory was evoked by several states during the International Conference, including Argentina. IATA was

Montreal Protocol 2014 is the first-of-its-kind treaty to mention the role of in-flight security officers (or IFSOs), so called "sky marshals".[91] Article VII amending Article 6 of the Convention empowers them with certain rights aimed at effective restraint of unruly passengers. The most important changes implemented into the Convention include: a right of aircraft commander to request (not require) assistance of an IFSO in restraint; a right of an IFSO to take preventive action against passengers, even without prior request of an aircraft commander, if they have reasonable grounds to believe that offence is about to be committed; attribution of the same immunity as the aircraft commander and passengers [see sub-chapter 2.2.2., section (d)].[92]

But perhaps the most distinctive element of the Protocol is its Article X adding Article 15 *bis* to the Convention. It entitles (but does not oblige) states to initiate relevant proceedings (either criminal, administrative or of any other kind) against unruly passengers, particularly when they commit any of the following acts:

> "a) physical assault or a threat to commit such assault against a crew member; or
> b) refusal to follow a lawful instruction given by or on behalf of the aircraft commander for the purpose of protecting the safety of the aircraft or of persons or property therein."[93]

---

supportive towards that, too, stating that according to airlines, nearly 60 percent of prosecutors cite the lack of jurisdiction as the primary reason for not pursuing charges against an offender.

J. A. Urban, "The Protocol to Amend the Convention". p. 722.

91 In-flight security officer (hereafter "IFSO") is a person whose function is defined in Annex 17 (Security) to the Chicago Convention:

"A person who is authorized by the government of the [s]tate of the [o]perator and the government of the [s]tate of [r]egistration to be deployed on an aircraft with the purpose of protecting that aircraft and its occupants against acts of unlawful interference. This excludes persons employed to provide exclusive personal protection for one or more specific people travelling on the aircraft, such as personal bodyguards."

Annex 17 to Convention on International Civil Aviation, done at Chicago, 7 December 1944 – Security, Tenth Edition, 2017, Definitions.

92 T. S. Huay, The Montreal Protocol 2014 - What Changes Will It Bring?, PowerPoint Presentation on ICAO Legal Seminar, on 28 November 2017, Nairobi, Kenya (https://www.icao.int/Meetings/LegalSeminar/Documents/TSH_Montreal%20Protocol%202014%20%2828Nov17%29.pdf) (9 March 2021).

93 Protocol to Amend the Convention on Offences and Certain Other Acts Committed on Board Aircraft, done at Montreal on 4 April 2014 (hereafter referred to as: "Montreal Protocol 2014"), Article X.

Would any of those acts be classified as a terrorist attack? If we look at the traits of terrorism [see sub-chapter 1.2.3.] and compare them to the above-mentioned acts, we would probably receive a negative answer. It is difficult to imagine a mere assault against a crew member, or refusal to follow aircraft commander's instructions as act with a political or religious motive, targeted at a government or international organisation. What is more, a terrorist attack should account for an offence. And according to provisions of the Montreal Protocol of 2014 or the Tokyo Convention, those acts do not necessarily must be regarded by state parties as offences. Nevertheless, physical assault or refusal to follow instructions of an aircraft commander might be an element of a greater terrorist operation. If a perpetrator wields a melee weapon and plans to approach a flight deck for a purpose of hijack, he might first attack any of crew members to facilitate himself the task. If then a state entitled to exercise jurisdiction decides to criminalise such behaviour, the offender might be punished already for that, even if he is subsequently incapacitated by an IFSO.

c) Commentary

The Montreal Protocol of 2014 is indeed an important instrument in the legal framework of aviation security, but fails to address essential issues in fight against terrorism. Its main purpose is to prevent occurrence of minor acts of undisciplined passengers that may jeopardise the safety of flight, rather than terrorist attacks of a greater magnitude.

Nevertheless, the Protocol itself might be praised for introducing a regulation of a problem that recently became disturbing for aviation industry, caused many delays and put health and life of passengers and crew in danger. What is more, it vested on IFSOs an accurate set of powers to restrain troublesome passengers, or in some cases, even terrorists before they commence an actual attack.

However, in contrast to The Hague and Montreal Conventions, as well as the Beijing instruments, the Montreal Protocol of 2014 does not introduce new solutions on extradition of offenders, or extension of catalogue of offences. More significant changes consist in turn of broadening of jurisdiction (by the state of operator and the state of landing). In general, the role of the Montreal Protocol of 2014 in global war against terrorism is marginal.

2.3. United Nations

Since its establishment in 1945, the United Nations has been taking efforts to fulfil its principal, somewhat uneasy task of maintaining international peace and security. During turbulent times of the Cold War, the UN was primarily concerned with local armed conflicts across the globe in which hostilities were conducted between supporters of the Soviet Union and countries backed by the United States and its western allies. But the growing threat from international terrorism forced the UN to include fight against it on its agenda. The importance of the actions taken was considerable and related to the fact that it is a single international organisation of a true universal character.[94]

The role the United Nations plays in the global war on terror evolves with time and is dependent on the capabilities of its organs (attributed thereto by the provisions of the UN Charter) and other agencies created within it. Currently, there exist 6 main organs: the General Assembly, the Security Council, the Economic and Social Council (ECOSOC), the International Court of Justice, and the Secretariat and Trusteeship Council. Apart from the Trusteeship Council, whose leading task was already realised[95], all organs have the particular competences vital for effective conduct of fight against terrorism (including aerial terrorism). Of course, within the organs function also other subsidiary bodies, including the United Nations Office on Drugs and Crime (UNODC), the United Nations Office of Counter-Terrorism (UNOCT), etc. Finally, a large spectrum of functions is executed by specialised agencies of the UN, being *de iure* separate and independent international organisations, but cooperating with the UN on the basis of an agreement with the ECOSOC and under its coordination.[96] One of such specialised agencies is the ICAO [discussed in previous sub-chapter].

The present sub-chapter aims primarily at presenting mechanisms functioning within the United Nations (mostly of legislative character) that are intended to prevent and eliminate threats of aerial terrorism. Firstly, the role of the General Assembly in the process shall be analysed, followed by an overview of Security Council achievements.

---

94 M. Lech, Ochrona prawna społeczności międzynarodowej, p. 111.

95 M. Marcinko, ONZ, p. 17. The author evokes words of then-Secretary-General of the UN, Kofi Annan, who proposed in his report In Larger Freedom: Towards Development, Security and Human Rights for All to remove Chapter XIII (on Trusteeship Council) from the UN Charter.

96 J. Menkes, A. Wasilkowski, Organizacje międzynarodowe. Prawo instytucjonalne (Wolters Kluwer Polska: Warszawa, 2010), p.120-121.

2.3.1. General Assembly

The General Assembly of the United Nations is a plenary organ, consisting of representatives of all Member States, whose primary function is to be a forum for the exchange of views and political discussions on most serious matters for international community, including world terrorism. Due to its institutional attributions, provided in the UN Charter, UNGA is unable to implement binding instruments (except for internal matters, like adoption of budget), but only acts being if fact soft law.[97] However, due to its role as a main arena for discussion between nearly all nations of the world, the General Assembly's resolutions should not be underestimated.

a) Pre-9/11 Resolutions

The UNGA expressed its interest in international terrorism not earlier than in 1970s. Its first resolution treating thereon was marked 3034 (XXVII) and adopted on 18 December 1972. Its draft was prompted by tragic events that occurred in Munich during Summer Olympics the same year – terrorists affiliated with the organisation called Black September held eleven representatives of the Israel Olympic team captive and eventually killed them.[98]

The Resolution was the first to address UN Member States with a call to accede to international conventions on the fight against terrorism and find peaceful solution to the problem of those acts of violence. However, its wording was not as much critical towards perpetrators themselves, as it was towards the States holding colonial powers. In paragraph 4, it states that "colonial, racist and alien regimes are repressive and terrorist", and deny peoples "their legitimate right to self-determination".[99] Therefore, the UNGA signalled that the problem with terrorism lies more within colonial powers rather than direct offenders and therefore blamed for occurrence of terrorist attacks should be States themselves. Nevertheless, the UNGA reasonably assumed that terrorism became an urgent problem and via paragraph 9 established an *Ad Hoc* Committee on International Terrorism consisting of 35 members appointed by the President of the General

97 Karta Narodów Zjednoczonych, in: Encyklopedia prawa międzynarodowego i stosunków międzynarodowych, Wiedza Powszechna, Warszawa 1976.

98 M. Marcinko, ONZ, p. 27.

99 United Nations General Assembly Resolution 3034 (XXVII), 18 December 1972, para 4.

Assembly. Its principal task was preparation of effective methods to prevent terrorist attacks and eliminate its fundamental causes.

Although Resolution 3034 (XXVII) did not effectively deal with the problem of international terrorism growing at that time, it acted as an impulse for further similar acts, adopted later by the General Assembly proposing more concrete measures against terrorism, including aerial terrorism.

Resolution 34/145, adopted on 17 December 1979 was the first one to be undertaken following the publication of the *Ad Hoc* Committee report. The report itself refers to aerial terrorism repetitively, particularly pointing at aircraft hijacking as one of most serious terrorist crimes.[100] Committee also criticised States for reluctance to accede into Conventions related to aerial terrorism (at that time: the Tokyo Convention, Hague Convention and Montreal Convention) and constant refusals to prosecute or extradite offenders responsible for hijackings.[101] Recommendations for the General Assembly to urge UN Members States to become parties to anti-terrorist Conventions were also inserted. Generally, the Resolution follows the instructions expressed in the report and calls States to cooperate in the field of prevention and elimination of terrorism, particularly in exchange of relevant information.

Similar wording was present in subsequently issued Resolutions on Measures to prevent international terrorism adopted in following years. The problem of aerial terrorism was more visibly emphasised not earlier than in 1985 when UNGA adopted without the vote Resolution No. 40/61 (on 9 December). The year itself was a true harvest of death for aerial terrorists – several planes were hijacked (including EgyptAir 648)[102], and Air India flight 182 was blown up from the skies.[103] Moreover, brutal attacks at airports were also recorded, with

---

100 See Report of the Ad Hoc Committee on International Terrorism, United Nations General Assembly Official Records, Thirty-Fourth Session, Supplement No. 37 (A/34/37), para 46 & 48.

101 Report of the Ad Hoc Committee on International Terrorism, United Nations General Assembly Official Records, Thirty-Fourth Session, Supplement No. 37 (A/34/37), para 96.

102 A Boeing 737 belonging to EgyptAir en route to Cairo from Athens on November 24th was seized by members of the extremist group Abu Nidal who ordered the flight crew to fly to Libya or Tunisia. The plane ultimately stopped to refuel on Malta and was stormed by Egyptian military who successfully killed the hijackers; https://aviation-safety.net/database/record.php?id=19851124-0 (9 March 2021).

103 On 23 June Air India flight 182 (Boeing 747) was on its way from Montreal to Delhi with stopover at London Heathrow Airport. When above Atlantic Ocean, close to Irish coast, it suddenly disappeared from radars. Investigation determined that bombing

two most notable at Rome – Fiumicino and Vienna – Schwechat. That tragic death toll prompted UNGA to encourage States through the Resolution to apply measures recommended by ICAO stated in relevant international conventions "to prevent terrorist attacks against civil aviation transport".[104] Furthermore, the ICAO was addressed with the request to "continue […] efforts aimed at promoting universal acceptance of and strict compliance with the international air security conventions".[105]

Resolution 42/159, adopted on 7 December 1987 refers directly to Resolution 41/60 (in its Preamble) and expresses positive attitude of the UNGA towards measures undertaken by ICAO in the field of aviation security. That is probably due to significantly lower number of victims of terrorist attacks that occurred in 1986 and 1987 in comparison with fatalities of attacks in 1985 (including attacks on civil aviation)[106]. The ICAO was also praised for having been preparing the Montreal Protocol for the purpose of prevention and elimination of attacks at international airports.[107] Vital is to notice here that Resolution 42/159 is the first one to comprise precise measures on elimination of terrorism addressed to States. They are enumerated in paragraph 5:

1) prevention of preparation and organisation of terrorist attacks directed against other States and their citizens;
2) assurance of the apprehension and prosecution/extradition of perpetrators;
3) endeavour to conclude agreements on bilateral, regional and multilateral basis dealing with fight against terrorism;
4) mutual cooperation in exchange of information concerning preventing and combatting terrorism;
5) harmonisation of domestic legislation with international conventions to which they are parties.[108]

The stress on the role of the ICAO in elimination of terrorism is featured also in Resolution No. 44/29 adopted by the UNGA on 4 December 1989. Most of its

---

was a cause – explosives were planted on board by Sikh militants from Babbar Khalsa; https://aviation-safety.net/database/record.php?id=19850623-2 (9 March 2021).

104 United Nations General Assembly Resolution 41/60, 9 December 1985, para 11.

105 United Nations General Assembly Resolution 41/60, 9 December 1985, para 12.

106 See diagram on numbers of victims of terrorist attacks from 1970 to 2015; (9 March 2021). https://www.datagraver.com/case/people-killed-by-terrorism-per-year-in-western-europe-1970-2015

107 United Nations General Assembly Resolution 42/159, 7 December 1987, para 9.

108 United Nations General Assembly Resolution 42/159, 7 December 1987, para 5.

provisions are similar or even identical in wording with those present in Resolution 42/159, but are formulated to reflect the status of global efforts at the time in the fight against terrorism. The UNGA appreciated in the Resolution adoption of the Montreal Protocol by the ICAO and furthermore urged the organisation to carry on its works on convention on marking plastic explosives for the purpose of detection. That call was not without a particular reason: just one year before Resolution 44/29 was adopted, the world was shocked by a terrible accident with a terrorist background: the Lockerbie bombing. On 21 December 1988, a Boeing 747 belonging to Pan American World Airways (or Pan Am) performing a flight 103 from London/Heathrow Airport to John F. Kennedy Airport in New York, exploded in mid-air, above the small town of Lockerbie, Scotland killing all 259 people on board, including 243 passengers and 16 crew members. 11 other persons were killed on the ground. The investigation conducted shortly afterwards revealed that the cause was a bomb hidden in a bag loaded into the plane in Frankfurt where the flight had originated [the case shall be discussed in detail later in this chapter]. The catastrophe is one of the most tragic events in aviation history.

The Lockerbie bombing was a key factor in the ICAO's process of drafting a convention on marking plastic explosives. The convention (eventually concluded on 1 March 1991)[109] would prohibit the manufacture and storage of plastic explosives without proper markings, so that they are identified easier during security checks at the airports and in consequence the risk of loading a bag containing an IED would be much reduced.

The contents of Resolution 44/29 clearly show that the UNGA deepened its interest in aviation security. Although the document did not refer directly to the Lockerbie disaster, the message arising from it is vivid: the UNGA supports all efforts aimed at the elimination of aerial terrorism and welcomes all juridical initiatives aimed at pursuing perpetrators of terrorist attempts.

The resolutions adopted in late 1980s and early 1990s signal the change of perception of the UNGA towards terrorism; the UN body rarely evokes the right of peoples to self-determination and no longer points at state regimes as those responsible for terrorist behaviour. Instead, the balance shifted to perpetrators

109 Officially named the "Convention on the Marking of Plastic Explosives for the Purpose of Detection done at Montreal on 1 March 1991". It entered into force on 21 June 1998. As of March 2021, there are 156 parties to the convention. The full list can be found on this website: https://www.icao.int/secretariat/legal/List%20of%20Parties/MEX_EN.pdf (9 March 2021).

themselves – they are not treated any more as fighters seeking liberty from oppression, but as offenders whose persecution should be prioritised by all states of the world. It is especially visible in Resolution 49/60 from 17 February 1995, whose core constitutes the Declaration on Measures to Eliminate International Terrorism (referred to as "Declaration" subsequently in this section). Through the Declaration, the UNGA again condemned all forms of terrorism, regardless of their ground (political, ideological, philosophical, racial, ethnic, religious, etc.) and encouraged States to accede into international conventions on prevention of terrorism (including the Tokyo, Hague, Montreal Conventions and the Montreal Protocol). Also, the measures to eliminate terrorism are repeatedly enumerated, as stated in paragraph 5 of the Resolution 42/159 with the inclusion of recommendation to ensure that before asylum is granted for a demanding person, all measures have been taken to verify if such a person had a terrorist background.[110] M. Marcinko affirms that the Declaration is very pragmatic and finally reflects the reality of terrorism, as it does not refer to "freedom movements" nor does it justify any kind of terrorist violence.[111]

On 16 January 1997, the UNGA adopted another Resolution, closely related to the Declaration. Resolution 51/210 as a main goal had an establishment of an Ad Hoc Committee that would elaborate conventions on suppression of terrorist bombings and suppression of acts of nuclear terrorism.[112] It also further supplements the Declaration by provisions that before granting an asylum-seeker refugee status, states need to make sure that such a person has not participated in terrorist acts and that after receiving the status granted, they would not use it for the purpose of committing a terrorist act against another state or its citizens.[113] Moreover, the Resolution called for treating terrorist offences as non-political for the purpose of extradition treaties between states and the general facilitation of extradition proceedings against terrorists.[114] By adopting this Resolution, the UNGA again showed pragmatism and emphasised essential problems related to fight against terrorism, proposing accordingly effective measures to counter the growing threat therefrom. Positive was also a decision to establish the Ad Hoc

110 United Nations General Assembly Resolution 49/60, 17 February 1995, Annex, para 5.
111 M. Marcinko, ONZ, p. 38.
112 United Nations General Assembly Resolution 50/210, 16 January 1997, para 5.
113 United Nations General Assembly Resolution 50/210, 16 January 1997, para 3.
114 United Nations General Assembly Resolution 50/210, 16 January 1997, para 6 & 7.

Committee on drafting two conventions dealing with terrorist bombings and nuclear terrorism.[115]

b) Post-9/11 Resolutions

When the United States, and along with them, the whole international community, was struck by the violent act of terrorism on 11 September 2001, the UNGA could not stay silent. On the first plenary meeting that occurred the next day, it adopted Resolution No. 56/1, being one of the shortest documents ever issued by the UN body. In the opening paragraph, the General Assembly condemned "the heinous acts of terrorism, which have caused enormous loss of human life, destruction and damage in the cities of New York, host city of the United Nations, and Washington, D.C., and in Pennsylvania".[116] Subsequently, all states were called to take all efforts to bring perpetrators before justice and to cooperate for suspension and prevention of terrorism. The Resolution also contained a clear message that those harbouring, financing or aiding terrorist shall be held accountable.

Resolution No. 56/1 was probably the first document enacted by the UNGA that referred directly to a particular terrorist attack. That Resolution initiated also a period of greater devotion of the General Assembly to the problem of terrorism – the body ever since has adopted way more Resolutions on measures against terrorism than before attacks on WTC, including some that were of a significant character.

Inarguably the most remarkable one is Resolution No. 60/288, adopted on September 8th, 2006, entitled "The United Nations Global Counter-Terrorism Strategy" (referred to as the "Strategy" subsequently in the present chapter).

---

115 Both conventions were subsequently adopted. The International Convention for the Suppression of Terrorist Bombings was adopted by the UNGA Resolution No. 52/164, on 15 December 1997. Its structure is analogical to one featured in the Tokyo-Hague-Montreal-Beijing system treaties; it defines the offence of bombing, introduces provisions on jurisdiction and extradition, describes relevant duties of state parties etc. It entered into force on 23 May 2001 and currently there are 170 parties thereto. In turn, by Resolution No. 59/290 (on 13 April 2005), the UNGA adopted the International Convention for the Suppression of Acts of Nuclear Terrorism. Its structure is also similar to other terrorist conventions and describes the elements of offences related to usage of radioactive material and stipulates on the role of International Atomic Energy Agency. The Convention became effective on 7 July 2007 and at present there are 114 parties thereto.

116 United Nations General Assembly Resolution No. 56/1, 12 September 2001, para 1.

The document is, as the UN declares on its official website, "a unique global instrument to enhance national, regional and international efforts to counter terrorism".[117] Reviewed every two years, the Strategy is structurally composed of a main body an annex named "Plan of action", which is its essential part, featuring 4 pillars (each of them is covered by a separate chapter):

I. Addressing the conditions conducive to the spread of terrorism;
II. Measures to prevent and combat terrorism;
III. Measures to build States' capacity to prevent and combat terrorism and to strengthen the role of the United Nations system in that regard;
IV. Measures to ensure respect for human rights for all and the rule of law as the fundamental basis for the fight against terrorism.

The Strategy contains many general provisions, characteristic for previously adopted Resolutions, as well as more practical solutions, including those related to civil aviation. Particular issues in that matter are featured in chapters II and III. Paragraph 14 of chapter II encourages states to undertake administrative and legal measures to implement terrorist travel-related obligations on the basis of what was prepared by technical organisations, such as the ICAO. Typically, such travel-related obligations would consist of proper security checks at airports, implementation of aircraft security programmes, etc. In paragraph 1 of Chapter III, the UNGA turned its attention to financing ant-terrorist initiatives in civil aviation and encouraged States to invest more, and with the assistance of private sector entities, in capacity-building programmes, particularly in the areas of port, maritime and aviation security. In turn, in paragraph 12, the ICAO, along with the World Customs Organisation and the International Maritime Organisation, was requested to cooperate with states in the manner of detecting shortfalls in national transport security systems and provide assistance in eliminating them.

The UNGA also referred to signature of both the Beijing Convention and Beijing Protocol, as instruments aimed at improving combat against aerial terrorism. In its Resolution 66/178 (adopted on 19 December 2011), the body addressed all UN Member States with a call to consider accession into international anti-terrorist conventions and protocols, including Beijing instruments. Another important addressee of the Resolution, beside Member States is the UNODC, requested to provide states a technical assistance with ratification and legislative incorporation of those acts.

117 https://www.un.org/counterterrorism/ctitf/un-global-counter-terrorism-strategy (9 March 2021).

c) Commentary

The United Nations General Assembly definitely contributed to global actions carried out against international terrorism. Although the body expressed its interest in the matter relatively late, in the beginning of the 1970s, since then it adopted numerous resolutions in response to growing threat from terrorists. Multiple times, it also emphasised the necessity to enhance measures to protect civil aviation from terrorist attacks, particularly by encouraging nations to become parties to treaties of the Tokyo-Hague-Montreal-Beijing system. We need also to positively rate the evolution of approach to terrorism taken by the UNGA. Although in earlier Resolutions, the body was seeking a main cause of terrorism within States' behaviour, mostly colonial powers provoking peoples under their regime to "fight for freedom", with time it changed its view by 180 degrees and focused on perpetrators themselves.

In fact, the General Assembly usually do not refer to particular events directly (the attack on WTC on 11 September was an exception), but often do not stay indifferent in regards to serious terrorist attacks (like Lockerbie bombing) and adopts relevant Resolutions in response to them. Some may argue that Resolutions themselves rarely contain concrete and precise measures that would eliminate threat of terrorism. But we need to remember that General Assembly, unlike Security Council has no competence of adopting binding norms, but only political declarations whose observance is not required by Member States. Still, UNGA should be praised for having drafted several dozens of Resolutions related to terrorism, as represented there are nearly all States of the world, devoted to different values and exercising different policies. In addition to that, on the forum of General Assembly concluded were several anti-terrorist conventions to which vast majority of States are nowadays parties, including Convention on the Prevention and Punishment of Crimes against Internationally Protected Persons, including Diplomatic Agents (signed 14 December 1973), International Convention against Taking of Hostages (signed 17 December 1979) or International Convention for the Suppression of Terrorist Bombings (signed on 15 December 1997). Solely a fact that Resolutions and conventions adopted by UNGA are so numerous only proves that combat against terrorism has a truly global character.

Truthful would be a statement that despite high number of documents issued by UNGA treating on terrorism, relatively few focus on aerial terrorism. On one hand that is quite understandable, as the principal role in improving aviation security was vested in the ICAO and most legal documents related to protection of civil aviation from terrorist threat have been drafted by the latter one. On the other hand, some of terrorist attempts directed at civil aviation were particularly violent and deserved to be discussed on the forum of the UNGA and subsequently mentioned in its Resolutions, not just referred indirectly [see above]. That would be an additional signal from the whole international community that any kind of violence stemming from terrorists is unacceptable.

2.3.2. Security Council

The main role of the UNSC, its powers and composition are subject of Chapter V of the UN Charter. According to its Article 24, the body is responsible for the maintenance of international peace and security. The UNSC is composed of 15 members, out of which 5 are permanent (China, France, Russia, the United Kingdom and the United States) and others are non-permanent, elected for the period of two years.

In the realisation of its powers, the Security Council, in similarity with the General Assembly, adopts specific decisions, like Resolutions. In order to effectively adopt them, an affirmative vote of at least nine members is required (under Article 27 of the UN Charter), provided that none of the permanent members veto it. Absence or abstention from voting does not count as a veto.[118]

Throughout the history of the UN, the Security Council adopted dozens of documents related to international terrorism, mostly in a form of Resolutions. In contrast to acts issued by the UNGA, the Security Council's decisions are binding upon all members of the UN and usually take a more concrete character – they refer to a particular situation that may pose a threat to international peace and security.

The present sub-chapter shall examine the Resolutions adopted by the UNSC in reaction to acts of aerial terrorism and comment their effectiveness.

118 J. Menkes, A. Wasilkowski, Organizacje międzynarodowe, p. 271.
In the Advisory Opinion of 21 June 1971, the International Court of Justice pointed out that at the time of voting over Resolution 276 (1970), already crystallised was a customary law norm that voluntary abstention by a permanent member does not constitute a bar to the adoption of resolutions. "By abstaining, a member does not signify its objection to the approval of what is being proposed; in order to prevent the adoption of a resolution requiring unanimity of the permanent members, a permanent member has only to cast a negative vote. See Legal Consequences for States of the Continued Presence of South Africa in Namibia (South West Africa) notwithstanding Security Council Resolution 276 (1970)", Advisory Opinion of 21 June 1970: ICJ. Reports 1971 Advisory Opinion, I.C.J. Reports 1971, p. 16, para 22.

a) Resolutions adopted before the 1990s

The UNSC reacted to a terrorist attempt for the first time in 1948. During the early days of the Israeli-Palestine conflict, a group of Israeli-born terrorists called Sterna murdered Count Folke Bernadotte, a mediator in the pending conflict.[119] In response, on September,18th, 1948, the Security Council unanimously adopted Resolution 57 (1948) in which it briefly affirms how shocking the death of the official was and denounces the act of assassination as "cowardly". But apart from that, no condemnation is expressed, neither was the act itself called "terrorist". Two more decades needed to pass before the Security Council's voice on terrorism was heard again.

At the turn of the 1960s and 1970s, a massive increase of aircraft hijackings prompted the UNSC to take the floor in the matter. On September 9th, 1970, it adopted Resolution 286 (1970) expressing its grave concern at the threat to innocent civilians who became victims of hijackers. The document ordered the states to release all passengers and crew being held as a result of hijackings, as well as call to take all possible legal steps to prevent further hijackings and other acts of unlawful interference against civil aviation.[120] Although the merits of the Resolution were more concrete than in previous one, the UNSC still did not take a proper approach against the threat. Of course, not all kinds of skyjackings having occurred at that time were of terrorist character, but all put the lives of passengers and crew into danger. Therefore, the body should have affirmed its condemnation of those attacks and request States to take more complex actions.

A bolder approach was taken by the UNSC in Resolution 337 (1973), adopted on 15 August 1973, which, paradoxically, was a reaction to counter-terrorist measures undertaken by Israel. On 10 August 1973, Israeli fighter jets intercepted a Middle East Airlines (Lebanon's flag carrier) Sud Aviation Caravelle plane en route from Beirut to Baghdad. The Israeli air force ordered the plane to land at a military airfield in Israel just a few minutes after take-off. After two hours of passenger check, the airliner was let free and allowed to continue for Baghdad. Eventually, Israeli authorities explained publicly that their aim was to intercept another plane, also bound for Baghdad, on board which one of the PFLP leaders, responsible for several terrorist attempts, George Habash, was present.

---

119 M. Marcinko, ONZ, 110.

120 United Nations Security Council Resolution 286, 9 September 1970, para 1 & 2.

Israel however, made a mistake and intercepted the wrong machine.[121] The Resolution itself strongly criticises Israel as a member of the UN and states that its actions violated Lebanon's sovereignty and territorial integrity, as well as constituted a breach of multiple international law documents, including the Lebanese-Israeli Armistice Agreement.[122] However, the Security Council abstained from imposing any real sanctions on Israel and only issued a warning not to repeat such actions under threat of "adequate steps or measures to enforce [the Security Council's] resolutions".[123] The UN body totally omitted the question of the counter-terrorist nature of the operation; there was no evoking of justification towards such action, even if the main aim was to pursue a person responsible for terrorist attacks (in this case George Habash). Nevertheless, Resolution 337 was a clear message to the international community that civil aviation must be free from third state interference, even in the name of the latter's security.

A slightly different attitude was taken by the UNSC in Resolution 496 (1981) from 15 December 1981. It concerned an event that occurred in November of the same year. In the Seychelles, a coup d'etat was being prepared against the then-president France-Albert René by a group of mercenaries under South African supervision. When they reached the Seychelles Airport in Mahé, security forces attempted to halt them and a shootout ensued. The mercenaries were losing and sought to escape the island. When Air India flight 224, a Boeing 707, on its way from Harare to Mumbai, landed at the airport for its scheduled refuelling, mercenaries embarked it and ordered the crew to fly to Rhodesia. Ultimately, the hijacked plane landed in Durban, South Africa.[124]

The UNSC responded to a complaint filed jointly by the Seychelles and Botswana and condemned the attacks and the subsequent hijacking in the Resolution. The body did not hesitate to call the attack "an aggression".[125] At that time, it was unknown that South Africa was the main organiser of the coup d'etat. In order to investigate the background and origins of the operation, an inquiry

---

121 T. Smith, "Israeli Jets Over Lebanon Force Down Arab Airliner", The New York Times, 11 August 1973 (9 March 2021) https://www.nytimes.com/1973/08/11/archives/israeli-jets-over-lebanon-force-down-arab-airliner-military-says-it.html

122 United Nations Security Council Resolution 337, 15 August 1973, para 1 & 2.

123 United Nations Security Council Resolution 337, 15 August 1973, para 4.

124 C. Mitchell, "Mercenaries to stand trial on coup attempt", UPI Archives, 14 June 1981. (9 March 2021) https://www.upi.com/Archives/1982/06/14/Mercenaries-to-stand-trial-on-coup-attempt/4805392875200/.

125 United Nations Security Council Resolution 496, 15 December 1981, para 2.

commission was formed.[126] It is evident that the UNSC undertook more definitive steps against the attempt on a state's sovereignty than in the case of Israel. The mercenaries' act was not, in fact, called "terrorist" (despite reasons to do just that), but the Security Council did not abstain from imposing measures that would lead to incurring responsibility by those accountable.

b) Post-Lockerbie bombing Resolutions

The tragic events of December 1988 that brought down Pan Am flight 103 and caused the death of 270 people [see sub-chapter 2.3.1. section (a)] ignited a lively discussion within the UNSC on aviation security and aerial terrorism prevention. The body adopted a series of Resolutions referring directly to that problem and consequentially naming violent acts against civil aviation "terrorist".

Just half a year after the Lockerbie bombing (on 14 June 1989), the Security Council enacted Resolution 635 (1989), in which it condemned "all acts of unlawful interference against the security of civil aviation".[127] Furthermore, the Resolution stated praised the actions taken by the ICAO and Member States that eliminate acts of international terrorism in the field of civil aviation. Analogically with Resolution 496, some practical measures were also recommended. The Security Council urged both the ICAO and the Member States to intensify their works on drafting the convention on marking plastic explosives for the purpose of detection (the UNGA adopted Resolution No. 44/29 in the same year with similar objectives) and make such markings easily detectable at airports.[128]

The Lockerbie disaster echoed in 1992 again, when the Security Council adopted two relevant Resolutions, concerning mostly Libya's political responsibility for the catastrophe. The investigation conducted in the aftermath of Pan Am flight 103 and the Union des Transports Aériens flight 772[129] revealed that Libyan special services were involved in both accidents.[130] In Resolution 731

---

126 United Nations Security Council Resolution 496, 15 December 1981, para 3.

127 United Nations Security Council Resolution 635, 14 June 1989, para 1.

128 United Nations Security Council Resolution 635, 14 June 1989, para 4-6.

129 On 19 September 1989, a McDonnell Douglas DC-10 belonging to the French airline UTA was performing flight 772 on the Brazzaville-N'Djamena-Paris/Charles de Gaulle route. Less than an hour after take-off from N'Djamena, the plane was struck by an explosion and eventually crashed in the Ténéré desert. All 156 passengers and 14 crew were killed; https://aviation-safety.net/database/record.php?id=19890919-1 (9 March 2021).

130 M. Marcinko, ONZ, p. 118.

(1992) issued on 21 January the Security Council once more condemned all terrorist acts targeting civil aviation and called the international community to eliminate all its forms. Additionally, the body referred to "state terrorism" as a phenomenon deleterious for international relations.[131] But more importantly, Libya was called to respond to the claims made by France, the United Kingdom and the United States on taking responsibility for both acts of aerial terrorism.

As Libya remained silent about the claims, the Security Council reacted more severely by adopting Resolution 748 (1992) on 31 March 1992. For the first time in history, the body evoked in its Resolution provisions of Article 2(4) of the Charter of the United Nations, thereby affirming that terrorist attacks might be regarded as the use of force threatening international peace and security. The consequence of this approach was the decision to act under Chapter VII of the UN Charter. Apart from a strict call to observe requests addressed to Libya by France, the United Kingdom and the United States and to promptly cease the support of any forms of terrorism, Libya was charged by non-military sanctions. In the foreground was the ban on aircraft taking off from or landing in Libya to fly over territories of all other Member States of the UN and the prohibition of supply of aircraft or their components to Libya[132]. Other sanctions included: suspension of arms trade, withdrawal of diplomats, denial of entry into territory of UN members by Libyan nationals involved in terrorist acts.[133] Furthermore, the UNSC established a special Committee to monitor the observance of mentioned coercive measures and draft reports to the Council.[134]

The Libyan government was reluctant to follow the requests, which caused the UNSC to impose even more severe sanctions. Resolution 883 (1993) from 11 November 1993 obliged states to freeze assets belonging to the Libyan government or other Libyan undertakings located in their territories, restrict economic transactions with Libyan Arab Airlines and significantly reduce crude oil and natural gas trade with Libya.[135]

It is worth to notice here that although in the past, states were called on by the Security Council to hold responsibility for acts of aerial terrorism [see above], the case of Libya was a first in which a responsible state incurred such harsh sanctions, affecting both economic and social affairs. The case proved that the

---

131 United Nations Security Council Resolution 731, 21 January 1992, preamble.
132 United Nations Security Council Resolution 748, 31 March 1992, para 4.
133 United Nations Security Council Resolution 748, 31 March 1992, paras 5 & 6.
134 United Nations Security Council Resolution 748, 31 March 1992, para 9.
135 United Nations Security Council Resolution 883, 11 November 1993.

Security Council is capable of responding accurately and unanimously to the cruelty of terrorism supported by states. What is more, the UNSC did not remain passive against Libya's continual rejection of requests made by France, the United Kingdom and the United States to take responsibility for the attack and imposed further, even more harmful sanctions.

The investigation on the Lockerbie bombing eventually resulted in indicating two suspects, both of Libyan nationality. The pressure from the international community forced the state's government to hand them over for trial to another state. The League of Arab states proposed three different solutions to this issue. Either the suspects were to be judged in a neutral state, in The Hague by a court composed of Scottish judges, or by a special tribunal based in The Hague.[136] The proposal was supported by many entities and brought to life in 1998, when the United Kingdom and the United States decided to judge the suspects in the Netherlands in front of a court seating only Scottish judges. The Security Council also condoned the initiative in Resolution 1192 (1998) from 27 August 1998. The body decided to suspend all sanctions imposed on Libya under Resolution 748, provided that both suspects would arrive in the Netherlands for the trial. The Libyan government finally accepted the request and delivered both persons before the court on 5 April 1999, which resulted in waiving the sanctions. Both suspects were sentenced on 31 January 2001 and the Security Council never adopted another Resolution related directly to the Lockerbie case.[137]

By the end of the twenty-first century, the UNSC adopted several more Resolutions on international terrorism, including Resolution 1067 of 26 July 1996. It concerned two American-registered civil aircraft which were shot down by the Cuban Air Force. Although the incident was not a terrorist act *per se*, it concerned the Security Council as it involved the use of a weapon against a civil aircraft by a state, which is strictly prohibited under the Chicago Convention.[138] Two more

136 M. Marcinko, ONZ, p. 121.

137 One of the accused, Abdel Basset al-Megrahi was found guilty and sentenced to life imprisonment, while the other one, Al Amin Khalifa Fhimah, was acquitted due to lack of proper evidence. See more: M. Marcinko, ONZ, p. 122, after: M. L. O'Sullivan, Shrewd Sanctions: Statecraft and State Sponsors of Terrorism (Brookings Institution Press: Washington D. C., 2003), pp. 184-185.

138 Both machines were small Cessna 337s operating on behalf of the Brothers to the Rescue organisation and were flying above Cuban territory to drop leaflets. They were hit by air-to-air missiles fired by MiG-29 fighters of the CAF while crossing international airspace. All four pilots died in the accident. See Inter-American Commission on Human Rights, Armando Alejandre Jr., Carlos Costa, Mario de la Pena y

Resolutions referring to international terrorism were issued on 13 August 1998 and 19 October 1999, numbered 1189 and 1269 respectively. The former one expressed the Security Council's condemnation of Al-Qaeda's terrorist attacks on US embassies in Nairobi, Kenya and Dar es Salaam, Tanzania and encouraged states to provide assistance to institutions investigating the attacks. The latter one, in turn, was oriented at international terrorism *in genere*. The Security Council instructed states to cooperate through international agreements to prevent terrorism, accede to international conventions on the suppression of terrorist attacks, cease financing terrorist activities, and exchange information on an administrative and international level to prevent the commission of terrorist crimes.

c) Resolutions on the 11 September attacks

The vileness and brutality of the attacks on the World Trade Center and Pentagon on 11 September could not have gone unnoticed by the Security Council. In response, the body issued a series of Resolutions that drastically changed the global attitude towards terrorism and put the question of combat against it in the new light.

Resolution 1368 (2001) adopted on the day following the attacks delivered a very symbolic message. The Security Council condemned the horrifying attacks and affirmed that they constituted a threat to global peace and security and expressed the deepest sympathy with all victims.[139] Moreover, the body pointed at the necessity of unifying the efforts in the fight against world terrorism by convincing all states "to work together urgently to bring to justice the perpetrators, organisers and sponsors of these terrorist attacks".[140] Accordingly, any kind of support, aid or harbouring of perpetrators, organisers or sponsors of those acts would incur responsibility.[141] But of a historical significance was a *passus* of the Resolution's recitals, in which the UNSC invoked the right of an individual and collective self-defence exercised to counter the armed attack. Although there was no clear signal that the Security Council regarded terrorist attacks as entitling to

---

Pablo Morales v. Republica de Cuba, Case 11.589, Report No. 86/99, OEA/Ser.L/V/II.106 Doc. 3 rev. at 586 (1999), United Nations Security Council Resolution 1067, 26 July 1996.

139 United Nations Security Council Resolution 1368, 12 September 2001, paras 1 & 2.

140 United Nations Security Council Resolution 1368, 12 September 2001, para 3.

141 United Nations Security Council Resolution 1368, 12 September 2001, para 3.

apply self-defence, reference to that issue in the Resolution completely changed the perception of the fight against global terrorism [see sub-chapter 1.4.3.].

Resolution 1373 (2001), directly related to Resolution 1368, was adopted a few days later (on September 28th 2001). It imposed more concrete measures on the states to try and facilitate the prevention and elimination of terrorism, related also to domestic legislature of Member States. Some key provisions include the suppression of financing terrorism; criminalisation of a wilful collection of funds for the purpose of carrying out terrorist acts; freezing of funds and economic assets of persons that committed or attempted to commit terrorist acts; refraining from providing recruitment of trainees and supplying arms to terrorist organisations; preventing entities that finance, support or engage in terrorism from conducting activities on their territories against other states or their citizens; criminalising terrorist acts in domestic legal and bringing perpetrators to justice, strengthening border control and during issuance of official documents, exchanging operational information related to the organisation of terrorist networks and the movement of their members, and ensuring that granting refugee status would not make it easier for the person in question to commit terrorist offences.[142]

The implementation of all of the above-mentioned provisions would be monitored by a special Counter-Terrorism Committee (CTC) composed of all members of the Security Council. The Committee would receive reports on the implementation of the provisions from all Member States according to a precise timetable.[143]

One could easily notice that the provisions of Resolution 1373, in contrast to all the previously adopted resolutions regarding terrorism, are legislative in nature and even affect the domestic legislation of Member States, which sparked many controversies in the international law doctrine. Some of its representatives, such as S. Talmon, indicated that the language used in the Resolution significantly differs from the wording of ones adopted previously, and resembles the language normally used in international treaties (as it included phrases such as "the states shall" that are "reserved" for the conventions), which might suggest that the Security Council is aiming to take over the of individual states.[144] However, we should bear in mind that the problem covered by the Resolution does

142 United Nations Security Council Resolution 1373, 26 September 2001, paras 1-3.

143 United Nations Security Council Resolution 1368, 12 September 2001, para 6.

144 S. Talmon, "The Security Council as World Legislature", American Journal of International Law, Vol. 99 (2005), pp. 176-177.

not, in contrast to many previously adopted documents, respond to a particular event endangering international peace and security only, but above all aims to repel a global threat, that being international terrorism, which requires the effective implementation of international standards.[145] Hence the need for a uniform network of measures to be implemented by states.

Moreover, Talmon underlined that the Security Council, by acting under Chapter VII of the UN Charter, imposed very strict obligations on Member States, whose observance and control thereof is a difficult task.[146] This is primarily due to the CTC being comprised by representatives of only a few states despite its objective being the supervision of all states and their progress in implementing the provisions of the Resolution, which Talmon claimed interfered in their domestic legislation. He also alleged the Committee's tasks were formulated rather vaguely. Nevertheless, the CTC acted like a platform for cooperation between the states rather than a body judging their efforts.[147] This resulted in several significant achievements in the global counter-terrorism policy. Most Member States of the UN have already implemented or considered enacting new counter-terrorism legislation, and became parties to most anti-terrorist conventions.[148] Recently, its executive directorate also published a technical to guide to effective implementation of Resolution 1373 by States.[149]

Also worth mentioning here is Resolution 1377 (2001) adopted on 12 November 2001. Although its core text is very short, an annexed declaration constitutes a main of it and requires attention. First of all, the Security Council affirmed that acts of international terrorism "constitute one of the most serious threats to international peace and security in the twenty-first century", which in fact would justify measures requested to be taken by the states in order to eliminate this threat (in accordance with Article 41 of the UN Charter). Furthermore, the Resolution urges states to implement Resolution 1373, underlining the

---

145 Simlarly: J. E. Stromseth, "An Imperial Security Council? Implementing Security Council Resolutions 1373 and 1390", American Society of International Law Proceedings, Vol. 97 (2003), p. 43.

146 S. Talmon, "The Security Council as World Legislature" pp. 192-193.

147 J. E. Stromseth, "An Imperial Security Council?", p. 44.

148 J. E. Stromseth, "An Imperial Security Council?", p. 44.

149 See United Nations Security Council Counter-Terrorism Committee Executive Directorate, Technical guide to the implementation of Security Council Resolution 1373 (2001) and other relevant resolutions; https://www.un.org/sc/ctc/wp-content/uploads/2017/08/CTED-Technical-Guide-2017.pdf (9 March 2021).

obligation to deny any support and safe haven to terrorists.[150] Also noted should be here that the Security Council addressed a message to the CTC by requesting its assistance to UN Member States in implementing the provisions of Resolution 1373. That message proved that the UNSC took a pragmatic approach on anti-terrorist policies. By creating the CTC, it allowed states to cooperate and exchange ideas on the fight against terrorism so that the goal of eliminating it would be achieved more effectively. One of the tools helpful for the implementation of Resolution 1373 was the Directory for International Best Practices, Codes and Standards, published by the CTC and regularity updated to provide detailed and broad guidelines for the application of measures present in paragraphs 1-3 of the Resolution.[151] The Directory guidelines refer to international conventions, UN documents, EU legislation, and more.

d) Post-11 September Resolutions

The attacks on the WTC acted as a catalyst for the UNSC that, as pointed out in Resolutions 1368, 1373 and 1377, treated terrorism as one of the threats to international peace and security. Henceforth, we observed an influx of Resolutions related to terrorism adopted by the Security Council with one particular dedicated solely to the problem of aerial terrorism. They will be analysed in the present sub-chapter.

The UNSC made a prompt response to an attempt of shooting down Boeing 757 belonging to Arkia Israel Airlines on 28 November 2002. The plane had just taken off from Mombasa Airport Moi, Kenya for a flight to Tel Aviv, when two missiles were fired in its direction. Fortunately, the projectiles missed the target and the captain continued safely to the final destination.[152] The Security Council subsequently adopted Resolution 1450 (2002) on 13 December, referencing the attack and calling the states to implement Resolution 1373 measures as well as fulfil their obligations arising from the Montreal Convention.[153]

---

150 United Nations Security Council Resolution 1377, 12 November 2001, Annex.

151 The Directory for International Best Practices, Codes and Standards is published on the UN website: https://www.un.org/sc/ctc/resources/databases/recommended-international-practices-codes-and-standards/united-nations-security-council-resolution-1373-2001/ (9 March 2021).

152 https://aviation-safety.net/database/record.php?id=20021128-1 (9 March 2021).

153 United Nations Security Council Resolution 1450, 13 December 2002, paras 1 & 3. The Security Council also encouraged all Member States to become parties to all international conventions (therefore also those on aerial terrorism, including Resolution 1456 (2003)) in several later Resolutions.

Another remarkable Resolution, marked with number 2166, was adopted on 21 July, 2014, in response to a terrible air accident that shocked the international community – the downing of Malaysia Airlines flight 17 above Ukraine. The plane, a Boeing 777-200 was on its route from Amsterdam to Kuala Lumpur, when it was shot down by pro-Russian separatists controlling the eastern parts of Ukraine. Due to the tense political climate related to the case, the Security Council underlined two essential issues in the Resolution:

1. its support for establishing a full, thorough and independent international investigation team in accordance with international law standards and request for other states to provide their assistance in both civil and criminal investigations[154];
2. the demand addressed to the armed groups controlling the crash site territory not to interfere with the wreckage, bodies of victims or aircraft equipment and enable investigating authorities, as well as members of international organisations, to access the site and the surrounding area.[155]

The Security Council, by having expressed the above mentioned, proved again its ability to react to various circumstances in appropriate way. As the crash site was located in the territory of an active armed conflict between Ukrainian government forces and pro-Russian rebels, the possibility to conduct an independent investigation by authorities of only one of the states seemed quite low. In order to ensure an unbiased and proper investigation of the accident's cause, a team consisting of experts from different countries not involved in the political tensions was needed. What is more, the Security Council was aware that in a conflict zone, unexpected interference with debris or the victims' bodies potentially negatively affecting the investigation was a definite probability. Therefore, it pointed out the necessity to secure the crash site for the purpose of reducing the risk of such interferences [the case of Malaysia Airlines 17, its juridical background and facts on investigation shall be discussed in sub-chapter 3.2.3.]. Notably, Resolution 2166 was adopted unanimously.

A major breakthrough in the discussion on aerial terrorism was made in 2016. On 22nd September, the Security Council published Resolution 2309 (2016) devoted in full to the matter. The document is a large and concrete set of instructions provided by the UNSC for the states that would improve the security of air passengers and improve protection from terrorist attacks. Already in

154 United Nations Security Council Resolution 2166, 21 July 2014, paras 3 & 4.
155 United Nations Security Council Resolution 2166, 21 July 2014, para 6.

the recitals, the Security Council underlined the role that civil aviation plays in world economy and progress, as well as noting that "secure air services in this regard enhance transportation, connectivity, trade, political and cultural links between states, and that public confidence in the security of air transport is vital".[156] By using such wording, the Security Council emphasised that civil aviation, by linking societies around the globe and strengthening ties between them acts as a vital component for a global peaceful coexistence of nations, which only defends the argument that an attack thereon might disrupt the international peace and security. The Security Council accordingly pointed out that a risk of terrorist attack therefore affects all Member States.[157]

The body also turned its attention to the security measures used in civil aviation – in order to prevent unintentional transportation of terrorists on board aircraft, it called States to refer to Annex 9 – *Faciliation* to the Chicago Conventions that provides standards and recommended practices helpful in detection of terrorist fighters willing to embark aeroplanes. Moreover, it noted that terrorists keep on detecting and exploiting flaws and mistakes in aviation security system (circumvent detection facilities at airports, carry clandestinely biological or chemical weapons) which makes it necessary for States to constantly monitor the evolution of this threat. And finally, in recitals, the Security Council affirmed the key role of the ICAO in assisting States in improving aviation security[158] and urged Member States to become parties to all conventions of the Tokyo-Hague-Montreal-Beijing system.

In the main body of the Resolution, the UNSC recalls the States' duty to maintain safety and security of their citizens provided that solutions they introduce are in accordance with international law (in particular human rights law and humanitarian law) – here the body touched an important question of the limits that states must respect when applying security measures. Aerial terrorism, although a serious threat to international peace and security requiring unified actions to

156 United Nations Security Council Resolution 2309, 22 September 2016, Preamble.
157 United Nations Security Council Resolution 2309, 22 September 2016, Preamble.
158 The UNSC mentioned here the adoption at the 37th Session of the ICAO Assembly the Declaration on Aviation Security and referred to ICAO Comprehensive Aviation Security Strategy, naming them both key instruments of leadership and engagement for the Organization in carrying out its aviation security programme. The Security Council also made a remark on ICAO's intention to develop a Global Aviation Security Plan as the future global framework for progressive aviation security enhancement. See United Nations Security Council Resolution 2309, 22 September 2016, Preamble.

be eliminated, should not push governments to implement measures that would infringe basic freedoms and rights every person is entitled to.[159]

Furthermore, the role of the ICAO as a principal organisation setting standards in aviation security is highlighted again. The UNSC affirms that the ICAO should constantly review their performance and adapt to the current global picture. The organisation is also called to provide assistance and control effective application of those standards in Member States.[160]

Paragraph 6 of the Resolution consists of set of precise guidelines for Member States that should be undertaken to counter terrorist threats in civil aviation: effective systems used at airports within the states' jurisdictions, involving screening, security checks and facility security; application of security measures on the ground through quality control and oversight procedures, as well as promotion of security control among all interested entities; attention given to persons with privileged access to some areas or information valuable for terrorists; addressing any deficiencies or flaws within security systems to the ICAO; usage of advanced technologies in screening and detecting explosive materials and sharing knowledge related thereto; exchange of information vital for upgrading security system on the basis of bilateral agreements; submission of advanced passenger information by airlines to state authorities for the purpose of detecting and detaining persons pursued for involvement in terrorism.[161]

Following paragraphs further call the states to transfer to other states technology, training and other resources necessary to achieve the above-mentioned results (paragraph 7), strengthen border controls and law enforcement to effectively counter terrorists (paragraph 8) and assure that internal bodies and agencies work closely for the purpose of combatting terrorism (paragraph 9). In the final provisions, the Security Council asks the CTC to organise a special meeting on aerial terrorism with the participation of the ICAO within the 12 following months.[162]

A step taken by the Security Council to issue a Resolution totally devoted to terrorism in civil aviation deserves appreciation. First of all, by dedicating one document to the problem, the body emphasised that aerial terrorism constitutes a "separate" form of terrorism, requiring special attention and a slightly different approach that its other incarnations. It also made the very clear and accurate

159 United Nations Security Council Resolution 2309, 22 September 2016, paras 1 & 2.
160 United Nations Security Council Resolution 2309, 22 September 2016, paras 4 & 5.
161 United Nations Security Council Resolution 2309, 22 September 2016, para 6.
162 United Nations Security Council Resolution 2309, 22 September 2016, para 10.

point that civil aviation itself is an essential factor in the peaceful coexistence of nations. Linking distant parts of the world makes people feel more connected to each other and also boosts the world economy. In that way, the Security Council showed that civil aviation is a sector worthy of protection.

Moreover, the UNSC reminded the governments that in the fight against terrorism, they cannot utilise whatever form of combat they deem necessary. Their efforts to repel terrorist threats should not compromise human rights and international law principles. But probably the most important part is paragraph 6, in which the body enumerated very concrete measures to be implemented or improved on the national level to counter the growing threat of terrorism in civil aviation. Just like in Resolution 1373, for example, the Security Council did not limit itself to condemning terrorism, but proposed accurate solutions to tackle the problem in a pragmatic way. That Resolution constitutes so far the most valuable tool published by the Security Council to fight against aerial terrorism.

The Security Council subsequently issued other Resolutions concerning terrorism in civil aviation, including several ones related to non-supplying terrorists with unmanned aircraft systems. But particular attention should be paid to two documents published on 21 December 2017 – Resolutions 2395 (2017) and 2396 (2017). In the former one, the Security Council once again mentioned the problem of circumventing security systems by terrorists and necessity that the ICAO and the UN should assist states in developing good standards in civil aviation, as well as eliminate gaps in aviation security systems. The UNSC accordingly welcomed the ICAO efforts in the creation of the Global Aviation Security Plan that aims to enhance the passengers' protection.[163]

In turn, in the latter Resolution, the Security Council pointed out the problem of using cargo by terrorists, both in order to transport clandestine material, or directly target civil aircraft. To tackle the problem, the body requested the Member States to follow the provisions of Annexes 9 and 17 to the Chicago Convention that deal with cargo screening. The Security Council also referred to the Global Security Plan and underlined the necessity of achieving five key priorities expressed therein, that being the enhancement of risk awareness and response, the development of security culture and human capability, the improvement of technological resources and innovation, the improvement of oversight and quality assurance, and increased cooperation and support.[164]

163 United Nations Security Council Resolution 2395, 21 December 2017, Preamble & para 30.

164 United Nations Security Council Resolution 2396, 21 December 2017, para 9.

Member States are further called on to implement the Global Security Plan and contribute to the ICAO's works on aviation security.

e) Commentary

The role the United Nations Security Council played in the global fight against aerial terrorism is not to be underestimated. The body's stance towards terrorism has been evolving from reluctant to mature and accurate. At the beginning of the rise of terrorism across the globe, the Security Council adopted several Resolutions in response to particular terrorist events without actually branding them as "terrorist", and mostly just expressed concern over the attacks and sympathy with their victims. Therefore, the main role in coordinating anti-terrorist actions in civil aviation was then totally left for the Member States of the United Nations. Positive change was observed after the Lockerbie bombing, when the Security Council actively joined the global fight against aerial terrorism. Not only did the body claim that a terrorist attack might constitute a breach of Article 2(4) of the Charter of the United Nations and thus be regarded as a threat to sovereignty, like an armed attack, the Security Council also showed its lack of tolerance for states that support attackers (in that case, Libya) and imposed sanctions thereon, related also to aerial transport, that were gradually increased as the state did not respond to them properly. That move was a vital lesson for the whole international community that supporting terrorism states would incur serious consequences. The UNSC should also be praised for having issued subsequent Resolutions in response to other terrorist attacks also targeting civil aviation. That only strengthened the position of the body and showed its unchangingly condemning stance on terrorism.

But undisputedly a true breakthrough was reached directly after the attacks on 11 September. The Security Council changed the concept of the fight against terrorism into a combat against an enemy that constitutes a threat to global peace and security and whose actions may be lawfully countered in the form of individual or collective self-defence. As it was mentioned before [see sub-chapter 1.4.3.], due to the approach expressed by the Security Council in Resolution 1373, the balance of eliminating large-scale terrorism shifted from enforcement units (like the police) to the military. States, by the unanimous decision of the Security Council, were then equipped with the right to engage in hostilities with states harbouring attackers, including cases of attacks carried out against civil aviation.

Finally, we should positively rate the idea of issuing a separate Resolution dedicated solely to terrorism in civil aviation. By publishing this document, the

UNSC has shown that the protection of air passengers from terrorist attacks requires slightly different practices than other kinds of terrorism. Some words of criticism should be addressed to the body that this instrument was adopted relatively late, merely 15 years after the attacks on the WTC, which only proves that even in fundamental issues like the protection of the international community against terrorism, the UNSC has difficulties in reaching compromise. Of course, to accurately assess the results of the measures proposed by the UNSC, we need to wait a couple of years, especially since several states are still incapable of implementing them due to financial or technical reasons.

In general, we might claim that the Security Council played a capital role in the global fight against terrorism by having built a system of real solutions and proving it fulfils its role of the guard of international peace and security. The Security Council has, in fact, strongly influenced the concept of combatting terrorism and shaped its form, motivating sovereign states to take appropriate measures.

2.4. The European Union

"Terrorism threatens our security, the values of our democratic societies and the rights and freedoms of European citizens. Fighting terrorism is a top priority for the EU and its Member States as well as its international partners"[165] – that statement is present in the heading of the Council of the European Union's webpage and gives a clear picture of the EU's stance towards terrorism. Fighting against this problem has been ranked as a top priority for the European Union institutions as well as its Member States. In recent years, their territories became crime scenes, as multiple terrorist attacks either occurred or were planned and costed many Europeans their health or life. A handful of those terrorist attacks also targeted civil aviation, causing massive damage and death tolls.

However, the approach to the fight against terrorism taken by European institutions was evolving with time and made a drastic change after 11 September. Instead of militarily engaging the forces of its Member States in the territories of states supporting terrorism (e.g. in Iraq), the Union focused more on constructing effective legal measures that would prevent attacks in the future.[166] However, in the second decade of the twenty-first century, Europe was struck dozens of

165 https://www.consilium.europa.eu/en/policies/fight-against-terrorism/ (9 March 2021).

166 J. Monar, "The EU's approach post-September 11", p. 267-268.

times the attacks organised by the Islamic State, which pushed European institutions to react more harshly to the threat. Outdated legislation was amended and the EU joined the Global Coalition against Daesh to support military forces in Iraq in their campaign.

The evolution of anti-terrorist legislation was boosted also by the ratification of the Treaty of Lisbon. Therefore, the Union was empowered by more competences in certain areas, including criminal policy, the forms of combatting terrorism slightly changed in comparison to the pre-Lisbon era. Effectively, institutions like Europol or Eurojust enhanced their scope of action.[167]

Currently, progress made by the European Union in the combat against terrorism has been impressive and contributed to the improvement of the safety of its citizens.[168] The present chapter shall focus on analysing the relevant EU legislation and the solutions implemented in relation to aerial terrorism.

2.4.1. Overview of early anti-terrorist EU policy

The European Union, being a bloc of cooperation between democratic states respecting the rule of law, has been an "attractive target" for terrorists since its first years of existence as the European Coal and Steel Community. The fact that the Old Continent has also been a place of constant growth of the civil aviation sector affected its vulnerability to aerial terrorism. Events like the Lockerbie bombing in 1988, the hijacking of Air France 8969 in 1994, or the massacre at the Brussels National Airport in 2016 left a grim mark in modern Europe's history. However, the stance of the European Union towards the problem of terrorism has been evolving with time. The general tendency prior to the 11 September attacks was that the Member States were responsible for adopting their own legislative norms on the fight against terrorism and, on the Union level, relevant regulations were rather modest.[169] The Rome Treaties, establishing the European

---

167 See M. Wade, "The European union as a counter–terrorism actor: right path, wrong direction?", Crime, Law and Social Change, Vol. 62 (2014), p. 361.

168 M. Lech, Ochrona prawna społeczności międzynarodowej, p. 157, after: C. Warbrick, "The European Response to Terrorism in the Age of Human Rights", The European Journal of International Law, Vol. 15(5) 2004, p. 989.
The data published on the webpage of the Council indicates that only in 2017 in the territory of Member States, 205 failed, foiled or successful terrorist attacks were carried out, and 1219 people were arrested for terrorist offences. See https://www.consilium.europa.eu/en/policies/fight-against-terrorism/ (9 March 2021).

169 C. Murphy, EU Counter-Terrorism Law, p. 17.

Economic Community and Euratom, were completely devoid of any provisions referring to terrorism. As C. Murphy points out, the cooperation between states on terrorism was too politically sensitive to be regulated by international legal acts. That resulted in the creation of the informal organisation called TREVI in 1976, a predecessor to the later Common Foreign and Security Policy.[170] The group functioned mostly as a forum to exchange ideas on the fight against terrorism and was reinforced in 1979 by the Police Working Group on Terrorism (or "PWGOT"). The body became a formal institution by 1990. Its main task was to inform police forces of requesting Member States of any kind of terrorist activities.[171]

The Treaty of Maastricht, signed by EU Member States (of which there were only 12 at the time) in 1992 extended the competences of the Union, adding two more pillars to its policies. The second pillar, called the Common Foreign and Security Policy, was focused on external security, whereas the third pillar, the Justice and Home Affairs, was oriented at common policies of asylum, immigration, and third country nationals.[172] Although none of the provisions of those pillars directly referred to terrorism, the Treaty featured some issues that could have been related thereto. C. Murphy presents here the "objective to strengthen the security of the Union in all ways" in Article 11(1) as an example.[173] The Treaty of Amsterdam (signed in 1997) was in fact the first legal act referring to terrorism *expressis verbis* and qualifying it as a crime of the same category as human trafficking, drug trade etc. in the third pillar[174]

In the pre-Lisbon era, the formation of the European Police Office, Europol, was also important for the fight against terrorism. Formally founded in 1995 under the Convention on the Establishment of a European Police Office, the institution's main goal (expressed in Article 2 paragraph 1 of the Convention) was "to improve [...] the effectiveness and cooperation of the competent authorities in the Member States in preventing and combating terrorism, unlawful drug

170 C. Murphy, EU Counter-Terrorism Law, p. 19.

171 J. Gierszewski, "Unia Europejska w walce z terroryzmem międzynarodowym", Acta Pomerania, Vol. 2 2009, pp. 137-138.

172 See more: P. Craig, G. de Burca, EU Law. Text, Cases and Materials (Oxford University Press: New York, 2011), p. 15.

173 C. Murphy, EU Counter-Terrorism Law, p. 20.

174 M. Lech, Ochrona prawna społeczności międzynarodowej, p. 158.

trafficking and other serious forms of international crime".[175] Moreover, Article 2 imposes on Europol the duty to deal with crimes committed in the course of terrorist action against life, limb, personal freedom or property.

The European Union's Judicial Cooperation Unit, also known as Eurojust functions as a key partner of Europol in preventing terrorism. Formed in 2000 under the Treaty of Nice, the organisation serves as a coordination body in the works of Member States' prosecutors in the fight against international crimes, like terrorism. Its main objectives include detecting, pursuing, arresting and forming indictments.[176]

However, despite the whole projection of an anti-terrorist shield structured by subsequent Treaties' provisions, terrorism has not been given a priority on the list of EU policies prior to the attacks of 11 September. Although Europe has been struggling against the death toll caused by massive terrorist attacks in the twentieth century, none of them impacted the continent so strongly as to make the EU institutions decide to adopt a sterner approach. But everything has changed in first years of the twenty-first century that were in some moments merciless for European societies.

The attacks carried out against the United States on 11 September were in reality targeted against the whole international community, with the "Western world" in the foreground. Therefore, the European Union also felt the impact of the attacks.[177] But the true impact of cruelty of terrorism was felt on the Old Continent in following years, when several terrorist attempts struck its largest cities. The most notable were the bombings in Madrid in March 2004 and in London in July 2005, as well as later attacks on civil aviation: the shooting at Glasgow Airport in June 2007, at Frankfurt Airport in March 2011, and the bombing at Brussels National Airport in March 2016.[178] All of these events ignited the discussion

---

175 Council Act of 26 July 1995 drawing up the Convention based on Article K.3 of the Treaty on European Union, on the establishment of a European Police Office (Official Journal of the European Communities C 316/1), art. 2(1).

176 M. Lech, Ochrona prawna społeczności międzynarodowej, p. 164.

177 According to C. Murphy, 67 Britons, 11 Germans, 10 Italians, 6 Irish, 5 Portuguese, 3 French and many other European nationals died in the attacks. See C. Murphy, EU Counter-Terrorism Law, p. 22.

178 Crucially, the EU institutions, although having expressed solidarity with the victims of the attacks and condemned them officially, their voice on the war on terror was much different than that of the United States administration under George W. Bush. After a series of attacks occurred on European soil, the Union changed its attitude towards terrorism to be more aggressive. See J. Monar, "The EU's approach post-September 11", p. 268.

on the combat against terrorism within European institutions that brought its effects in the implementation of concrete anti-terrorist measures, also in the field of civil aviation.

2.4.2. The role of EU Treaties

Unlike its predecessors, the Treaty of Lisbon that entered into force in December 2009 and abandoned the earlier system of the three pillars of the EU, consists of more precise provisions related to terrorism and prioritising the fight against it. The Charter of Fundamental Rights of the EU in its Preamble states that "[the Union is] founded on the indivisible, universal values of human dignity, freedom, equality and solidarity; it is based on the principles of democracy and the rule of law".[179] Terrorism inherently affects democratic states and endangers the freedom and lives of individuals, and as such, targets the very same values the Union swore to protect. Thus, Member States of the EU were forced to establish a legal framework that would enable them to repel the threat.

Both EU Treaties have an important place in that system. The Treaty on the European Union (or "TEU") describes the role of combatting terrorism within the Common Security and Defence Policy[180]. Under Article 43(1), the Union may engage military or civilian means, including peace-keeping operations, humanitarian aid and rescue tasks. And contribute to the fight against terrorism, also in the territories of third countries.

However, the more concrete provisions referring directly to the order within the Union Member States are present in the Treaty on the Functioning of the European Union (or "TFEU"), particularly in its Title V dealing with the area of freedom, security and justice. Article 67(3) stipulates that the Union "shall endeavour to ensure a high level of security through measures to prevent and combat crime [...]".[181] It is obvious that ensuring a high level of security in the territories of Member States would be impossible if no effective anti-terrorist solutions are provided. One such solution is provided in Article 75, equipping the European Parliament and the Council with the right to establish administrative

179 Charter of Fundamental Rights of the European Union (Official Journal of the European Union C 326/391), Preamble.

180 The Union's course of action triggered responses in the areas of defence and crisis management, an integral part of the Common Foreign and Security Policy.

181 Treaty on the Functioning of the European Union (Official Journal of the European Union Official Journal C 326/01), art. 67.

measures, including the freezing of the funds of both state and non-state entities in order to prevent the financing of terrorism.

Another important provision regarding the problem is Article 83 of the TFEU enabling the European Parliament and the Council to adopt directives defining criminal offences and sanctions in the area of cross-border serious crime activities. Those particular activities are: terrorism, human trafficking, sexual exploitation of women and children, illicit drug trafficking, illicit arms trafficking, money laundering, corruption, counterfeit means of payment, computer crime and organised crime. Such an approach to the problem of terrorism clearly shows the European Union considers terrorism a problem threatening all of its citizens on an equal level and it is unreasonable to leave its regulation entirely to the legislative bodies of the Member States themselves. Better results in anti-terrorism policy could be achieved if uniform regulations are implemented by the European Parliament and the Council as EU legislators.

2.4.3. Other anti-terrorist legislative tools enacted by the EU

a) *Counter-Terrorism Strategy: A milestone in the campaign against terrorism*

Even before the Treaty of Lisbon was adopted, the Council published a cornerstone document of the EU's anti-terrorist actions: the Counter-Terrorism Strategy (hereafter referred to as the "Strategy"). It is intended to shape the Community's main tasks in eliminating the problem of terrorism, but with respect to human rights. Already in its introduction, the Strategy identifies terrorism as "a threat to [the Union's] security, to the values of [the Union's] democratic societies and to the rights and freedoms of [the Union's] citizens, especially through the indiscriminate targeting of innocent people".[182] The Strategy's key priorities are:

1. to prevent;
2. to protect;
3. to pursue;
4. to respond.

182 Council of the European Union, The European Union Counter-Terrorism Strategy (14469/4/05), para 1.

To prevent.

The Union aims to prevent its citizens turning to terrorism and to stop further generations of terrorism from emerging. Every group should be free from radicalisation. Thus, it is necessary to examine the factors that seriously motivate radicalisation and turn people into terrorists and eliminate them. That requires both internal and external cooperation.[183]

To protect.

The urgent need to enhance the security of key infrastructure points (especially those involved in transportation) and collective EU Member States' actions towards the improvement of border security, the exchange of intelligence information, and so on.[184]

To pursue.

The Union must cooperate to disrupt terrorists' activities in Member States' territories, and to detect and eliminate their networks. All Member States shall collect necessary information and analyse them. Strict cooperation between Europol and Eurojust is also required.[185]

To respond.

Reducing the negative effects of terrorist attacks, providing necessary information and assistance (including military) upon occurrence, and the development of crisis cooperation agreements. Engaging efforts to help victims of the attacks.[186]

The Strategy is designed as a comprehensive and complex document reflecting the idea of cooperation between Member States in order to maintain security and freedom of their citizens. The EU version of the "war of terror" described in the Strategy features mostly engagement of non-military forces to minimise the risk of terrorist attacks. By developing them, the Union aims to wipe out terrorism root and branch. Through the cooperation of intelligence and enforcement services of particular Member States and the exchange of information, the

---

183 Council of the European Union, The European Union Counter-Terrorism Strategy (14469/4/05), paras 6-13.

184 Council of the European Union, The European Union Counter-Terrorism Strategy (14469/4/05), paras 14-21.

185 Council of the European Union, The European Union Counter-Terrorism Strategy (14469/4/05), paras 22-31.

186 Council of the European Union, The European Union Counter-Terrorism Strategy (14469/4/05), paras 32-38.

Community hopes to detect and disrupt terrorist cells. The Strategy also underlines some long-term ideas, like fighting extremism and radicalisation of their citizens. Such a decision would require education programmes and social campaigns focusing on groups at risk of being radicalised (like Islamic extremists). The Strategy also has a pragmatic character. It indicates the necessity to protect key areas from attacks, reflecting terrorist tendencies. They usually target densely crowded areas, such as airports, railway stations or hotels, to maximise the "resonance" of attack. Certainly, the effective application of the Strategy requires strict and unconditional cooperation between Member States.

b) Overview of key secondary law acts related to aerial terrorism

The task of assembling and enumerating all EU secondary law acts related to aviation security, particularly the fight against aerial terrorism, is highly challenging. The last years have been very fruitful in terms of adoption of new legislative acts by the European Parliament, the Council and European Commission. In this sub-chapter, we shall take into consideration some more important documents which have strongest influence on the Union's legal framework in the fight against aerial terrorism: Regulation (EC) No. 300/2008 of the European Parliament and of the Council of 11 March 2008 on the common rules in the field of civil aviation security and repealing Regulation (EC) No. 2320/2002 (hereafter referred to as "Regulation No. 300/2008"); Commission Regulation No. 272/2009 of 2 April 2009 supplementing the common basic standards on civil aviation security laid down in the Annex to Regulation (EC) No. 300/2008 of the European Parliament and of the Council (hereafter referred to as "Regulation (EC) No. 272/2009") (with amendments); Directive (EU) 2016/681 of the European Parliament and of the Council of 27 April 2016 on the use of passenger name record (PNR) data for the prevention, detection, investigation and prosecution of terrorist offences and serious crime (hereafter referred to as "PNR Directive"); Directive (EU) 2017/541 of the European Parliament and of the Council of 15 March 2017 on combating terrorism and replacing Council Framework Decision 2002/475/JHA and amending Council Decision 2005/671/JHA.

2.4.4. Regulation No. 300/2008

a) Scope of application

Regulation No. 300/2008, adopted in accordance with Article 80(2) of the Treaty establishing the European Community (current Article 100(2) of TFEU), is intended to replace Regulation (EC) No. 2320/2002 that entered into force shortly after the attacks of 11 September. As its title suggests, it sets out common rules to be observed by all Member States ensuring security of civil aviation on their territories. Its scope of application therefore includes, but is not limited to, aerial terrorism. According to its Article 2, the Regulation applies to:

a) all airports or parts of airports located in the territory of Member States, provided that they are not used for military purposes exclusively;
b) all operators, including air carriers, providing services at such airports;
c) all entities applying aviation security standards that operate from premises located inside or outside airport premises and provide goods and/or services to or through such airports.[187]

The application of security measures on board aircraft of air carriers registered in the EU Member States (like Air France, Alitalia, LOT Polish Airlines etc.) is without prejudice to provisions of the Conventions of Tokyo-Hague-Montreal-Beijing system.

b) Common basic standards

The essential part of the Regulation is enshrined in its Article 4 and establishes common basic standards that should safeguard civil aviation from acts of unlawful interference. Those common standards are contained in the Annex to the Regulation and are separated into 12 categories.[188]

---

187 Regulation (EC) No 300/2008 of the European Parliament and of the Council of 11 March 2008 on common rules in the field of civil aviation security and repealing Regulation (EC) No 2320/2002 (hereafter referred to as "Regulation No. 300/2008") (Official Journal of the European Union L 97/72), Article 2.

188 The following categories are listed:
Airport security;
Demarcated areas of airports;
Aircraft security;
Passengers and cabin baggage;
Hold baggage;
Cargo and mail;
Air carrier mail and air carrier materials;
In-flight supplies;
Airport supplies;
In-flight security measures;
Staff recruitment and training;
Security equipment.
Regulation No. 300/2008, Annex.

Airport Security provisions establish a system of airport areas and obligatory forms of surveillance and control. Each airport serving civil aviation in EU territory should consist of four areas: the landside (generally the whole part of the airport barring the airside), the airside (restricted parts of the airport), security restricted areas (parts of the airside in which additional aviation security standards are applied), and critical parts of security restricted areas (Article 1.1.). Everything but the landside area is subject to access restrictions and require a person to be checked *a priori* the security purposes (Articles 1.2.–1.3.). In addition to that, vehicles accessing security restricted areas should be checked for dangerous materials. Airports should also be under constant surveillance and physical control (Article 1.5.)

As for Aircraft Security provisions, they consist of a general clause that each civil aircraft should be searched or checked for the presence of dangerous items onboard prior to departure (Article 3.1) and protected from unauthorised interference (Article 3.2.).

Section 4 of the Annex introduces the general duty of screening departing and transferring passengers and their baggage with exemptions to those persons that arrive from another EU Member State or a state in which the applied safety standards are equivalent to those expressed in the Regulation, those that do not leave the aircraft during transfer (e.g. when the plane made a scheduled stop for refuelling), or those that do not mix with passengers boarding the same aircraft (Article 4.1.). Departing passengers shall be granted protection from unauthorised interference from the moment they are screened until their departure (due to the provisions not providing a precise definition specifying if such protection is dependent on the scheduled departure time, we can conclude it probably also applies when the flight is delayed or cancelled and the passengers are re-booked for another one) (Article 4.2.).

According to provisions stipulated in Section 5 of the Annex, hold luggage (commonly known as "checked baggage") should also be screened prior to loading, with similar exemptions as those enumerated above (Article 5.1.). It shall be subject to the same protection as passengers and their cabin baggage after screening (Article 5.2.). Article 5.3. provides rules on classification of pieces of baggage as "accompanied" or "unaccompanied". In the latter case, it is declined to be transported unless it had been separated from a passenger due to reasons beyond their reasonable control (e.g. the suitcase was stolen from a passenger when they were already in the terminal, then found later), or if it was made subject to appropriate security control.

Cargo and mail are not by any means free from controls before loading into an aircraft, which stems from Section 6 of the Annex. Control is either applied by the air carrier, or an appropriate agent or consignor. Exemptions apply only for transfer and transit cargo and mail (Article 6.1.). In similarity with passengers and their baggage, cargo and mail are subject to protection before departure (Article 6.2.).

Finally, Sections 7, 8 and 9 stipulate on security control of the following items: air carrier mail and materials, in-flight supplies, and airport supplies.

Section 10 of the Annex, unlike previous ones that mostly referred to security measures implemented at airports, deals with in-flight standards. Article 10.1. introduces a ban on unauthorised personnel to enter flight crew compartments (such as the flight deck or rest areas) and states further that potentially disruptive passengers shall be subject to "appropriate security measures" during the flight. Although the term "appropriate security measures" is not explained, the Annex in Article 10.2. mentions the training of flight crew and cabin staff for the purpose of preventing acts of unlawful interference. Therefore, we can indicate actions such as restraint, basic forms of self-defence, negotiation skills, etc. Furthermore, Article 10 imposes a general ban on carrying weapons outside the cargo hold of the aircraft. An exception to this rule constitutes carrying such items with prior authorisation from a state (Article 10.3.).

Section 11 briefly states the obligation to appropriately recruit and train staff responsible for implementing screening, access control and other security controls (as no precise provisions are expressed, a detailed programme of recruitment and training shall either be present in executive legal acts or national legislation). Equipment used for screening, access control and other security controls shall comply with relevant specifications in accordance with Section 12. Although that Section closes the Annex, future insertion of other common basic standards is made possible by the wording of Article 4(2) of the Regulation and is subject to rules of ordinary legislative procedure (Article 294 of TFEU). However, if a future amendment concerns non-essential elements of common basic standards, it might be implemented via a regulatory procedure provided in Article 19(3). List of measures that can be covered by such an implementation is featured in paragraphs 2 and 3 of Article 4.

c) Other provisions

Crucially, those common standards expressed in the Annex to the Regulation are a certain minimum required from Member States. They are permitted to implement more stringent measures under Article 6. However, Member States must observe certain limits of such policy. According to the provision, those measures must be "relevant, objective, non-discriminatory and proportional to the risk that is being addressed".[189]

Article 7 in turn establishes a procedure in case of requests submitted by third countries to any EU Member State concerning different security standards than those in force within the Union. When such a situation arises, the Commission, with relevant demand from a Member State or its own, examines the application of any measures being subject to the request and on that basis provides a response. The procedure serves as an assurance that when air carrier based in the EU launches a scheduled flight from a Union Member State to a third country, it might expect that similar measures are applied at airports on both entities' territories.

As for the monitoring of the application of common standards, Member States are obliged under Article 9 to select the appropriate institution (if on their territory more than two are responsible for aviation security).

Other provisions of the Regulation deal with establishing security programmes by Member States, their air carriers, their airports, etc., inspections conducted by the Commission, penalties imposed, and other similar issues.

d) Commentary

Unlike the provisions present in, e.g., the Tokyo-Hague-Montreal-Beijing system Conventions, Regulation No. 300/2008 is oriented more at preventing attacks on civil aviation than their definition and cooperation between states in pursuing and eventual prosecution of offenders. By shaping those common safety standards in aviation security, the European Parliament and the Council expected that all Member States observe technical requirements necessary to prevent carriage of dangerous items on board aircraft and therefore reduce the risk of terrorist attacks. On the global level, that uniformity in security standards is somewhat difficult to achieve, as not all states of the world have enough funds or are technically prepared to such solutions at all of their airports. Given that Member States of the EU are characterised by a relatively high level of economic development and significant funds reserved for aviation safety and security, a common implementation of standards is easier to achieve.

A weakness of the Regulation lays within the construction of certain provisions. Their understanding might seem too vague and would need an accurate interpretation either from the side of legal doctrine or EU institutions themselves

189 Regulation No. 300/2008, art. 6(1).

that would enact suitable guidelines for unclear terms. On the other hand, laying down very detailed security measures that would have a universal application on the whole Community is a very difficult task. The role of the European Commission is to adopt delegated acts giving more accurate norms on security procedures at airports.

Doubtlessly, Regulation No. 300/2008 is a good tool for shaping the general framework of security measures necessary to reduce the risk of aerial terrorism throughout the European Union. Passengers travelling within or from the Community would then be sure that regardless of where they depart, each piece of baggage and every other person boarding the same aircraft is properly checked and would bring no dangerous items on board. The effectiveness of the Regulation's mechanisms can be proved by the fact that since its adoption, there has been no single terrorist accident within the EU involving civil aircraft. All terrorist attacks directing civil aviation that occurred afterwards were committed at airport premises at their landside.

2.4.5. Commission Regulation (EC) No. 272/2009 and its amendments: A supplement to the aviation security system

a) General remarks

As was pointed out in the previous sub-chapter, the Commission was granted the right to amend provisions of Regulation No. 300/2008 in "non-essential" matters, which, in accordance with Article 290 of TFEU, entitles the Commission to implement delegated acts (regulations, directives and decisions) on the basis of delegation provided in a legislative act (such as Regulations adopted by the European Parliament and the Council).[190] Regulation No. 272/2009 is a great example of such an action from the side of the European Commission, as it supplements the mentioned Regulation No. 300/2008 with some general measures related to common basic standards. The document's Preamble stipulates that those measures are embodied in the field of "screening, access control and other security controls as well as in the field of prohibited articles, third country recognition of equivalence, staff recruitment, training, special security procedures and exemptions from security controls".[191]

190 J. Barcz, Źródła prawa Unii Europejskiej (Instytut Wydawniczy EuroPrawo: Warsaw, 2012), p. 23.

191 Commission Regulation (EC) No 272/2009 of 2 April 2009 supplementing the common basic standards on civil aviation security laid down in the Annex to Regulation (EC) No 300/2008 of the European Parliament and of the Council (hereafter

In similarity with Regulation No. 300/2008, the act is also built of a main part and an Annex. However, the main part consists of just 3 Articles, dealing with the Regulation's primary objectives, definitions of terms and the date of entry into force respectively, whereas the Annex is in fact the core of the Regulation and features its key provisions.

We need to point out here that the Regulation has been amended several times for the purpose of adapting it to current issues arising in civil aviation security. The following amendments to Regulation No. 272/2009 have been adopted so far: the Commission Regulation (EU) No 297/2010 of 9 April 2010 amending the Commission Regulation (EC) No. 272/2009 of 2 April 2009 supplementing the common basic standards on civil aviation security laid down in the Annex to Regulation (EC) No. 300/2008 of the European Parliament and of the Council (hereafter referred to as "Regulation No. 297/2010"); the Commission Regulation (EU) No 720/2011 of 22 July 2011 amending Regulation (EC) No. 272/2009 supplementing the common basic standards on civil aviation security regarding the phasing-in of the screening of liquids, aerosols and gels at EU airports (hereafter referred to as "Regulation No. 720/2011"); the Commission Regulation (EU) No 1141/2011 of 10 November 2011 amending Regulation (EC) No. 272/2009 supplementing the common basic standards on civil aviation security regarding the use of security scanners at EU airports (hereafter referred to as "Regulation No. 1141/2011"); the Commission Regulation (EU) No 245/2013 of 19 March amending Regulation (EC) No. 272/2009 regarding the screening of liquids, aerosols and gels at EU airports (hereafter referred to as "Regulation No. 245/2013").

In the present analysis, we will jointly study the contents of all aforementioned documents, only indicating that particular provisions were inserted or modified by any of amending Regulations.

b) Issues covered by the Annex

The European Commission undertook to give precise guidelines on how to exercise security measures provided by the Regulation No. 300/2008. In Part A of the Annex, eligible methods of screening passengers and their baggage are listed, as well as items carried by persons other than the passengers (like journalists visiting the airside of the terminals), air carrier mail and air carrier materials,

---

referred to as "Regulation No. 272/2009") (Official Journal of the European Union L 91/7), Preamble, para 3.

in-flight supplies, and airport supplies. Enumerated methods consist of x-ray checks, hand searches, explosive detection dogs, liquid scanning, etc.[192]

Although the list is headed with the word "allowed", we can conclude that it constitutes a *numerus clausus* of methods to be legally applied by security personnel at the airports. However, the Commission, aware of the rapid technological progress, left some space for future possible forms of screening that were unknown at the time of implementation of Regulation 272/2009. In the last paragraph of part A of the Annex, the possibility of using other methods of screening is mentioned "on a trial basis and for a limited period of time on condition that such trials do not prejudice the overall levels of security".[193] In practice it would mean that if, as a result of scientific research, a new technology is developed and able to perform more detailed screening of liquids, electronic devices, etc., then it might be installed at the airport for a short period of time in order to evaluate if it improves the screening standards. However, that action needs to be preceded by a sophisticated procedure at the Commission level (explained in Article 19(2) of the Regulation No. 300/2008 in relation to Article 4(3) thereof).

Part B describes the categories of objects that may not be carried in security restricted areas or on-board. Therefore, those items can be regarded as "potentially prohibited", as without the prior implementation of rules prohibiting carrying them (adopted under Article 4(3) of the Regulation No. 300/2008), persons entering security restricted areas or boarding aircraft are allowed to bring them. Listed here are following types of objects: devices discharging projectiles (like guns or firearms), stunning devices, objects with sharp points or edges, workmen's tools, blunt instruments, and explosives.

Part B1, introduced into the Annex by Regulation No. 297/2010 is a section dealing with the screening of liquids, aerosols and gels (LAGs) carried in hand luggage. Its addition into the Annex text was based on the failure to employ effective technologies capable of detecting explosive liquids at airports across the EU before 29 April 2010 (on that day Regulation No. 297/2010 entered into force).[194] Part B1 originally established that on 29th April 2011 all EU airports

192 See full list of methods: Regulation No. 272/2009, Annex, part A.

193 Regulation No. 272/2009, Annex,, part A.

194 From the Preamble to Regulation No. 272/2009 it follows that the Commission primarily wanted to have the technology to detect explosive liquids employed at airports across the EU no later than on 29 April 2010. Regulation No. 272/2009, Preamble, para 6. See more: https://ec.europa.eu/transport/modes/air/security/aviation-security-policy/lags_en (9 March 2021).

should be fit for the screening of LAGs obtained at a third country airport or on board an aircraft of a non-Community air carrier. Moreover, it stated that on 29th April 2013, such a screening system should be applied to all LAGs. However, due to progress not being as swift as originally planned, Regulation No. 720/2011 deleted the first date. Regulation No. 245/2013 moved even further and replaced the second date. As a result, the Commission decided not to give exact dates of the necessary universal implementation of LAGs screening technology and instead a gradual lifting of restrictions on their carriage should be inserted. The final and currently enforceable version of part B1 only provides that "[LAGs] shall be permitted to be taken into security restricted areas provided they are screened or exempted from screening in accordance with the requirements of implementing rules adopted pursuant to Article 4(3) of Regulation (EC) No. 300/2008". In consequence, into the list of eligible screening methods, present in part A, point 2 the usage of a liquid explosive detection system was added.

The next parts of the Annex, C and D, are devoted to the control of access to the airside and security restricted areas, respectively, and also describe the methods allowed for the examination of vehicles, as well as the performance of aircraft checks.

Part E of the Annex is particularly interesting, as it establishes the Commission's duty to recognise the equivalence of safety standards in third countries. The recognition is normally based on three factors:

(a) a good record of cooperation between a third country and EU Member States;
(b) application of satisfactory standards of aviation security, including quality control; and
(c) verification that a third country applies security measures in regard to passengers, their baggage, cargo and mail etc. equivalent standards as those expressed in the Annex to Regulation No. 300/2008.[195]

The provision itself vests upon the Commission wide powers, as its wording is quite vague. A term "good record of cooperation" between third countries and EU Member States is not explained in the Regulation and its interpretation belongs solely to the Commission. Typically, the organ would take into account cooperation in terms of pursuing terrorists, common conduct of research on technologies related to airport screening or exchange of information on aviation security. Similarly as with the expression "satisfactory standards", the Commission then

195 Regulation No. 272/2009, Annex, part E.

determines unilaterally whether a country successfully implemented norms of safety analogical to those in force in the EU.

Parts F–H provide detailed criteria for the screening of the following items: cargo and mail (part F), air carrier mail and air carrier materials (part G) and in-flight and airport supplies (part H). In turn, part I defines sets out criteria defining critical parts of security restricted areas for the purpose of preventing contamination of departing passengers and their luggage. The last two parts of the Regulation are: part J, on the recruitment of staff responsible for checking and screening passengers and their luggage, and part K, on the special procedures of security checks and relevant exemptions.

c) Commentary

The fight against terrorism, as it was underlined previously in the present monograph, not only requires military actions and engagement of special services, but should be also oriented at preventive actions, especially in areas such as civil aviation. Consequentially, effective methods of screening people and luggage were brought into the airside of airports on board aircraft. However, institutions like the European Union are fully aware that the implementation of too strict anti-terrorist measures might eventually be too harmful for the Member States' citizens and its main administrative body, the Commission, adopted Regulation No. 272/2009 in order to assess the limits of control and checks passengers and their luggage might be subject to.

Enlisting the methods of screening by airport officers ensures that any items that may be useful for terrorist purposes are detected without significant interference in an individual's freedoms, protected *inter alia* by the EU Charter of Fundamental Freedoms. Moreover, we should rate the Commission's practice of "updating" the list of eligible methods by Regulations positively. The solution provided in the last paragraph of part A of the Annex to Regulation No. 272/2009, which allows the employment of technologically advanced security measures on a trial basis also seems reasonable. The Commission opened the way for the introduction of future improvements in screening technology without compromising the safety of passengers. However, as the provision points out, such an introduction must follow the procedures enshrined in Article 4(3) of Regulation No. 300/2008, which refers to the Committee procedure in its Article 19.[196] The

196 Article 19 of the Regulation No. 300/2008 further refers also to Articles 5 and 7 of Decision 1999/468/EC, which is no longer in force. It was replaced by Regulation (EU) No 182/2011 of the European Parliament and of the Council of 16 February

procedure itself might be time-consuming and in consequence delay the implementation of a highly demanded new technology, as the Committee is normally composed of representatives of all Member States and requires observance of strict rules.

Separate comments should be made regarding carrying LAGs. Just to recall some facts, the introduction of the ban on carrying LAGs in containers of more than 100 ml volume was the result of a terrorist plot to blow up several planes en route from Heathrow International Airport in 2006.[197] From the continuous adoption of delegated acts amending Regulation No. 272/2009, we can clearly see the Commission had the ambitious plan of the swift elimination of that ban which is a major inconvenience for many passengers. But as the schedule of employing liquid-scanning technology failed, the organ decided to simply abandon the idea of imposing deadlines in acts amending Regulation No. 272/ 2009 and

only allowed liquid explosive detection systems to be applied at airports across the EU.

That only proved that strategy of "putting airports under pressure" to install those system is of low effectiveness. Legislation cannot by itself boost technological development, but only give it proper directions. Nevertheless, the fact that the Commission showed its great interest in employing universal LAGs detection system deserved approval. The 2006 plot to blow up planes during their transatlantic flights confirmed that terrorists are capable of making explosives of various types of material, including liquids. On the other hand, the convenience

---

2011 laying down the rules and general principles concerning mechanisms for control by Member States of the Commission's exercise of implementing powers (hereafter "Regulation No. 182/2011). In consequence, when reference to Article 5 of Decision 1999/468/EC is made, Article 5 of the Regulation No. 182/2011 shall apply, whereas in case of reference to Article 7 of Decision 1999/468/EC, Articles 10 and 11 of Regulation No. 182/2011 shall apply.

197 The objective of the plot was to blow up seven airliners departing within several hours of each other to fly to the other side of the Atlantic: two Air Canada planes bound for Toronto and Montreal, along with five other American Airlines and United Airlines vessels with destinations at New York, Chicago, Washington and San Francisco. Investigation revealed that terrorists linked with Al-Qaeda were planning to detonate small liquid explosives made of hydrogen-peroxide. Each of the targeted aircraft carried between 240 and 285 people.

See https://www.cbc.ca/news/world/montreal-toronto-flights-targeted-in-alleged-british-bomb-plot-1.747225 (9 March 2021).

of passengers flying within, out or into the EU is also necessary and if an appropriate device detecting composition of LAGs is widely used, the terrorist threat will both be minimised and the passengers' satisfaction improved. The Commission continues its works on successful legislation in that matter in close cooperation with international entities.[198]

2.4.6. The PNR Directive: A controversial tool to prevent and eliminate aerial terrorism

a) *The principal purpose of the Directive and the definition of PNR*

On April 2016, the European Union adopted a controversial Directive (EU) 2016/681 of the European Parliament and of the Council of 27 April 2016 on the use of passenger name record (PNR) data for the prevention, detection, investigation and prosecution of terrorist offences and serious crime (hereafter referred to as "PNR Directive"), whose main aim is expressed in Article 1: collection and processing of PNR "only for the purposes of preventing, detecting, investigating and prosecuting terrorist offences and serious crime".[199]

Before we conduct a deeper study on the document, we firstly need to define its central term – the passenger name record (or "PNR"). The ICAO in its Document No. 9940 entitled *Guidelines on Passenger Name Record (PNR) Data* defines it as "the generic name given to records created by aircraft operators or their authorised agents for each journey booked by or on behalf of any passenger".[200] The PNR Directive itself gives a legal definition for its purposes in Article 3(5): "a record of each passenger's travel requirements which contains information necessary to enable reservations to be processed and controlled by the booking and participating air carriers for each journey booked by or on behalf of any person, whether it is contained in reservation systems, departure control systems used to check passengers onto flights, or equivalent systems providing the same functionalities".[201] Simply speaking then, each record containing the data

198 More on the official website of the European Commission, Department General of Mobility and Transport: https://ec.europa.eu/transport/modes/air/security/aviation-security-policy/lags_en (9 March 2021).

199 Directive (EU) 2016/681 of the European Parliament and of the Council of 27 April 2016 on the use of passenger name record (PNR) data for the prevention, detection, investigation and prosecution of terrorist offences and serious crime (hereafter "PNR Directive"), art. 1.

200 ICAO, Guidelines on Passenger Name Record (PNR) Data, ICAO Doc 9944, para 2.1.1.

201 PNR Directive, art. 3(5).

and itinerary of a passenger that booked a flight ticket collected by an air carrier can be called a PNR. The air carriers normally use this data in order to manage passengers' reservations and check-in.

The main purpose of the PNR Directive is to establish rules on transferring the PNR by air carriers, their processing, and exchange between EU Member States for the purpose of detecting whether air passengers are linked to terrorist offences or other serious crimes and eventually prevent them from happening. As each PNR consists of information that strongly facilitates a passenger's identification (including their name, telephone number address, etc.), use of that kind of information raises concerns on the protection of fundamental rights, in particular to privacy and data protection.[202] The present sub-chapter shall be dedicated to analyse the basic aims of the PNR Directive from the perspective of the fight against terrorism and the potential conflict with the freedoms mentioned above.

b) *Conflict with the right to privacy*

The PNR Directive established the duty of Member States to designate a passenger information unit (or "PIU"), an authority competent in the matter of prevention, detection, investigation or prosecution of terrorist offences and serious crime. According to Article 4 of the Directive, there is no need that each Member State has one single PIU, as two or more of them may designate a common one. Its competences are enshrined in Article 4 of the Directive:

> "(a) collecting PNR data from air carriers, storing and processing those data and transferring those data or the result of processing them to the competent authorities [...];
> (b) exchanging both PNR data and the result of processing those data with the PIUs of other Member States and with Europol [...]".[203]

Importantly, although the primary objective of the PNR Directive is to oblige Member States to impose duties concerning personal data of passengers travelling on international flights between the EU and third countries on air carriers, Article 2 entitles Member States to extend their power over intra-EU flights. That discretion was ultimately adopted by 23 Member States.[204]

---

202 S. Villani, "Some Further Reflections on the Directive (EU) 2016/681 on PNR Data in the Light of the CJEU Opinion 1/15 of 26 July 2017", Revista de Derecho Politico, No 101 2018, p. 902.

203 PNR Directive, art. 4(2).

204 https://ec.europa.eu/home-affairs/news/list-member-states-applying-pnr-directive-intra-eu-flights_en (9 March 2021).

The flow mechanism of PNRs is relatively simple: once the data is received by an air carrier (e.g. when a passenger books a flight), it is transferred to the PIU and stored there. Then, a transfer is made through the so-called "push method", in which Member States make a request to the carrier for providing the passengers' data (as opposed to the "pull method" with which a Member State itself gains access to the air carrier's database). The PIU then analyses the data to "identify persons who were previously unsuspected of involvement in terrorism or serious crime". Such analysis enables competent authorities to update or establish new criteria for evaluating the involvement of any person in terrorist offences or serious crimes.[205] Article 12 adds that the data can be retained in the PIUs for a period of time not exceeding five years. With the lapse of that time, the data should be deleted and depersonalised through masking out of specific elements after a period of six months.[206]

The final stage in the transfer of the PNR is the exchange of relevant information between Member States and the potential delivery to Europol through exchange networks and electronic means (Article 9).[207]

If we then look at the chain of the PNR transfer, we would quickly conclude that state authorities have a massive amount of personal data under surveillance. First of all, the list of data that can be proceeded as PNR, present in Annex I to the Directive, is relatively long. State authorities not only gain access to details such as the name and address of a passenger, but even their frequent flyer programme number, or all forms of payment information.[208] Additionally, most flights in the EU are intra-EU (those accounted for 47% of total passengers in 2016), followed by extra-EU (36% in 2016) and domestic flights (17% in 2016).[209] N. Vavoula points out that such dynamic movement of persons increases the scope of state

205 The list of offences that can be regarded as "serious crimes" for the purposes of the PNR Directive are listed in Annex II. In turn, "terrorist offences" mean offences referred to in Articles 1-4 of the Framework Decision 2002/475/JHA. The latter document was however repealed and replaced by Directive (EU) 2017/541 of the European Parliament and of the Council of 15 March 2017 on combating terrorism and replacing Council Framework Decision 2002/475/JHA and amending Council Decision 2005/671/JHA (hereafter "Directive 2017/541). Therefore, "terrorist" offences are those actually listed in that directive.

206 S. Villani, "Some Further Reflections on the Directive", p. 913.

207 S. Villani, "Some Further Reflections on the Directive", p. 913.

208 See PNR Directive, Annex I.

209 https://ec.europa.eu/eurostat/statistics-explained/index.php/Air_transport_statistics (9 March 2021).

surveillance and in fact allows constant monitoring of people even if they were not previously involved in any serious crime or terrorist offence.[210]

Words of criticism are also addressed regarding the lack of rules concerning analysis of the data in the hands of the PIU. Although procedures on the collection and retention of data are clearly structured in the Directive (and are based on the much less intrusive "push method"), the document is completely silent on how the profiling of persons is organised. S. Villani indicates here that it should be based on the identification of behavioural patterns according to a probabilistic logic.[211] Nevertheless, no such criteria are provided and therefore authorities, are given a wide spectrum for analysing the data.

All those presented arguments permit to understand the concerns of many sceptics that the PNR Directive too much compromises EU citizens freedoms for the purpose of security.

c) Anti-terrorist context

The concept of collecting data of air passengers is not in any way a new one. Some developed countries, with the United States on the foreground have been having such regulations in force since many years. In the EU, the first draft of an act dealing with retention and analysis of PNR was presented by European Commission in the "pre-Lisbon era", in 2007. Subsequent drafts were either rejected or treated with lower priority, until 2015 when several Member States of the EU were struck by terrorist attacks and the death toll was rising in following years. Hence the rebirth of another anti-terrorist legal document.

The PNR Directive itself explains its role in fight against terrorism in Recital 7 of the Preamble. It stipulates as follows:

---

210 N. Vavoula, "'I Travel, therefore I Am a Suspect': an overview of the EU PNR Directive", EU Immigration and Asylum Law and Policy, 26 October 2016. http://eumigrationlawblog.eu/i-travel-therefore-i-am-a-suspect-an-overview-of-the-eu-pnr-directive/. The author expressed in her article a bold statement that such an approach to monitoring the data of passengers might be regarded as a reversal of the presumption of innocence. It is a somewhat exaggerated view, as the presumption of innocence, serving as a principle in criminal proceedings and being protected by Article 48(1) of the European Charter of Fundamental Rights, means that any person standing trial shall be presumed innocent until proved guilty in legal proceedings. None of the PNR Directive provisions stipulate that a person checked on the basis of data received in PNR shall be even regarded as a suspect.

211 S. Villani, "Some Further Reflections on the Directive", p. 917.

> Assessment of PNR data allows identification of persons who were unsuspected of involvement in terrorist offences or serious crime prior to such an assessment and who should be subject to further examination by the competent authorities. By using PNR data it is possible to address the threat of terrorist offences and serious crime from a different perspective than through the processing of other categories of personal data. However, to ensure that the processing of PNR data remains limited to what is necessary, the creation and application of assessment criteria should be limited to terrorist offences and serious crime for which the use of such criteria is relevant. Furthermore, the assessment criteria should be defined in a manner which keeps to a minimum the number of innocent people wrongly identified by the system.[212]

From this provision we can affirm that the key point established by the Directive is prevention. By using the data assembled by air carriers, Member States might identify persons that were never suspected of terrorism before, but their data suggest that they would have some connotations with terrorist actions. A typical example would be tracking a person living at exactly the same place and having the same surname as members of a family who were responsible for a terrorist attack that occurred some time before. European institutions then concluded that it is better to seize a person posing the risk of a terrorist attempt in advance than wait until they reveal their identity as a result of the attack.

However, there are many critical voices on how the PNR Directive reflects reality. One of the most prominent political figures openly negating the idea of its implementation is Guy Verhofstadt, the former prime minister of Belgium and current leader of the Renew Europe group (formerly known as "Alliance for Liberals and Democrats for Europe" or "ALDE") in the European Parliament. He admitted that most of people travelling within the EU use either rail or road transport, therefore collecting the data from air carriers is inefficient in the identification of terrorist suspects. Moreover, under the Directive, there are no plans to create one single EU-wide database with all records, but instead, dozens of single databases administrated by Member States individually. And above all, the exchange of data between them is voluntary, not compulsory.[213] In the light of that argumentation, it is doubtful whether the idea of enabling easy surveillance of air passengers really has any positive effect on minimising the terrorist threat.

The controversies provoked by the relatively high level of intrusion into fundamental freedom, which is the right to privacy, along with the low efficiency of real detection of terrorist threats, make the PNR Directive an inaccurate tool

---

212 PNR Directive, Preamble, para 7.

213 G. Verhofstadt, Europe's Last Chance. Why the European States Must Form a More Perfect Union (Basic Books: New York, 2017), para 321.

to fight terrorism within the EU. To some extent, it is however useful to prevent attacks on civil aviation. If a person plans to commit a terrorist offence on board aircraft (hijack it, blow it up, use it as a weapon etc.) or on airport premises, then police forces might detain them before they even enter the departure hall if data from PIU gives state authorities cause for concern that the person is involved in terrorism. But again, the question arises whether the provisions of the Directive would really imply a higher level of security and if that is worth reducing the citizens' freedom. This will probably be verified in the near future, as in May 2019, the Gesellschaft für Freiheitsrechte (or "GFF", Society for Civil Rights), a German non-governmental organisation supported several complaints brought forth by individuals before the District Court in Cologne against Lufthansa regarding transferring their data to the German Federal Criminal Police Office. As the Court had expressed its doubts over the Directive's provisions compliance with the Charter of Fundamental Rights, it suspended proceedings and brought a preliminary question on that matter to the CJEU. The case is yet to be decided.[214]

2.4.7. An accurate and up-to-date solution for the terrorist problem: Overview of Directive 2017/541

a) *Framework Decisions 2002/475/JHA: The first important instrument in anti-terrorist legislation*

Before the Treaty of Lisbon entered into force, the primary instrument used to regulate criminal law, police and judicial organs' matters common for the whole European Union was a framework decision, functioning within the Union's third pillar. In essence, it shared many commonalities with the directive as a legal instrument. Framework decisions were binding for Member States and outlined results to be achieved without instructing them on how to achieve it.[215] When the Treaty of Lisbon became effective, the institution of the framework decision was removed from the secondary legislation portfolio of the EU. Existing framework decisions were gradually replaced by appropriate directives.

When analysing EU legislation concerning terrorism, it is essential to mention the Council Framework Decision of 13 June 2002 on combatting terrorism (2002/475/JHA) (hereafter referred to as the "Framework Decision"). It was an

---

214 See https://edri.org/cjeu-to-decide-on-processing-of-passenger-data-under-pnr-directive/ (9 March 2021).

215 See J. Barcz, Źródła prawa Unii Europejskiej, pp. 49-50.
M. Osiecki, "Zamachy", p. 70.

instrument adopted in order to harmonise the definition of terrorism and establish its criminalisation within all EU Member States. Issues covered by the Framework Decision included penalties for terrorist offences, jurisdiction and prosecution, liability of legal persons, etc [to be discussed in the next section].[216]

The Framework Decision served for many years as EU's cornerstone for the common policy on the fight against terrorism. But, as the threat from terrorist organisations including the Islamic State grew and Europe suffered multiple terrorist strikes, Member States decided to adapt the provisions on combatting terrorism to the new reality. Hence the idea of drafting a new directive that would replace the obsolete Framework Decision. Directive (EU) 2017/541, adopted by the European Parliament and the Council on 15 March 2017 on combatting terrorism and replacing the Council Framework Decision 2002/475/JHA and amending Council Decision 2005/671/JHA (hereafter referred to as "Directive 2017/541") is an instrument aiming to strengthen the European Union's capabilities of eliminating all forms of terrorism, including air terrorism. The present sub-chapter shall discuss the structure of Directive 2017/541, its merit and present main differences that distinguish the Directive from its predecessor, the Framework Decision 2002/475/JHA.

b) Definition of terrorism common for all Member States

Directive 2017/541, analogically to the Framework Decision, introduces (in its Article 3) the duty for the Member States to define certain acts (being offences under their national legislations) as "terrorist". The approach to defining terrorism is then casuistic – the provision gives a "catalogue" of offences that should be regarded as "terrorist" provided that they fulfil certain conditions:

> a) seriously intimidate the population;
> b) unduly compel a government or an international organisation to perform or abstain from performing any act;
> c) seriously destabilise or destroy the fundamental political, constitutional, economic or social structures of a country or an international organisation.

The offences regarded then as "terrorist" are listed in points (a)-(j) and are all linked to the use of violence against a person or property. Therefore, the

216 See the text of Council Framework Decision of 13 June 2002 on combating terrorism (2002/475/JHA): https://eur-lex.europa.eu/legal-content/EN/TXT/?uri=celex:32002F0475 (9 March 2021).

definition of terrorism presented in sub-chapter 1.2.3. of the present monograph perfectly matches the one functioning in the Directive. The definition itself, although indeed casuistic, covers also offences related to aerial terrorism:

a) attacks upon a person's life which may cause death. A general term under which falls a large spectrum of attacks, like aircraft bombing, or using an aircraft as a weapon.
b) attacks upon the physical integrity of a person. An example might be attacks targeting passengers directly.
c) kidnapping or hostage-taking, or, in other words, other forms of attacks targeting passengers directly.
d) causing extensive destruction to a government or public facility a transport system, infrastructure facility including an information system [...], a public place or private property likely to endanger human life or result in major economic loss. This point accounts *inter alia* for attacks destroying airport infrastructure or any of its facilities.
e) seizure of aircraft, ships or other means of public or goods transport. Obviously, this point criminalises aircraft hijacking.
f) use of explosives or weapons, including chemical, biological, radiological or nuclear weapons [...]. This provision concerns also the destruction of aircraft with specific kinds of weapons (in similarity with the Beijing Convention that makes mandatory the criminalisation of using BCN weapons against aircraft).
g) causing explosions that endanger human life. A typical example of such an offence is aircraft bombing.[217]
i) illegal system interference, as referred to in Article 4 of Directive 2013/40/EU of the European Parliament and of the Council. The evoked provision criminalises illegal interference with information systems, which also includes cyberattacks on civil aviation.[218]
j) introduces a general clause criminalising threats to commit any of the offences enumerated in the provision.

Importantly, this list of offences is very similar to the one present in the Framework Decision, with the exception to offences stated in point i). But of utmost

217 Point h) criminalises the interference with or disruption of the supply of water, power or any other fundamental natural resource, and so has none or very little relation with aviation terrorism and is then omitted in the enumeration.

218 Article 4 of Directive 2013/40/EU stipulates that "Member States shall take the necessary measures to ensure that seriously hindering or interrupting the functioning of an information system by inputting computer data, by transmitting, damaging, deleting, deteriorating, altering or suppressing such data, or by rendering such data inaccessible, intentionally and without right, is punishable as a criminal offence, at least for cases which are not minor". See Directive 2013/40/EU of the European Parliament and of the Council of 12 August 2013 on attacks against information systems and replacing Council Framework Decision 2005/222/JHA (Official Journal of the European Union L 218/8), art. 4.

importance is that Directive 2017/541 indeed deals with the criminalisation of all kinds of terrorist attacks that in present times might target civil aviation. In consequence, all Member States shall adopt similar provisions concerning terrorism, including aerial terrorism to make sure that in the whole territory of the EU any terrorist offenders would be pursued. That aspect also encompasses a crucial advantage of EU law over international agreements – directives as sources of EU law are binding for Member States. Regardless of their political interests, all of them have to implement the Directive 2017/541 into their legal systems in any method to achieve a given result. In case of treaties, like the Tokyo-Hague-Montreal-Beijing system conventions, such an obligation is out of concern – states of the world decide on becoming parties thereto on voluntary basis, which *ab initio* reduces their potent.

c) Wider scope of offences

The Framework Decision extended the criminalisation on certain offences that although are not "terrorist" *per* se, have strong links to terrorism. Directive 2017/541 contains similar provisions, but in comparison to its predecessor, greatly extends the scope of criminalisation. It brings forth the offence of directing a terrorist group and participating in its activities, as defined in Article 4(b).[219] Interestingly, under the Directive's provisions, a definition for a "terrorist group" is given (unlike in the Tokyo-Hague-Montreal-Beijing system conventions) and that being at the head of one or participating in its activities (under certain conditions) is considered a crime regardless of whether any of the offences stated in Article 3 are actually committed. Solely the fact that a structured group is formed for continuous existence in order to commit terrorist attacks is sufficient to bring its directors or participants to justice. That solution puts a higher stress on the prevention of terrorist attacks. If a group is already formed and, according to the gathered evidence, makes preparations to commit a terrorist act, Member State

219 A "terrorist group" should be understood as follows: "a structured group of more than two persons, established for a period of time and acting in concert to commit terrorist offences; 'structured group' means a group that is not randomly formed for the immediate commission of an offence and that does not need to have formally defined roles for its members, continuity of its membership or a developed structure". Directive (EU) 2017/541 of the European Parliament and of the Council of 15 March 2017 on combatting terrorism and replacing Council Framework Decision 2002/475/JHA and amending Council Decision 2005/671/JHA (Official Journal of the European Union L 88/6) (hereafter "Directive 2017/541"), art. 2(3).

enforcement authorities would be able to detain its members before the strike is executed. However, some may argue that prioritising prevention could lead state authorities to abuse their position to dismantle groups seemingly dangerous for the state, without obtaining prior proof that they were really formed for terrorist purposes. Regardless, when the protection of society from terrorist attacks is at stake, the idea of prevention might be justified.

Offences enumerated in Title IV of Directive 2017/541 are commonly named "offences related to terrorist activities". The following acts are taken into account:

a) public provocation to commit a terrorist crime (Article 5);
b) recruitment for terrorism (Article 6);
c) providing training for terrorism (Article 7);
d) receiving training for terrorism (Article 8);
e) travelling for the purpose of terrorism (Article 9);
f) organising or otherwise facilitating travelling for the purpose of terrorism (Article 10);
g) terrorist financing (Article 11);
h) aggravated theft with a view to commit terrorist offence (Article 12 point a);
i) extortion with a view to commit terrorist offence (Article 12 point b);
j) drawing up or using false administrative documents with a view to committing terrorist offence (Article 12 point c).

Every provision of Title IV precisely defines the offence and obliges Member States to take necessary measures to ensure they are punishable in their domestic legal system. The Directive, however, does not give the Member States precise instructions on how severe the penalties for their commission should be, only stipulating that they should be "effective, proportionate and dissuasive [...], [may] entail surrender or extradition".[220] Nevertheless, all of those provisions share some commonalities. Certainly, all those offences have to be committed intentionally to be regarded as crimes and their purpose has to either contribute to a terrorist offence, as stated in Article 3, or, in some cases, other offence enshrined in that Chapter. In other words, all those offences on which treats Title IV have to be linked to commission of another terrorist offence if they are to be criminalised.

In comparison with Directive 2017/541, the Framework Decision featured a much narrower scope of protection of EU citizens from terrorism, as it did not criminalise offences dealt with in Title IV (with the exception of those enumerated in Article 12). Without a doubt, that is related to the fact that at the time, when the Framework Decisions were adopted in 2002, European Union Member

220 Directive (EU) 2017/541, Article 15(1).

States were less threatened by terrorism than in the second half of the 2010s. What is more, the knowledge about the functioning of terrorist groups has been growing constantly in recent years and the new legislation much more accurately reflects the true capabilities of terrorist networks and their supporters that organise recruitment, provide training, or publicly call for perpetrating terrorist acts.

The approach to terrorism featured in Directive 2017/541 is thus progressive. The act is more adapted to current conditions of the fight against terrorism and puts greater stress on prevention, as it criminalises the earlier stages of preparation of terrorist attacks, not only the attacks themselves.

d) Jurisdiction and prosecution, system of assistance to victims

Article 19 of Directive 2017/541 is devoted to aspects of jurisdiction. The provision stipulates that any Member State may claim the right to execute its jurisdiction where:

> (a) the offence is committed in whole or in part in its territory;
> (b) the offence is committed on board a vessel flying its flag or an aircraft registered there;
> (c) the offender is one of its nationals or residents;
> (d) the offence is committed for the benefit of a legal person established in its territory;
> (e) the offence is committed against the institutions or people of the Member State in question or against an institution, body, office or agency of the Union based in that Member State.[221]

The bases for jurisdiction enumerated in Article 19 resemble those featured in the Tokyo-Hague-Montreal-Beijing system conventions, but two new ones are present here: the base for the jurisdiction of a Member State in whose territory a legal person benefiting from the offence is based, and that of a Member State where an EU institution, body, office or agency is based. The former one is related to the fact that the Directive also established the liability of legal entities that benefit from offences committed by an individual having a leading position within that legal entity (Article 17). A typical example would be the decision of a chemical manufacturing company with ties with terrorist networks to release on toxic substances in a huge area. The latter one, in turn, is a kind of *sui generis* form of establishing jurisdiction based on the location of an institution, absent in most international treaties and arising from the nature of the European Union itself. According to this principle, if the premises of any of EU agency (like the European Aviation Safety Agency in Cologne) are attacked, then the Member

221 Directive 2017/541, Article 19(1).

State in whose territory the headquarters are based may institute criminal proceedings against the offender.

Article 19(3) also predicts the mechanism of solving conflicts between Member States concerning concurrent jurisdictions. Provided here is a mechanism of cooperation, under which interested states decide which one of them is ultimately responsible for prosecuting the offender. The idea of centralising the proceedings in just one Member State which might be achieved through recourse to Eurojust is definitely favoured here. Priority is given to Member States on the basis of territoriality (place where offence was committed), the nationality of the offender, the origin of victims, or the place where the offender is found. All provisions concerning the jurisdiction are analogical to those in the Framework Decision.

The Directive also provides a system of assistance to victims, regulated in Title V. Article 24 states that launching investigations concerning terrorist offences is not dependent on a report or the accusation of a victim, but normally is initiated *ex officio*. However, victims of any attack shall receive professional psychological and legal assistance free of charge, including advice on matters of victim compensation, exercising the right to information of terrorists, as well as healthcare services. Providing all that assistance requires the prior activation on the basis of local protocols. This is something natural, as in cases of terrorist attacks, the death toll might be immense and therefore, coordinating assistance services that help particular victims needs careful and effective planning. All Member States are also obliged to observe the provisions of Directive 2012/29/EU of the European Parliament and of the Council of 25 October 2012 establishing minimum standards on the rights, support and protection of victims of crime (Article 25). Important is also that residents of a Member State other than that on whose territory the offence was committed should have a full access to information regarding their rights, the available support services and compensation schemes in the Member State where the event occurred (Article 26).

e) Commentary

The global tendency to extend the legal measures concerning anti-terrorist solutions could not omit the European Union, especially in the perspective of the growing terrorist threat on the Old Continent in recent years. In fact, Directive 2017/541, being a replacement of "the ageing" and now obsolete Framework Decision, builds upon the solutions provided in the Tokyo-Hague-Montreal-Beijing system conventions, but has the particular advantage of being enforceable in a Member State regardless of their consent – norms protecting citizens under the Directive just need to be implemented by Member States to become effective. As a result, each Member States' citizen shall have a guarantee of the same level of protection in all Member States of the EU.

A strong point of the Directive is a real coverage of most terrorist offences known to humanity today, including cybercrime. As explained previously, its provisions are relevant for protection from offences relating to aerial terrorism (including aircraft hijacking, shooting down of aircraft, attacks at airport premises, etc.). Therefore, drafting a separate directive (or other legislative act) on aerial terrorism uniquely is unnecessary. Directive 2017/541 provides all mechanisms to effectively fight terrorism, at least on a juridical level. The fact that its provisions criminalise behaviours related to terrorism gives a green light for preventive actions and the possibility of dismantling terrorist networks before they actually attack. What is important on that note, Directive 2017/541, unlike the PNR Directive, does not implicate many controversies on its application. There are seemingly no provisions that would collide with the fundamental freedoms of EU citizens.

The instrument should also be praised for providing a system of support to victims of terrorist attacks –immediate assistance provided instantly after the event might save the lives of those severely wounded or assist psychologically those with their resulting trauma. Of course, the effectiveness of that system shall depend on the states and their resources themselves.

All of the above-stated arguments support the claim that Directive 2017/541 might serve as a modern solution for the fight against terrorism, at least on the EU level. It is enriched with elements that were absent in the Framework Decision and institutes a uniform system for the entire European Union, leaving Member States enough room to organise internal matters related to the fight against terrorism by themselves.

Chapter 3. Case study

3.1. Introduction

As was presented in the previous chapters, the international community has developed a vast framework of legal norms aimed at protecting air passengers from acts of aerial terrorism. The continuous development of international treaties that are being adapted to present conditions of this global trend proves that States of the world are seriously concerned with the problem and treat it with high priority on their agenda, although in many cases political interests prevail over a will to sacrifice some own state competences for increased protection of citizens from terrorist attacks.

This chapter is devoted to the case study of several aerial terrorism events that happened in the past and sparked a global discussion on the state of anti-terrorist system. The main purpose is to show the reader how the juridical framework protecting us, air passengers, from terrorist attempts functions in practice.

Each sub-chapter shall be composed of a description of facts related to a particular event, a wide analysis of legal consequences based on international legal provisions in force and a short commentary on their effectiveness. To show as large a spectrum as possible, the case study shall focus on attacks of various kinds: shooting down, hijacking, destruction of aeroplane by explosion, and attack of airport facilities. The following events shall be analysed:

–shooting down of Malaysia Airlines flight 17 above Ukraine on 17 July 2014;
–bombing of Metrojet flight 9268 above Sinai Peninsula on 31 October 2015;
–bombing at Brussels National Airport on 22 March 2016;
–hijacking of Air France flight 8969 on 24 December 1994.

3.2. Metrojet flight No. 9268: Terror above the Sinai Peninsula

3.2.1. Case facts and investigation

a) History of the flight

The following history is a visceral example of the brutality that emanates from extremist Islamic groups, such as the Islamic State. It all happened on 31 October 2015. An Airbus A321 jet registered as EI-ETJ belonging to the Russian airline Metrojet (also known as Kogalymavia) was scheduled to operate flight

No. 9268 (7K-9268) from Sharm el Sheikh Airport, Egypt to Pulkovo Airport in Saint-Petersburg, Russia. The plane was carrying 217 passengers, either of Russian, Belarusian or Ukrainian citizenship and 7 crew members, including captain Valery Nemov and first officer Sergei Trukhachev, both Russian nationals.[1] The Airbus took off as scheduled at 5:50 am local time (3:50 UTC) and headed north towards the Gulf of Aqaba. The plane climbed to its cruising altitude of 31,000 ft and should have made contact with Cyprus air traffic control, but never did. At 6:13 am (just 23 minutes after the plane took off), controllers based on the Sinai Peninsula received the last signal from the crew. As the aircraft was no longer visible on the radar, it was believed that it crashed.[2] Records of its last minutes show erratic readings of airspeed and altitude.[3]

Soon after the machine disappeared from the radar, rescue forces were launched to find the wreckage and help those who survived. The remnants of the Airbus were ultimately found 300 kms north of Sharm el Sheikh, scattered over a large area of 13 square kilometres which immediately gave a clue the machine could have broken up in mid-air. If an aeroplane is destroyed as a result of a crash on the ground, its wreckage is usually spread on a small area, but if the fuselage suffers from breakup in the sky, its remnants fall on a greater stretch of land.[4] When rescue forces arrived, they quickly understood there could not be any survivors. All 224 people on board were killed.

b) *Investigation*

The investigation on the causes was initiated on November 1st, just one day after the crash. The investigation team comprised specialists from the French Bureau

---

1 Ministry of the Russian Federation for Civil Defence, Emergencies and Elimination of Consequences of Natural Disasters, list of passengers and crew of aeroplane Airbus A321 "Kogalymavia" 7K-9268 (Министерство Российской Федерации по делам гражданской обороны, чрезвычайным ситуациям и ликвидации последствий стихийных бедствий, список пассажиров и экипажа самолета Airbus A321 авиакомпании «КогалымАвиа» 7К9268): http://www.mchs.gov.ru/operationalpage/Operativnaja_informacija/item/5216330/ (9 March 2021).

2 http://aviation-safety.net/database/record.php?id=20151031-0 (25 May 2020).

3 See the diagram of airspeed before the crash of 7K-9268: http://aviation-safety.net/photos/displayphoto.php?id=20151031-0&vnr=1&kind=G (9 March 2021).

4 https://www.france24.com/en/20151101-russian-plane-crash-sinai-egypt-broke-air-says-aviation-official (9 March 2021).

of Enquiry and Analysis for Civil Aviation Safety (French: *Bureau d'Enquêtes et d'Analyses pour la Sécurité de l'Aviation* Civile, or "BEA"), the German Federal Bureau of Aircraft Accident Investigation (German: *Bundesstelle für Flugunfaluntersuchung*, or "BFU"), the Irish Air Accident Investigation Unit (or "AAIU") and the Russian Interstate Aviation Committee (Russian: *Межгосударственный авиационный комитет*, or "MAK"), supported by representatives of Airbus Industrie, as well as officials from the Egyptian Ministry of Civil Aviation.

After more than two weeks of research, on November 16th, MAK investigators came to the conclusion that the breakup of the aircraft was a result of an explosion. In the wreckage, some pieces of explosives were found. Speculations arose that an IED was placed on board with force equivalent to 1kg of TNT. Soon after, the Sinai branch of ISIS claimed responsibility for the attack, posting a confession video on the Internet. Further research confirmed that the aircraft hull had been impacted by a strong force from within the cabin. The cause of the aircraft's destruction was certainly an explosion.

However, the stance towards the cause was divided. Egyptian authorities issued an interim statement on December 14th denying that the accident was of terrorist nature.[5] In response, one of the MAK staff members, Dmitry Peskov, publicly stated that the accident indeed had a terrorist background. The president of Egypt, Abdel Fattah el-Sisi, had the final word, and admitted that the crash of 7K-9268 was an act of terrorism committed for the purpose of worsening relations with Russia, who was involved in the war in Syrian territory, at the time mostly controlled by ISIS.[6] Later investigators' research revealed that the destruction of the Airbus in mid-air was indeed caused by an explosion of a tiny bomb located in the cargo hold. The tracks eventually led to the Islamic State which, some time before the catastrophe, published in its online bulletin a short guide on making an IDE programmed to explode on a desired altitude using an empty can of a Schweppes Gold tonic drink. Investigators then searched for any potential suspect among the Sharm el Sheikh Airport ground crew that could have had any links to the Islamic State, as only ground crew members are allowed

5 Ministry of Civil Aviation of Arabic Republic of Egypt, Issuance of the Preliminary Report for the Metrojet Russian Airplane accident.

6 See more on the consequences of Russia's involvement in the war in the light of 7K-9268:
T. Dunning, "Politics, economics and security: Implications of Metrojet Flight 9268", Daily Sabah, 21 November 2015. (9 March 2021) https://www.dailysabah.com/op-ed/2015/11/21/politics-economics-and-security-implications-of-metrojet-flight-9268

to put bags inside the cargo hold of an aeroplane. According to their findings, one of the employees had a cousin that had been recruited to the Sinai branch of Islamic State shortly before the accident. So far, this clue is not officially confirmed, but many states have already accepted that theory.[7]

The accident remains the deadliest in the history of Russian aviation and the most tragic that ever occurred in Egyptian aerospace.

3.2.2. Analysis of the terrorist context

a) *Presence of terrorist factors*

As seen from the reports and statements published by state officials [see above], opinions on the character of the 7K-9268 accident are divided. Organs investigating the event disagree on the key issue: did the tragedy have a terrorist background or not? To respond to that query, we firstly need to examine the circumstances surrounding the attack and then compare them to the criteria crucial for establishing the terrorist nature of an act.

First of all, today, the official cause of the crash is rather unquestioned: a bomb was smuggled by an ISIS affiliate's relative, and ultimately detonated and ripped the plane apart. We shall now verify that possibility in the light of terrorism.

As it was mentioned in the first chapter [see sub-chapter 1.2.3.], there are some criteria that an offence must fulfil to be qualified as a terrorist attack:

1) Intentional use of violence or threat thereof,
2) Conduct against the law,
3) Realisation of particular ideological or political goals,
4) The aim to spread fear or danger throughout society,
5) Affecting entities such as states or international organisations.

Intentional use of violence or threat thereof.

If an intentional bombing scenario is declared officially to be true, then the catastrophe might be absolutely considered "terrorist". The first criterion is therefore obviously fulfilled: planting a bomb with the intent to kill the passengers of the plane is an act of physical violence.

---

7 P. Graff, "Exclusive: EgyptAir mechanic suspected in Russian plane crash", Reuters, 29 January 2016. (9 March 2021) https://www.reuters.com/article/us-egypt-crash-suspects/exclusive-egyptair-mechanic-suspected-in-russian-plane-crash-idUSKCN0V712V

Conduct against the law.

Involvement of the second element is also indisputable: the destruction of an aircraft in service (which also means aircraft bombing) is a type of offence outlined by Article 1 point (b) of the Montreal Convention [see sub-chapter 2.2.3. section b)]. At the precise moment the 7K-9268 was destroyed, the Arab Republic of Egypt was one of the parties and therefore, was obliged to criminalise the act.[8] Egypt, like most states, by supporting the Montreal Convention's criminal provisions, decided to implement them in its Penal Code. The provisions that are most relevant to the destruction of aircraft are Articles 167 and 168. They read as follows:

[Article 167] "Whoever deliberately exposes to risk the safety, or interrupts the traffic and course, of the land, water, or air transport means and system, shall he punished with temporary hard [labour] or imprisonment."

[Article 168] "Temporary hard [labour] shall be the penalty if the deed mentioned in the previous Article results in injuries as those prescribed in Article 240 or 241. If the deed results in the death of some person, the perpetrator shall be punished with execution or permanent hard [labour]."[9]

Those Articles state the severity of the penalty dependent on the scale of offence. As in the case of 7K-9268, all persons on board were killed, the offender is punishable by either hard labour or capital punishment (which in Egypt is executed in the form of hanging[10]). Doubtlessly, these penalties satisfy the criterion provided in Article 3 of the Montreal Convention obliging state parties to punish offenders by "severe penalties".

Realisation of particular ideological or political goals.

The third element of terrorist character of offence, the realisation of ideological or political goals, is also present in the hypothesis that ISIS was responsible for the attack. The Islamic State of Iraq and Al-Sham is a terrorist organisation

8 The country became a party to the Convention 20 May 1975; see Convention on the Suppression of Unlawful Acts Against the Safety of Civil Aviation, ICAO Doc. 8966, List of parties. Retrieved from: https://www.icao.int/secretariat/legal/List%20of%20Parties/Mtl71_EN.pdf. (9 March 2021).

9 Law no. 58 01 The year 1937 Promulgating the Penal Code, Egyptian Government Bulletin, 1937-08-05, No. 71, art. 167 & 168.

10 See Law no. 58 01 The year 1937 Promulgating the Penal Code, Egyptian Government Bulletin, 1937-08-05, No. 71, Article 13.

that (despite seeing its influence diminish in recent years), several years ago was a powerful and cruel formation that held authority over large portions of the territory of Syria and Iraq. Its main goal was to establish a caliphate over lands traditionally inhabited by Muslims and beyond.[11] Blowing up 7K-9268 would be an "instrument" to realise their political ambitions. The Russian Federation is one of the few allies that the government of Syria has in their struggle against ISIS on their territories. By killing more than two hundred Russian nationals, ISIS manifests their will that Russia should withdraw from the fight and stop supporting Syria.[12]

The aim to spread fear or danger throughout society.

The criterion of spreading fear over society is quite clear in this case. Egypt, a country highly dependent economically and socially on tourism, recorded a big drop in tourist traffic shortly after the attack. The fear of falling victim to another terrorist attack caused people to abandon planning their holidays at the Red Sea or among the Giza Pyramids, which strongly affected the country's industry. The Egyptian tourist sector showed signs of recovery no sooner than in late 2017/ early 2018.

Affecting entities such as states or international organisations.

Finally, the question of affecting political entities, such as States or international organisations has to be raised. The accident of 7K-9268 was an event that shocked the international community and provoked many political decisions, especially among European states. Several large airlines, including Lufthansa, Air France or Emirates decided to suspend their scheduled flights over Sinai (or fly around the peninsula) for the safety of their passengers, until causes of the crash are officially revealed.[13] Moreover, KLM declined on 5 November to check the passengers' luggage for the cargo hold on flight KL553 from Cairo, which resulted in refusals of more than half of passengers to fly. President Vladimir

---

11 J. D. van der Vyver, "The ISIS Crisis and the Development of International Humanitarian Law", Emory International Law Review, Vol. 30(4) 2016, p. 532-533.

12 Agence France-Presse reported that the Egyptian branch of ISIS confessed to have downed the jetliner in retaliation for air strikes in Syria carried out by the Russian air force. See S. Al-Atrush, M. Antonova, "Experts explain why it's 'unlikely' that ISIS is responsible for the Russian plane crash", Business Insider, 1 November 2015. (9 March 2021) https://www.businessinsider.com/afp-russia-holds-day-of-mourning-after-224-die-in-sinai-plane-crash-2015-11?IR=T

13 S. Al-Atrush, M. Antonov, "Experts explain".

Putin imposed a ban on flights between Russia and Egypt and British authorities chartered several "repatriation flights" for United Kingdom citizens who at the time resided in Egypt.

If we combine all arguments presented above, then it would be unreasonable to argue with President el-Sisi, who stated that the explosion of 7K-9268 had a terrorist character. Despite initial disputes over the character of the attack between Russian and Egyptian investigation organs, today hardly anybody questions that ISIS is to blame for that terrorist-orchestrated tragedy.

b) Context of the Egyptian Penal Code

Since legal aspects of terrorism are being discussed in the context of this case, we should briefly analyse how the Penal Code of Arab Republic of Egypt defines terrorist offences. The definition itself is quite wide and can be found in Article 86. It reads as follows:

> […] all use of force, violence, threatening, or frightening, to which a felon resorts in execution of an individual or collective criminal scheme, with the aim of disturbing public order, or exposing the safety and security of society to danger, if this is liable to harm the persons, or throw horror among them, expose their life, freedom or security to danger, damage the environment, causes detriments to communications, transport, property and funds, buildings, public or private properties, occupying or taking possession of them, preventing or obstructing the work of public authorities, worship houses, or educational institutions, or interrupting the application of the constitution, laws, or statutes.[14]

Like in most legal systems of the world, Egypt decided to "differentiate" criminal offences in the Penal Code, and divide them into those of a terrorist character and those of a non-terrorist character. However, according to Egyptian law, there is a kind of *numerus clausus* of terrorist crimes. The Penal Code *expressis verbis* names those offences that might be regarded as such. Accordingly, if a particular offence is committed in terrorist character, higher penalties are predicted. Typical examples of such crimes include destruction of public property (Article 90), violation of sacredness or sanctity of cemeteries or graves (Article 160), killing a person deliberately (Article 234), etc. Interestingly enough, offences described in Articles 167 and 168 (see above) do not fall under that classification; it means

---

14 Law no. 58 01 The year 1937 Promulgating the Penal Code, Egyptian Government Bulletin, 1937-08-05, No. 71, Article 86; unofficial translation of the document from Arabic into English published by the UNODC.

that regardless of the fact whether they have a terrorist character or not, they are punishable with the same kind of penalty.

If we then have a complete view on the terrorist aspect of the attack on 7K-9268, we should affirm whether it should be classified as state terrorism. As was pointed out above, the responsibility for the attempt was claimed by the Islamic State, an organisation that at the time of downing Metrojet Airbus A321, controlled a large portion of Syrian and Iraqi territory. The organisation evidently calls itself a "state" and exercises many state competences over controlled territories, but would that be sufficient to qualify an offence committed under its auspices as "terrorist?" The answer is negative. The Islamic State of Iraq and Al-Sham does not even fulfil the "classical" criteria of statehood set out by the Montevideo Convention on the Rights and Duties of States in its Article 1. It does not have a permanent population, a defined territory, a government, or the capacity to enter into international treaties. As for the population criterion, the Islamic State has never established "a bond" between itself and the people inhabiting the lands they control through citizenship. Therefore, it is even difficult to assess whether a person living under ISIS regime is a citizen, or an alien. What is more, neither any country in the world nor any international organisations recognise any such thing as "Islamic State citizenship". The territory on which ISIS executes its powers, belonging originally to Syria and Iraq, has been acquired by force, so in contradiction to international law. And then, those territories might not be regarded as attributed to ISIS. The only element that likens that organisation to a state is the government. The Islamic State has a structured and hierarchically organised structure of authorities conceptually resembling the government of a caliphate with military council, judicial organs, defence, and security bodies. However, the organisation lacks the capacity to enter into international treaties, as it cannot act independently on the international arena. It lacks proper representation and is considered a "terrorist organisation" by most states of the world. It makes it totally unable to sign treaties, establish embassies, join international organisations, and so on.[15]

It is therefore clear that the Islamic State by no means would incur state liability for the attack on Metrojet 9268 as a state. But it does not mean that the organisation would be totally free from responsibility. The Egyptian Penal Code provides a system of penalties for members of terrorist groups for their activities taken for the benefit of the group or supporting its causes. Article 86 *bis* criminalises establishing, founding, running or organising any kind of group that

15 See more on issue of ISIS statehood: M. Osiecki, "ISIS vs. the world"., pp. 107-109.

has the purpose of "interrupting the provisions of the constitution or laws, or preventing any of the Slate's institutions or public authorities from exercising its works, or encroaching on the personal freedom of citizens or other freedoms and public rights as guaranteed by the constitution or the law, or impairing the national unity or social peace".[16] The punishment for an offender is normally imprisonment. However, Article 86 *bis* A introduces an even more severe penalty, if one of the methods used by the group to achieve their goals is terrorism. In such a case, the Penal Code allows for the offender to be sentenced to capital punishment or permanent hard labour. What is more, a person joining such a group would also be subject to being sentenced to temporary hard labour.

3.2.3. Aspects of the attack in the light of sector Conventions

a) Montreal Convention

As we pointed out in the above section, the *modus* of downing 7K-9268 (aircraft bombing) justifies the application of the provisions of the Montreal Convention from 1971, as at the time of the attack, it was the only international convention in force whose provisions covered the destruction of aircraft (the Beijing Convention, intended to be its "successor", was not yet enforceable). The present section shall be dedicated to the analysis of the accident in the light of the provisions of the Montreal Convention, whereas the subsequent ones shall feature the perspective of other Conventions.

First of all, it is rational to assess whether the application of the Montreal Convention is indeed justified. The answer can be found in Article 4. Paragraph 1 stipulates that aircraft used in military, customs or police services are outside of the Montreal Convention's application. The destroyed Airbus A321 was, of course, performing a civil flight, and operating under civil aviation rules. Therefore. It matches the criterion of application. The same principle applies in relation to paragraph 2 of Article 4. Under its provisions, the Convention shall apply only if an aircraft's place of take-off or landing (actual or intended) is located outside its state of registration, or if the offence is committed in the territory of a state other than the state of the aircraft's registration. In fact, both criteria are fulfilled in the case of 7K-9268. The plane bore the markings EI-ETJ, which, in accordance with ICAO standards, means that its state of registration was the

16 Law no. 58 01 The year 1937 Promulgating the Penal Code, Egyptian Government Bulletin, 1937-08-05, No. 71, Article 86 bis.

Republic of Ireland.[17] And, obviously, the place of take-off was located on a different state's territory (Egypt), as was the place of intended landing (Russia).

Regardless of the nature of the accident (terrorist or not), certain norms that decide which states are eligible to conduct the investigation apply. In that matter, Annex 13 to the Chicago Convention entitled *Aircraft Accident and Incident Investigation* is relevant, as it explains the competences of the state of occurrence, so the state in whose territory an accident happens, in regard to other interested states. Article 4.1. stipulates that the State of Occurrence (in this case – Egypt) is obliged to notify the following entities about the accident with minimum delay:

a) the state of registry (here – Ireland);
b) the state of operator (Russia);
c) the state of design (Germany);
d) the state of manufacture (France);
e) the ICAO, if the maximum mass of aircraft involved is over 2,250 kg (as was the case with 7K-9268).[18]

The Arab Republic of Egypt fulfilled its duties, as all of the above-mentioned states and the ICAO were notified about the accident. In turn, the initiation and execution of the investigation itself is by default the responsibility of the state of occurrence, in accordance with Article 5.1. of Annex 13. Nevertheless, delegating the entire investigation or just a part of it to another state by mutual arrangement and consent is possible. Egypt benefited from that right and conducted the investigation along with Russia.

Now we shall turn our attention to the question of jurisdiction. As was explained in sub-chapter 2.2.3. section c), the Montreal Convention provides multiple bases for jurisdiction of the interested states. In the case of 7K-9268, the question of jurisdiction would mostly concern which state's law would apply in regards to the pursuit of the person responsible for planting the bomb in the Airbus.

According to Article 5 of the Convention, the following states would be eligible to establish their jurisdiction: Egypt (as the state of occurrence), Ireland

17 ICAO, Aircraft nationality marks and common marks; https://www.icao.int/safety/airnavigation/NationalityMarks/alpha_state.pdf, 9 March 2021.

18 Annex 13 to Convention on International Civil Aviation, done at Chicago, 7 December 1944 – Aircraft Accident and Incident Investigation, Eleventh Edition, July 2016, Article 4.1.

(the state of registry of an aircraft against whom the offence was committed) and Russia (the state which an aircraft lessee considers to be their principal place of business). The known facts about the accident suggest that the person that planted the bomb was one of the ground crew members – an EgyptAir mechanic whose cousin had joined the Egypt branch of ISIS branch some time before the tragedy. A baggage handler and two police officers are believed to have assisted him with this task.[19]

Article 6 imposes on any state party the obligation to detain the alleged offender if they are found in its territory and keep them in custody until criminal or extradition proceedings can be instituted. The Egyptian authorities observed this provision and detained both the mechanic who is believed to have planted the bomb, as well as the baggage handler and the two police officers. So far, no formal proceedings have been initiated against them, nor is any extradition expected. However, if Egypt does not decide to deliver those suspects to another state by extradition, it will have to submit their case to competent authorities for the purpose of prosecution, in accordance with the principle *aut dedere aut iudicare* expressed in Article 7 of the Montreal Convention. However, very few states have a real interest in judging the offenders responsible for blowing up 7K-9268, and so it is improbable that Egypt would receive multiple requests for extradition. In any case, the Montreal Convention itself might be considered the basis for extradition in absence of a "regular" extradition treaty between Egypt and another interested state (which is stipulated in Article 8 paragraph 2 of the Convention).[20]

b) Possible application of Beijing Convention provisions

The Beijing Convention, a legal instrument intended to improve global efforts in the fight against terrorism, was not yet in force at the time of the accident, nor was it even ratified by any state involved in the accident of 7K-9268 (currently, only France and Germany have signed the Convention, with only France ratifying

---

19 T. Gumrukcu, "Exclusive: EgyptAir mechanic suspected in Russian plane crash", Reuters, 29 January 2016. (9 March 2021) https://www.reuters.com/article/us-egypt-crash-suspects/exclusive-egyptair-mechanic-suspected-in-russian-plane-crash-idUSKCN0V712V

20 Currently, the Arab Republic of Egypt has extradition treaties signed with following states (as provided by the Egyptian Ministry of Foreign Affairs): Albania, Armenia, Malta, and Ukraine.

it).[21] However, in order to present how this Convention could re-shape the proceedings in the case, we shall examine the hypothetical situation, assuming the Convention were in force at the time and all relevant states were bound by it.

First of all, there would be no difference in the qualification of the act of blowing up the Airbus, as the Beijing Convention (in Article 1 point (b)) requires the criminalisation of the destruction of aircraft in service just as the Montreal Convention does. But, the criminalisation is extended over those persons that organise the commission of an offence or direct others to commit it (Article 1 paragraph 4). That construction opens a way for prosecuting not only the person that planted the bomb on board and their accomplices (which is also stipulated in the Montreal Convention), but also those persons, who were organised the whole operation or ordered to plant the bomb. Theoretically, that could mean the prosecution of prominent figures of the Islamic State, if criminal investigation revealed their involvement in the bombing. What is more, all other persons that made any contribution to allowing the crime to happen would have also been considered to be accomplices (Article 2 paragraph 5 of the Beijing Convention). Thus, the people who handed the bomb over to the mechanic, built the explosive device (and so on) would also be included in the list of suspects.

Article 4 of the Beijing Convention would bear importance in this case only if it was discovered in the investigation that a legal entity was engaged in the commission of the offence (offered financial support, supplied the perpetrators with illegal explosive materials, intentionally sheltered the offenders, etc.). So far, the investigation has revealed no such fact, so the provision would be irrelevant.

In turn, Article 8 of the Beijing Convention would have had a slight influence on the investigation itself, as according to the jurisdiction bases enumerated as part of said Article, the right to establish jurisdiction would have been vested also in Ukraine and Belarus. That results from paragraph 2 of that Article, entitling the states whose nationals were targeted by the offence to exercise their jurisdictions. And as we pointed out in section a), apart from the Russian citizens, Belarusian and Ukrainian citizens were also on board Airbus A321. The question remains, how would the current turbulent relations between Ukraine and Russia have affected the investigation itself? It is unlikely that the authorities of both states would have cooperated during the investigation on the causes of the crash in such a negative political climate.

---

21 Convention on the Suppression of Unlawful Acts Relating to International Civil Aviation, ICAO Doc. 9960, List of parties. (9 March 2021). https://www.icao.int/secretariat/legal/List%20of%20Parties/Beijing_Conv_EN.pdf

The question of extradition in the hypothetical application of the Beijing Convention would remain rather unchanged. Neither state conducting the investigation signalled an intention to have the alleged offenders extradited to their territory, and therefore, the provisions concerning extradition are irrelevant. Crucially, in accordance with Article 13, if a request for extradition of offenders from Egypt to another state had been formed, Egypt could not have declined to proceed with the extradition on the basis of political motives.

3.2.4. A reason for retaliation?

In previous sections, we mentioned many times that the tragic events from 11th September, 2001 totally changed the perception of the fight against terrorism and convinced the states of the world to take a different approach in regard to terrorist attempts which nowadays can be treated as armed attacks that threaten a states' sovereignty.

How does such an approach affect the case of 7K-9268? First of all, we need to recall the stance of the UNSC expressed in Resolutions adopted shortly after the attacks on the WTC (numbered 1368, 1373 and 1378). Their interpretation leads to a conclusion: a terrorist attempt might be regarded as a threat to international peace and security; such an attack might be treated as an aggression under art. 51 of the UN Charter, and therefore constitute a legitimate reason for an attacked state to respond in self-defence that might be directed against a non-state actor, such as a terrorist organisation, and/or against a state in whose territory located are main organisation units, or one that harbours them, or even tolerates their activities, even when it does not exercise effective control over them.[22]

Moreover, the Security Council reaffirmed in Resolution 2309 (2016) that states have an interest in protecting their citizens and nationals against terrorist attacks targeting civil aviation.

From that interpretation and all arguments presented in the previous sections on the terrorist character of the attack on Metrojet 9268, we can clearly see that it constituted a threat to international peace and security and therefore justified acting in self-defence by state-victims. It should be assessed then how wide is the circle of those state-victims? As we explained in sub-chapter 1.4.4., in accordance with the principle arising from Article 1 of the Chicago Convention, a state in whose airspace an attack is carried out faces a breach of its sovereignty, and therefore should be treated as a state-victim. However, if a strike hits an

22 T. Aleksandrowicz, "Zamach terrorystyczny", p. 570.

aeroplane flying above a state's territory, it is difficult to deprive the state of that aircraft's registry (or the state in whose territory an aircraft lessee's principal place of business is located) the status of state-victim as well. But also, if in consequence of the attack passengers of the plane are killed, then also their state of nationality might be considered a victim.

So, the scope of potential state-victims in the attack on Metrojet 9268 is quite large: definitely we can count Egypt, Russia and Ireland as targeted states, as well as Ukraine and Belarus. In practice then, all of those states may resort to self-defence against the terrorist organisation (ISIS) and any states harbouring it or tolerating its activities, as Article 51 of the UN Charter authorises them to do so. And that, in fact strongly relates, to the armed conflict in the Middle East. In 2015, Syria and Iraq were experiencing the hell of war. The Islamic State, at that time, controlled a significant part of the territory of both states, and had acquired access to strategic, economic, and military points, such as oil refineries, bank assets, and tanks.[23] The Global Coalition, a large military alliance of international organisations and countries, including Egypt, Ireland and Ukraine, and led by the United States, opposing Daesh's claims, was a principal armed force countering ISIS under Iraq's consent.[24] However, the Syrian government headed by president Bashar Al-Assad did not condone any hostilities of the Global Coalition in its territory under the consideration that it violated international law.[25] Instead, only the Russian armed forces were allowed to engage in the fight on Syrian territories. Irani troops ultimately provided the Russians with support.[26]

The legal mechanism of legitimate self-defence gives the state-victims of the Metrojet attack an opportunity to retaliate against ISIS in the form of armed attack both on the lands of Syria and Iraq, as the two states hold the terrorist organisation's main command centres.[27] Theoretically, state-victims could, for

---

23 M. P. Scharf, "How the War Against ISIS Changed International Law", Case Western Reserve Journal of International Law, Vol. 48 2016, p. 2.

24 For the full list of the Global Coalition partners see http://theglobalcoalition.org/en/partners/ (25 May 2020).

25 M. P. Scharf, "How the War Against ISIS Changed International Law", p. 3.

26 K. B. Sælebakke, Into the Quagmire? Explaining Russia's Military Intervention in Syria, University of Oslo, Oslo 2016, p. 47.

27 In 2015, the Islamic State exercised effective control of numerous cities in Syria and Iraq, but its main centres of operations were located in Raqqa (Syria), which served as the organisation's de facto capital. See M. J. Stephan, "Civil Resistance vs. ISIS", Journal of Resistance Studies, Vol. 1(2) 2015, p. 133.

example, perform air strikes on Daesh bases in both countries. However, an approach to that solution should be pragmatic, first and foremost. If we consider Ireland, Ukraine, Egypt, Russia and Belarus to be the victims of the destruction of flight 7K-9268, we need to remember that the armed forces of those states vary in strength. In 2015, Ukraine was already engaged in conflict with Russia due to the annexation of Crimea, and would have needed to direct its forces to Syrian territories for the purpose of retaliation. The risk of clashing with Russian troops on Syrian soil would have been a dramatic turn of events for Ukraine and another escalation of conflict between those two countries, which in the long-term, would cost Ukraine too much, especially in relation to the fact, that "only" four of its citizens died in the accident.[28] Ireland in turn, as a neutral state, does not have a strong army and moreover is not even part of NATO. Its direct engagement in the hostilities in Syria would likely be harmful, especially if its forces encountered resistance from Russian and Irani troops. Taking also into account that Ireland had low involvement in the accident (although the destroyed Airbus A321 was registered in Ireland, it had been leased to foreign operators in Russia)[29], its decision to retaliate would be ultimately counter-productive. As for the Arab Republic of Egypt, potential strikes on Syrian territory would have damaged relations between Egypt and Russia, its partner in the accident investigation. Cooperation between both countries' investigation teams was essential for finding the causes of the catastrophe and their face-off would negatively affect the investigation itself. And most importantly, all three states mentioned are members of the Global Coalition, and therefore officially fight against Daesh, mostly on Iraqi territory, since as was pointed above, Iraq permits its allies to fight on its territory.

Other key cities for the Daesh included: Mosul (Iraq), Palmyra (Syria), or Tikrit (Iraq). For current maps showing the real control of ISIS over territories in Middle East: https://isis.liveuamap.com/ (9 March 2021).

28 Ministry of the Russian Federation for Civil Defence, Emergencies and Elimination of Consequences of Natural Disasters, list of passengers and crew of aeroplane Airbus A321 "Kogalymavia" 7K-9268 (Министерство Российской Федерации по делам гражданской обороны, чрезвычайным ситуациям и ликвидации последствий стихийных бедствий, список пассажиров и экипажа самолета Airbus A321 авиакомпании «КогалымАвиа» 7K9268): http://www.mchs.gov.ru/operationalpage/Operativnaja_informacija/item/5216330/ (9 March 2021).

29 For the history of aircraft operations, see https://www.airfleets.net/ficheapp/plane-a321-663.htm (9 March 2021).

Russia was in the opposite situation. Its strategic partnership with the Syrian regime gave it a convenient way to continue and even intensify its air strikes over its allies' territory. Importantly, the Russian Federation's investigation authorities were the first to declare that 7K-9268 was brought down in a terrorist attack, therefore the state justified *ab initio* its enforced campaign to counter the Daesh. That stance was even enhanced by the fact that Russia was arguably the most serious victim of the attack, losing more than two hundred of its nationals. As for Belarus, there were no signs of direct involvement in the investigation, not to mention the war in Middle East, so the question of this state's recourse to self-defence is rather out of discussion.

The above analysis greatly proves that even a violent terrorist attack does not awaken in a state the will to resort to self-defence automatically when political issues are at stake. Sometimes, states would prefer to join forces with international actors of a greater military power (which is why the Global Coalition was form under the leadership of the United States), or conduct non-military policy against terrorists than engage in armed conflict whose long-term forecast is not promising for the attacked entity. This only strengthens the argument for effective application of sector conventions (in this case, the Tokyo-Hague-Montreal Beijing system), which assure that an offender or even all involved terrorist group members do not escape from justice. To say it more trivially, they still keep a way open for anti-terrorist proceedings other than air strikes on states harbouring offenders.

3.3. The downing of Malaysia Airlines flight 17: Another step towards the intensification of the conflict in eastern Ukraine

Very few aviation accidents have sparked as intense an international debate as the tragedy of Malaysia Airlines flight 17 (MH 17). The crash played a significant role in the worsening already at this time tense relations between Ukraine and Russia, and dealt a grave blow to the reputation of one of the most successful air operators in Southern Asia. Although one of the official reports on the accident was already released, controversies still arise and new facts are being discovered. What is more, a MH 17 criminal case has been opened in District Court of The Hague and investigations are still ongoing. The horrific history of MH 17 also shows how political issues negatively affect the fight against terrorism.

3.3.1. Factual background

a) History of the flight

On 17 July, 2014, a Boeing 777-200 jet belonging to the Malaysian national air carrier, Malaysia Airlines, registered with the number 9M-MRD, took off at 12:31 local time (10:31 UTC) from Amsterdam-Schiphol Airport for a scheduled flight to its home base in Kuala Lumpur, Malaysia.[30] On board were 283 passengers representing 10 nationalities. Most of them were Dutch (193 persons), Malaysian (28 persons) and Australian (27 persons). The others held either Indonesian, British, German, Belgian, Philippine, Canadian or New Zealand passports. The crew consisted of four pilots and eleven flight attendants, all of Malaysian nationality.[31]

Upon its departure, MH 17 reached its cruising altitude of 31,000 feet at 10:53 UTC and headed south-eastward, to fly above Germany and then Poland. Ninety minutes into the flight, just before entering Ukrainian airspace, the plane was at the altitude of 33,000 feet. It was scheduled to enter the Dnipropetrovsk air traffic control area and climb further to 35,000 feet. MH 17 continued according to the flight plan into the airspace above the eastern part of Ukraine, where armed conflict was on-going. Ukrainian government forces were battling pro-Russian rebels on those lands, which put any airliners flying over at risk of being hit by a surface-to-air missile. In the past, several military aircraft had already been shot down. Therefore, Ukrainian authorities set up a no-fly zone in the airspace up to 32,000 feet. one thousand feet lower than the cruising altitude of MH 17 at that moment.[32]

At 13:19 UTC, the radar showed the air traffic controller that the plane deviated to the left from its scheduled track. He requested the pilots to alter their route due to incoming traffic and seconds after received an acknowledgement. At 13:20, when the plane was above the town of Hrabove, the controller transmitted further clearance and demanded a report back. But this time, no reply was given by the pilots and the plane vanished from the radar.[33]

---

30 https://aviation-safety.net/database/record.php?id=20140717-0 (9 March 2021).

31 Dutch Safety Board, Crash of Malaysia Airlines flight 17, p. 27.
Some sources published information on a different number of flight occupants than indicated by the Dutch Safety Board. That resulted from the fact that 24 passengers had more than one nationality.

32 J. Nicas, R. Wall, "Height of Ukraine No-Fly Zone Faces Scrutiny", The Wall Street Journal, 17 July 2014. (9 March 2021) https://www.wsj.com/articles/height-of-ukraine-no-fly-zone-faces-scrutiny-1405639624

33 https://aviation-safety.net/database/record.php?id=20140717-0 (25 May 2020).

As the aeroplane debris fell from the skies on the soil of Hrabove, it became nearly clear that MH 17 was destroyed. Shortly after the moment of tragedy, the National Bureau of Air Accidents Investigation of Ukraine officially commenced the investigation on the facts and sent notifications on the aircraft's disappearance to the following entities as required by Annex 13 to the Chicago Convention: Malaysia (the state of aircraft's registry and the state of operator), the United States (state of manufacturer) and the ICAO, as well as the Netherlands and Australia, as those states lost the most nationals.[34] In the meantime, the Ukrainian State Traffic Service Enterprise closed the whole airspace above the eastern part of Ukraine.[35]

b) *Investigation on the crash*

Already on the following day of the MH 17 catastrophe, the pro-Russian rebels' emergency forces arrived on the crash site and located 181 bodies of the passengers. A search for flight data recorders (so called "black boxes") was also launched and after some time, the separatist officials recovered them from the wreckage. Despite early concerns by Australian and Ukrainian authorities that the devices might have been transferred to Russia, Sergei Lavrov, the Foreign Minister of the Russian Federation, declined that his country would have had such an interest. Ultimately, on 21 July, the recorders were handed over to a Malaysian official in Donetsk and then transported to Kyiv under his supervision. The devices were later sent to the Dutch Safety Board and then examined in the laboratory of the Air Accidents Investigation Branch of the United Kingdom in Farnborough.[36]

On 23 July, Ukraine officially delegated the power to conduct the accident investigation to the Dutch Safety Board (or "OVV", Dutch: *Onderzoeksraad Voor Veiligheid*), under the relevant right expressed in Article 5.1. of Annex 13 to the Chicago Convention. Just a few days later, on 28 July, a coordinated meeting at Eurojust was initiated and finalised by drafting an agreement on the formation of a Joint Investigation Team (or "JIT"), signed by Dutch, Belgian, Australian and Ukrainian authorities for the purpose of a common criminal investigation in the MH 17 case. All four states were involved, with Malaysia and Eurojust as co-participants. The investigation is coordinated by the Dutch Public Prosecutor's

34 Dutch Safety Board, Preliminary report. Crash involving Malaysia Airlines Boeing 777-200 flight 17, p. 7-8.

35 Dutch Safety Board, Crash of Malaysia Airlines flight 17, p. 101.

36 Dutch Safety Board, Preliminary report, p. 18.

Office.[37] The establishment of the JIT constituted a response to the UN Security Council Resolution No. 2166, which emphasises the need to set up an independent international investigation team [see sub-chapter 2.3.2., section d)].

Within several months, the OVV investigators confirmed that a projectile must have brought down the plane, as many 9M38-series missile fragments were found amongst the wreckage. It was later established that the missile was fired by a Buk surface-to-air missile system, a self-propelled military device produced on the territory of Russia.[38] That discovery only fuelled political accusations both from the Ukrainian and Russian side. The President of the Russian Federation, Vladimir Putin, blamed the government of Ukraine for allowing tensions to break out in the eastern parts of the country, which eventually must have caused a tragedy. Moreover, Putin regarded the Ukraine government's decision not to close the whole airspace above its eastern territory as negligent in regards to the ongoing armed conflict.[39] In turn, the then-Ukrainian Prime Minister, Arseniy Yatsenyuk, called the accident an "international crime", and claimed that Russia

37 Dutch Public Prosecution Service, The criminal investigation by the Joint Investigation Team (JIT); https://www.prosecutionservice.nl/topics/mh17-plane-crash/criminal-investigation-jit-mh17 (25 May 2020).
The JIT was formed as a body separate from the Dutch Safety Board investigating the causes of the MH 17 crash, as according to Article 3.1. of Annex 13 to the Chicago Convention, the sole objective of such an investigation (conducted by appropriate state authorities) shall be the prevention of accidents and not the apportion of blame or liability. Therefore, for a criminal investigation, a different body should be set up.

38 Dutch Safety Board, Crash of Malaysia Airlines, pp. 82, 149-150. Interestingly, Russian authorities have been denying that a missile could have been fired at the aircraft, as flight radar images from the Ust-Donetsk radio station did not show any trace of a projectile having been launched. But experts from the JIT did not accept such a version of events, as in their opinion, a 9M38-series missile normally flies at much higher speed than an average civil aircraft, and therefore might not have been registered by the flight radar. See Dutch Public Prosecution Service, Status of the investigation and position on the progress of the trial - part 2 (10-3-2020). (9 March 2021)
https://www.prosecutionservice.nl/topics/mh17-plane-crash/prosecution-and-trial/status-investigation-and-position-on-progress-trial---part-2

39 In the final report on the crash published by the Dutch Safety Board, it was indicated that the closure of airspace by the Ukrainian government was a reasonable precaution measure. However, the emergence of a conflict zone constitutes in the opinion of investigators a sufficient reason for the closure of the whole airspace above such a zone, and states in general should be encouraged to do so, as normally they rarely use that option. See Dutch Safety Board, Crash of Malaysia Airlines, p. 11.

was to be held accountable.[40] The President of Ukraine, Petro Poroshenko, publicly affirmed that the crash was the result of an act of terrorism.

However, a years-long investigation has ruled out any possibility of a terrorist attack. But the JIT established that the missile was launched from a Buk system in an agricultural field near the village of Pervomaiskyi, controlled at that time by pro-Russian rebels. In addition to that, it was transported to the location from Russian territory.[41] In May 2018, investigators from the JIT also confirmed that it originated from the 53rd Anti-Aircraft Missile brigade, a unit of the Russian army stationing in Kursk.[42] But Russian authorities again declined any responsibility for the crash and rejected the statement that the missile system originated in their country.

The criminal investigation goes on and, according to official sources, is now aimed at finding the perpetrators and assessing whether there was any direct relation between them and any state's government. So far, evidence delivered by the JIT has served as the basis for the initiation of prosecution of four individuals believed to be responsible for the crash, on 19 June, 2019, by the Netherlands Public Prosecution Service.[43] Among those persons is Igor Girgin alias Strelkov, a Russian military veteran and a self-declared rebel commander who immediately after MH 17 was shot down, posted on social media a statement that the rebel forces successfully downed an Antonov An-26, a Ukrainian military aircraft, and later deleted said post. Thus, many came to speculate that the separatists mistakenly targeted MH 17 having been convinced that they were aiming at the Antonov.[44]

---

40 https://nationalpost.com/news/malaysia-airlines-mh17-black-boxes-reportedly-recovered-russia-denies-it-will-take-them-from-rebels (9 March 2021).

41 Dutch Public Prosecution Service, Status of the investigation and position on the progress of the trial - part 2 (10-3-2020). (9 March 2021) https://www.prosecutionservice.nl/topics/mh17-plane-crash/prosecution-and-trial/status-investigation-and-position-on-progress-trial---part-2

42 Dutch Public Prosecution Service, Status of the investigation.

43 More information can be accessed through official MH 17 criminal case website: https://www.courtmh17.com/en/timeline/timeline-mh17-trial.

44 S.-D. Bachmann, "Malaysia Airlines flight MH17: the day Russia became a state sponsor of terrorism", Amicus Curiae, 97/2014, p. 14,
T. Lachowski, "Kto strzelał – kto odpowie?", p. 197.

3.3.2. Was the attack really a terrorist attempt?

After studying the investigation reports and experts; opinions on the circumstances of the crash, the answer to the question of whether terrorism was involved in the shooting down of MH 17 seems to be negative. However, we need to point out here that accident reports are not drafted for purposes of apportioning liability, especially in regards to state actors. The issue of state liability for air accidents is, in other words, simply excluded from the area of interest of investigators. Reports mostly focus on improving the safety of air travels in the future. Thus, if an accident report states that terrorism might be ruled out as the cause of the crash, we need to interpret it more narrowly – as an "individual" or "classical" form of terrorism, not state terrorism. The task of indicating what entity should be held liable for having caused the crash is attributed to the criminal investigation team, which, in the case of MH 17, is the JIT. And although it presented valuable evidence that allowed to already prosecute four persons involved in the downing, official hearings before the Dutch court were only conducted on 9 March 2020 and the case itself is far from over (not to mention that the proceedings were suspended amid the COVID-19 pandemic).[45] Therefore, the involvement of state terrorism cannot be totally discarded at that point. Additionally, among the opinions of prominent political figures, the notion arose that terrorism was indeed a factor related to the crash. As was mentioned in a previous section, Ukrainian President Petro Poroshenko claimed that the downing had indeed a terrorist nature. In turn, Tony Abbott, the then-Prime Minister of, Australia, strongly considered calling the tragedy "terrorist," which would have resulted in triggering the payment of high compensation to the families of Australian victims.[46] The state usually indicated as potentially responsible for the catastrophe is the Russian Federation. But to what extent it is possible that Russia could incur liability for an act of state terrorism? A relevant study shall be presented below.

45 https://www.courtmh17.com/en/timeline/timeline-articles/first-hearing?referrer=3f920eb7-ba11-443e-8836-29d596ba61b0 (9 March 2021).

46 J. Ireland, "MH17: Abbott government may declare downing of plane a terrorist attack, triggering payments to families", The Sydney Morning Herald, 21 July 2014. (9 March 2021) https://www.smh.com.au/politics/federal/mh17-abbott-government-may-declare-downing-of-plane-a-terrorist-attack-triggering-payments-to-families-20140721-3cajb.html

a) *Attribution of attack to a state*

First of all, we need to assess whether the act of shooting down MH 17 could be attributed to a state. The known facts of the case point at a pro-Russian separatist unit as those who actually fired missile at the Boeing 777 [see the above section]. At the time of the accident, the territory of eastern Ukraine was doubtlessly under the effective control of rebels who consider those lands as the "Luhansk People's Republic" (or "LPR") and the "Donetsk People's Republic" (or "DPR"), commonly known as "Novorossiya".[47] However, there is no legal basis to recognise those "republics" as independent state actors; to some extent they might only be regarded as "quasi-states", dependent on Ukrainian domestic law.[48] Therefore, separatists would be treated as non-state actors under international law.

However, there is plenty of evidence suggesting that the separatist forces were not acting independently, but were receiving strong support from Russia. The country was constantly providing them with military supplies and combat personnel which made the effective occupation of LPR and DPR possible. Russian officers were also commanding the rebelling forces, as was the case with Igor Strelkov, who led the unit that fired the missile from the Buk system [see the section above].[49] But are all those circumstances sufficient to claim that Russia was responsible for the shooting down of the plane? To answer that question, we need to examine the concept of a state's responsibility itself.

In accordance with Article 3 of the document entitled *Responsibility of States for Internationally Wrongful Acts* (hereafter referred to as the "Articles on Responsibility") adopted by the International Law Commission (ILC) during its fifty-third session, which codifies customary law norms related to states' responsibility, a state may incur responsibility for a wrongful act when its conduct (an

---

47 An argument that the territory of the Donetsk Oblast, where the Boeing wreckage was found, was being under effective control of the separatists was confirmed when international investigators struggled to reach the crash site. Rebel forces prevented them from accessing the debris and declined to transfer the black boxes to the relevant authorities. That constituted one of the reasons for the Security Council to adopt Resolution 2166 in which the body called for allowing an undisrupted access to the crash site. The Ukrainian government itself had a little or no de facto control over the area. See R. Abeyratne, "Flight MH 17 and state responsibility for ensuring safety and security of air transport", Journal of Transportation Security 7/2014, p. 351

48 See more: T. Lachowski, "Kto strzelał – kto odpowie?", p. 199.

49 B. ter Haar, "Lessons from the MH17 Disaster", Security and Human Rights 25/2014, p. 457.

action or omission): (I) is attributable to the state under international law, (II) constitutes a breach of international obligations binding that state.[50] Importantly, this concerns breaches of any kinds of obligations (including contractual), which was confirmed *inter alia* by the France-New Zealand Arbitration Tribunal in the *Rainbow Warrior* case.[51]

The most troublesome aspect here is deciding on the fulfilment of the first condition. As the pro-Russian separatist believed to have shot down MH 17 are not by any means state organs, their behaviour may be qualified as a state activity only if they, in accordance with Article 5 of the Articles on Responsibility, are empowered by the law of such a state to exercise some of its government authorities. Furthermore, Article 8 of the Articles on Responsibility stipulates that the conduct of a group of persons (in our case: the pro-Russian rebels) would be considered an act of a state if that group "acts on the instructions of, or under the direction or control of, that [s]tate in carrying out the conduct".[52] That provision should be interpreted in the light of the ICJ judgement in the *Nicaragua vs. USA* case from 1986; it concerned the support provided by the United States' government to a guerilla group *contras* which at the time fought against the then-overpowered president.[53] Although it was proven that *contras* were receiving financial resources, training and military equipment, the Court held that such activities could not have been regarded as attributed to a state, as a necessary condition here would be the existence of *effective control* over *non-state actors* activities, including the act of breaching international law itself. In the case of downing MH 17, it would entail that pro-Russian separatist units were not acting independently, but were under *effective control* of the Kremlin and the act of shooting down was, in fact, conducted under Russian instructions.[54]

At the early phase of the criminal investigation, it was only verified that the relation between the Kremlin and the separatists was indeed very vivid [see above],

---

50 M. Shaw, International Public Law, p. 569.

51 Case concerning the difference between New Zealand and France concerning the interpretation or application of two agreements, concluded on 9 July 1986 between the two States and which related to the problems arising from the Rainbow Warrior Affair, 30 April 1990, United Nations Reports of International Arbitral Awards, vol. XX, 1990, p. 251.

52 Draft articles on Responsibility of States for Internationally Wrongful Acts, UN Doc A/56/10, Article 8.

53 Militarv and Puramilitary Activities in und aguinst Nicaragua (Nicaragua v. United States of America), Judgement of 27 June 1986: ICJ Reports 1986, p. 65.

54 See more: T. Lachowski, "Kto strzelał – kto odpowie?", p. 201-203.

much like the situation of *contras* and the US government, which would have excluded the attribution of the rebels shooting down the plane to a state and in consequence, freeing Russia of responsibility. But ever since, progress in the JIT research has been disclosing facts suggesting that the Kremlin could have had a more significant role in shooting down the plane than was originally thought. For instance, investigators concluded that the Buk missile system from which the projectile was fired had originated from the 53rd Anti-Aircraft Missile Brigade of the Russian army, which suggests that Russian military officials could have been involved. Nevertheless, there is too little evidence disclosed to the public to definitely prove the act itself could have been attributed to any state. Support provided by the Russian Federation to the rebels in LPR and DPR does not itself constitute an instance of state conduct *per se* and therefore does not fulfil the first condition expressed in Article 3 of the Articles on Responsibility.

However, if later in the investigation circumstances sufficient to claim that the act of shooting down the plane would be attributable to a state were to be revealed, then the fulfilment of the second condition from Article 3 would be much easier to prove. The attack on MH 17 would be a clear breach of Article 3 *bis* of the Chicago Convention, which stipulates that "[…] every State must refrain from resorting to the use of weapons against civil aircraft in flight […]".[55] The Chicago Convention is a document of a nearly universal application, with 192 parties, including the Russian Federation, Ukraine, and other states involved in the case. The act of firing a missile at an aeroplane, provided it is committed by a state actor or a non-state actor under a state's instructions, is an infringement of the provision enshrined in the international treaty, and therefore probably entails the state's responsibility.

b) Character of the shooting: Terrorist or not?

After analysing the issue of responsibility in regards to the MH 17 catastrophe, we have to turn our attention back to the primary question: would shooting down the plane constitute an act of state terrorism? The answer to that question is not totally clear, at least in the current state of knowledge of the facts. First of all, to call a particular conduct "state terrorism", we have to be certain that it can be attributed to a state. As was presented above, such an attribution would be premature, as neither the ongoing investigation nor the already instituted criminal case before the Dutch court have given a clear answer so far. But even if that

55 Chicago Convention, Article 3 bis.

were to happen and a state (most probably Russia) were to incur responsibility for the accident, the problem of whether the act qualifies as terrorist remains. Providing a definition of terrorism itself would certainly be helpful, or more precisely, the criteria of a terrorist act:

1) Intentional use of violence or threat thereof,
2) Conduct against the law,
3) Realisation of particular ideological or political goals,
4) The aim to spread fear or danger throughout society,
5) Affecting entities such as states or international organisations.

Intentional use of violence or threat thereof.

In regards to the first criterion, the use of violence is unquestionable –downing a jet with the usage of a surface-to-air missile constitutes an act of violence in itself. But the involvement of intent is not that obvious. The facts revealed in the investigation show that the pro-Russian separatists, under the command of Igor Strelkov, were indeed aiming to shoot down a jet, but a military one, an Antonov An-26 [see section b)]. If the investigation reveals that MH 17 was in fact targeted by mistake, then the intent of those who fired the missile would most probably be excluded.

Conduct against the law.

As for the second element, there is no need for a thorough examination. As we already explained [see above], the usage of a weapon against civil aircraft is strictly prohibited under international law. That would strengthen the argument of a terrorist character of the downing of MH 17.

Realisation of particular ideological or political goals.

Political interests have been present in the conflict in eastern Ukraine since its beginning and the passengers and crew of MH 17 became their victims. The pro-Russian separatists in LPR and DPR have been engaged in conflict in order to build their own states independent from Ukraine, as both territories had solid economic and social ties with the Russian Federation, and even local population spoke the Russian language on an everyday basis.[56] Thus, the rebels' military activity might be read as having political context, including shooting down aircraft that occurred at least several times on the territories of LPR and DPR during armed the conflict.

56 B. ter Haar, "Lessons from the MH17 Disaster", p. 456.

The aim to spread fear or danger throughout society.

The aim of spreading fear throughout society, if even present in the case of MH 17, is quite weak. Although the accident itself shocked the international community and pushed Ukraine to close all of its airspace above the eastern parts of the country, it is rather doubtful that the separatists that fired a surface-to-air missile at MH 17 really wanted to spark fear in society, especially if there are no clear indications that their intention was to strike down a civil airliner, and not a military one.

Affecting entities such as states or international organisations.

Fulfilment of the last element is in turn strongly manifested in the case. As we mentioned already, the downing of the plane ignited a reaction from many states and international organisations. The UNSC adopted Resolution No. 2166 which condemned the attack and called for the establishment of an international investigation team [see sub-chapter 2.3.2. section d)], whereas the ICAO sent a team of experts to assist Ukraine in the investigation process in its territories.[57] Authorities of those states whose nationals died in the crash also expressed their support in the investigation proceedings or even publicly called the accident "terrorist" [see above]. But above all, shooting down an aircraft performed by pro-Russian rebels was part of their campaign to achieve independence from Ukraine and to eventually become part of the Russian Federation. Such behaviour in itself affects a state that risks losing part of its territory and population.

Are we then able, after having taken into account all the aforementioned arguments, to affirm that striking down MH 17 was an act of state terrorism? A positive answer to that question would be rather premature, or generally doubtful. The act of shooting down the plane itself did not meet all the criteria necessary to call it "terrorism", at least not on the basis of the currently known facts. In addition, until now, there has been no clear evidence showing that shooting down the Boeing was the act of a state. Therefore, although the accident of MH 17 could be perceived as a breach of international law, known facts do not let us consider it as a form of state terrorism.[58]

---

57 https://www.icao.int/Newsroom/Pages/Ukraine-requests-ICAO-assistance-in-MH17-accident-investigation.aspx (9 March 2021).

58 Not everyone shares the same opinion. Apart from the then-Ukrainian President, Petro Poroshenko, who called the shooting down of MH 17 an act of terrorism, some authors are also convinced that the act could be regarded as terrorist. Dr Sacha-Dominik Bachmann argues that the pro-Russian separatists might be put on a terrorist organisation list which would result in recognizing their activities (such as the downing of MH 17)

3.3.3. The offence under the Tokyo-Hague-Montreal-Beijing system conventions

Regardless of how we qualify the accident of MH 17 (terrorist or not), it needs to be assessed whether it could be regarded as a crime under international law and accordingly, how would the perpetrators be treated for their act.

a) Applicability of the Montreal Convention

First of all, we have to assess whether it fulfils the criteria of an unlawful act against civil aviation. As the Montreal Convention was a single convention regulating the offence of shooting down aircraft in force when the accident occurred, it is reasonable to conduct research on its basis. It should be noted that all states involved were at that time (and still are) parties to the Convention.[59]

We shall here recall wording of Article 1(1) of the Convention:

> "Any person commits an offence if he unlawfully and intentionally:
> (a) performs an act of violence against a person on board an aircraft in flight if that act is likely to endanger the safety of that aircraft; or
> (b) destroys an aircraft in service or causes damage to such an aircraft which renders it incapable of flight or which is likely to endanger its safety in flight".[60]

It does not require further explanation that the shooting down of MH 17 would match point b) of the provision stipulating on the destruction of aircraft in service. However, as we mentioned in the previous section, it would be problematic to assign to the perpetrators the intent of committing the act, as some evidence shows that the rebels who fired the missiles were aiming at military aircraft, not at the Boeing 777. If indeed a military plane had been hit, that would have automatically excluded the application of the Convention, as it stipulates in its Article 4 that it does not apply to aircraft used in customs, police and military.

The question of proving the intent of the perpetrators is in the case a *sine qua non* condition of qualifying their act as an offence under the Montreal Convention. As of today, it has not been clearly proven in the course of the investigation that the separatists using the Buk missile system really intended to strike MH 17

---

as terrorist as well. The author also points out that the domestic law of both Ukraine and Russia criminalises such activities as terrorist.

S.-D. Bachmann, "Malaysia Airlines flight MH17", pp. 2-3.

59 https://www.icao.int/secretariat/legal/List%20of%20Parties/Mtl71_EN.pdf (9 March 2021).

60 Montreal Convention, Article 1.

down from the skies. If that remains unchanged and even in the final stage of the criminal proceedings it is revealed that the Boeing was shot down because of a mistake in the identification of aircraft, the perpetrators would probably incur criminal responsibility, but not under the provisions of the Convention.

However, as long as the criminal investigation is pending, the perpetrators might be regarded as "alleged offenders" under the Montreal Convention, and in consequence its provisions concerning jurisdiction and extradition might be applied. According to Article 4(2), its applicability is justified due to the fact that MH 17 originated in the Netherlands and was hit over the territory of Ukraine, both being states different than the one in which the aeroplane performing the flight was registered (Malaysia).[61] The catalogue of states entitled to establish jurisdiction (under Article 5) is quite narrow and consists of:

a) Ukraine (state of occurrence);
b) Malaysia (state of aircraft registration).

If an alleged offender is found on a territory of a different state party, the latter one should establish their jurisdiction, at least if it decides not to extradite them (Article 7 in relation to Article 5 paragraph 2). In any case, such a state shall either take the alleged offender into custody or exercise appropriate measures to ensure their presence, as Article 6 stipulates. Interestingly, Igor Strelkov, the then-leader of the pro-Russian separatists in DPR who commanded the group that fired the missile from the Buk system, went back to his homeland of Russia and became more engaged in political affairs shortly after the accident. So far, no restraint measures were imposed upon him, but at the same time, no extradition request was submitted to the Russian Federation regarding his person. [62]

As for the extradition itself, the Russian Federation has extradition treaties signed with multiple countries, but even if it were to receive a request for

---

61 The Boeing was marked 9M-MRD, which signifies the nationality of Malaysia according to the official list published by the ICAO. See ICAO, Aircraft nationality marks and common marks; https://www.icao.int/safety/airnavigation/NationalityMarks/NationalityMarks%20WEB%20en.pdf (9 March 2021).

62 More on Strelkov's activities post-MH 17:
N. Waller, "Ex-Separatist Leader Launches Party Aimed at Restoring Russia's Empire", Georgia Today, 2 June 2016. (9 March 2021) https://web.archive.org/web/20160602041435/http://georgiatoday.ge/news/3927/Ex-Separatist-Leader-Launches-Party-Aimed-at-Restoring-Russia%E2%80%99s-Empire

transmitting an alleged offender from a state with whom it does not have any such treaty signed, the Convention might serve as a basis (Article 8).[63]

b) Hypothetical application of the Beijing Convention

The Beijing Convention, whose provisions prevail over the Montreal Convention, was not yet in force when the tragedy of MH 17 occurred. Moreover, among all the interested states, only the Kingdom of the Netherlands is a party to the Beijing Convention.[64] However, we shall analyse the potential consequences of its applicability in order to present how they would differ from those that arise under the force of the Montreal Convention.

First of all, there would be no difference in the interpretation of the accident itself. Shooting down aircraft would be equally considered an offence under the Beijing Convention, provided that the intent of the offenders to strike the plane down is proven (Article 1 paragraph 1 point d). Moreover, the investigation did not indicate that any party was threatened with the commission of the act before the accident actually happened. Therefore, there are no legal grounds to consider that Article 1(3) of the Beijing Convention would be applicable.

However, in the light of the subsequent provisions of the Beijing Convention, the situation of the perpetrators could have been much different. Paragraph 4(b) of Article 1 criminalises the organisation and the direction of others to commit offences against civil aviation. Hypothetically, if the act of downing MH 17 had been qualified as an offence (committed intentionally), those that were in charge of organising the attempt, so possibly even the Russian officers that held commanding positions in the rebel units, would have incurred responsibility for a criminal offence under the mentioned provisions. Furthermore, the members of separatist groups could have faced criminal liability for other offences enshrined in Article 1(5). The provision obliges to criminalise in point b) the contribution to commit attacks against civil aviation by a group of persons with the aim of fostering general criminal activity of the group concerning attacking civil aviation. That provision would have been relevant in the case as the group that fired

---

63 According to information provided by the VisaSam.ru website, currently, the Russian Federation has extradition treaties signed with around 65 states, whereas countries that refuse to extradite their citizens to Russia are: the United Kingdom, Lithuania, Latvia, Estonia, Japan, China, Sweden, Ukraine, and the United States; https://visasam.ru/emigration/vybor/strany-bez-ekstradicii-v-rossiyu.html (9 March 2021).

64 Beijing Convention, list of parties; https://www.icao.int/secretariat/legal/List%20of%20Parties/Beijing_Conv_EN.pdf (9 March 2021).

the missile at the Malaysian Boeing was forming a part of a larger community of separatists whose military activities were oriented against the Ukrainian government. The group had previously destroyed several military aircraft flying over territories under their control and thus striking down MH 17 could have been regarded as fostering its general activity (if committed intentionally). Taking all of the above into account, we can state that the configuration of responsibility for the offences under the Beijing Convention differs significantly.

A provision whose context is particularly visible in the case of MH 17 is Article 6 of the Beijing Convention. It stipulates in paragraph 2 that activities of armed forced during an armed conflict that are normally governed by international humanitarian law are outside of the scope of the Convention. At the same time, paragraph 3 states that provisions of the preceding paragraph shall not be interpreted as condoning or making lawful any otherwise unlawful acts, or precluding prosecution under other laws. It serves as a sort of declaration that conditions of armed conflict would not by any means justify committing an offence against civil aviation.

The subsequent provisions of the treaty do not significantly influence the legal consequences of the downing of MH 17. Under Article 8, the right to establish jurisdiction would have been extended to and included the following states: (possibly) the Russian Federation (state of offender's nationality); all states of nationals against whom the offence was committed: the Commonwealth of Australia; the Kingdom of Belgium; Canada; the Federal Republic of Germany; the Republic of Indonesia; the Netherlands; the United Kingdom; the Republic of the Philippines.

As for the question of extradition, it is important to mention here the solutions introduced by Article 13 of the Beijing Convention, which prohibits the refusal to extradite on the basis of political motives. Technically, if a state on whose territory an alleged offender was present had received an extradition request, the state could not decline to hand over the alleged offender only because the offence was concerned to be political. Taking into account that the case of MH 17 has a political background involving tensions between Russia and Ukraine, any request of extradition submitted by one of those states to another could have been declined and the requested state could have preferred to prosecute the offender on its own territory. The refusal to extradite could have also been justified by reasons expressed in Article 14. This provision entitles to decline handing over an offender to a requesting state if the requested state has substantial grounds for believing that the offender would be prosecuted or punished solely on the account of his race, religion, nationality, ethnic origin, political opinion or gender.

3.4. The 2016 Brussels Airport bombing: Europe as a target of the Islamic State

In the wake of Islamic terrorism in the EU in the years 2015-2017, Members States of the Community were struck several times by violent terrorist attacks, organised and carried out mostly by perpetrators associated with the Islamic State. As we noted in a previous chapter [sub-chapter 2.4.], they served as an impulse for EU institutions to implement more strict legal provisions on the fight against terrorism in the territories of its Member States.

One of those attacks, the attack at Brussels Airport in March 2016, struck at the very heart of Europe, and heavily influenced EU institutions in their efforts of adopting new legal measures on terrorism, while simultaneously being harmful for civil aviation. In this sub-chapter we shall present the known facts about the attempt and analyse its legal background with focusing particularly on the provisions of *acquis communautaire.*

3.4.1. Circumstances of the attack and the subsequent investigation

On Tuesday morning on 22 March 2016, when Brussels, the capital of Belgium, was waking, the morning routine was interrupted by three massive explosions.

The first place struck was the Brussels National Airport of Zaventem. Shortly before 8.00 am, a bomb exploded in one of the facilities' departure halls, instantly killing 11 people and injuring a further 76. A recording from CCTV footage revealed that the explosions were caused by two suicide bombers – Ibrahim el-Bakraoui and Najim Laachraoui. A third person accompanying them, Mohamend Abrini, fled from the airport shortly after the detonation.

Just an hour later, at 9.10 am, another huge explosion occurred, this time at metro station Maelbeek in central Brussels, just a few hundred meters from European Union buildings. The brother of Ibrahim el-Bakraoui, Khalid, detonated himself in the second carriage of a metro train that just approached the station. The attack caused 21 persons to be killed and more than 100 injured.[65] In total,

65 J. Fioretti, "Brussels Attacks Death Toll Lowered To 32", Huffington Post, 29 March 2016. (9 March 2021) https://www.huffingtonpost.com/entry/brussels-attacks-death-toll-lowered_us_56facaa4e4b0a372181b27ed,
K. Yournish, et al., "What Happened at Each Location in the Brussels Attacks", The New York Times, 22 March 2016. (9 March 2021) https://www.nytimes.com/interactive/2016/03/22/world/europe/brussels-attacks-graphic.html?_r=1.

the attacks brought a death toll of 32 victims, of whom most were Belgians (including André Adam, a former Belgian Permanent Representative to the United Nations and later Ambassador of Belgium to the United States), and others were of American, Dutch, Swedish, German, Chinese or other nationalities.

On the day of the attack, a police investigation was launched, in which it was quickly concluded that the Islamic State of Iraq and Al-Sham was behind the attacks. Soon after the bombings, ISIS figures publicly claimed responsibility for the massacre and expressed their enthusiasm about the fact that the capital of Belgium suffered from explosions.[66] As a result of the investigation, many people affiliated with ISIS were arrested.

3.4.2. Terrorist character of the bombing

a) Analysis on the basis of definition

Nearly all media reports from the attack at Brussels National Airport unanimously called that incident "terrorist". Although *prima facie* it seems that all conditions for such a claim have been fulfilled in that particular case, we shall make a careful juridical analysis on the question whether the attack has all traits of terrorism?

First of all, we shall again recall the criteria of qualification of an act as terrorist and describe how they relate to the case of the bombing:

1) Intentional use of violence or threat thereof,
2) Conduct against the law,
3) Realisation of particular ideological or political goals,
4) The aim to spread fear or danger throughout society,
5) Affecting entities such as states or international organisations.

Intentional use of violence or threat thereof.

This point does not require extensive explanation. Detonating bombs by suicide attackers constitutes an act of physical violence that caused either injury or the death of many people. The investigation revealed that the attempt was carefully planned and organised by ISIS activists.

---

66 L. Dearden, "Isis supporters claim group responsible for Brussels attacks: 'We have come to you with slaughter'", The Independent, 22 March 2016. (9 March 2021) https://www.independent.co.uk/news/world/europe/isis-supporters-claim-responsibility-for-brussels-attacks-bombings-belgium-airport-maalbeek-metro-we-a6945886.html

Conduct against the law,

For an analysis of that criterion, we shall turn our attention to the Belgian Criminal Code from 1867. Crucially, its Article 137 defines a "terrorist offence" in paragraph 1 by enumerating its criteria. It stipulates the following:

> [c]onstitutes a terrorist offence, an offence […] that given its nature or its context may seriously damage a country or an international organisation and is committed intentionally for the purpose of seriously intimidating population or unduly compelling public authority or an international organisation to perform or abstain from an act, or seriously destabilising or destroying fundamental political, constitutional, economic or social structures of a country or an international organisation.[67]

It is vital to note here that the wording of this provision also reflects the definition of terrorism present in Article 3 of EU Directive 2017/541. The Belgian Criminal Code, like most of its equivalents in the EU, in some way categorises offences into two types: terrorist and non-terrorist. That categorisation relates to the penalties provided for the offences, being higher in case of those of a terrorist type, whereas typical crime is regulated by Article 138 of the Penal Code. In the Penal Code, provided is the *numerus clausus* of offences that can be regarded as terrorist. Among them is one described in Article 137§1 point 3: "destruction or massive degradation, or causing flooding of an infrastructure, a transportation system, a public or private property, aimed at endangering human life or causing considerable economic losses […]".[68] The bombing of Brussels Airport perfectly matches the traits of an offence stipulated in this provision and therefore can be regarded as a crime under Belgian law.

Realisation of particular ideological or political goals.

The aim to realise a political goal is evident in the case. The Islamic State, which claimed responsibility for the attack in Brussels, is a powerful terrorist organisation whose main goal is the establishment of a caliphate in the occupied territories in the Middle East and conducting jihad, a "sacred war" in the most violent way, in order to make Islam conquer the world.[69] The attempt was just

67 Law of 8 June 1867 – Belgian Penal Code, number 1867060850, page 3133, Article 137§1 (author's personal translation from French language).

68 Law of 8 June 1867 – Belgian Penal Code, Article 137§1 (author's personal translation from French language).

69 W. Sacharczuk, "Islam – Religia, a terroryzm", in: Problemy prawno-organizacyjne zwalczania terroryzmu w Polsce, eds. K. Liedel, J. Szafrański, (Wydawnictwo Wyższej Szkoły Policji: Szczytno, 2011), p. 55.

one in a series of many others that occurred in Asia and Europe, which only reflects the scope of ISIS' political ambitions [see sub-chapter 1.1.5., section c)].

The aim to spread fear or danger throughout society.

The attack, in similarity to other attacks carried out in other European, cities caused massive fear among the population. ISIS figures openly claimed that their aim was to slaughter people and bring death to Brussels [see section above].

Affecting entities such as states or international organisations.

Apart from causing the death or injury of many people and massive damage to property, the attack had a significant impact on the Belgian government, as well as other states' authorities and international organisations. All public transport in Brussels was shut down in the aftermath[70], identity checks were re-established temporarily on the Belgian-French border[71], and the National Security Council raised the terror alert level to the highest possible.[72] The Brussels National Airport passengers and cargo operations were suspended for a period of time, and the facility experienced a short-term drop in operational numbers.[73] Instantly after the attacks, the European Union premises were evacuated. The EU institutions themselves adopted several documents on anti-terrorist measures on an internal level.[74] In reaction to the incident, in several countries similar security measures were also enforced at airports.

70 L.-M. Eleftheriou-Smith, "Brussels Metro system shut down after station explosion as Belgium terror alert raised to maximum", The Independent, 22 March 2016. (9 March 2021) https://www.independent.co.uk/news/world/europe/brussels-metro-system-shut-down-following-explosion-at-station-near-eu-institutions-leaving-several-a6945431.html

71 E. Magdelaine, "Attentats à Bruxelles: contrôles renforcés à la frontière franco-belge", Franceinfo, 22 March 2016. (9 March 2021) https://france3-regions.francetvinfo.fr/hauts-de-france/explosions-bruxelles-controles-renforces-la-frontiere-franco-belge-957629.html

72 T. Reals, "Deadly explosions rock Brussels airport, subway", CBS News, 22 March 2016. (25 May 2020) https://www.cbsnews.com/news/reported-explosions-at-brussels-airport-in-belgium/

73 Official statistics published on Brussels Airport website show 7% decrease of passeger traffic in 2016, in comparison with previous year. See https://www.brusselsairport.be/pressroom/brussels-airport-welcomed-21-8-million-passengers-in-2016/ (9 March 2021).

74 See e.g.: European Commission, Communication from the Commission to the European Parliament, the European Council and the Council delivering on the European

All the aforementioned arguments combined strongly support stating that the bombing at the Brussels National Airport in 2016 had a purely terrorist character. It therefore justifies the application of criminal law provisions related to terrorism to the accident directly.

b) *Perspective of European Union law*

As the attack occurred on the territory of the Kingdom of Belgium, one of the founding members of the European Union[75], it is rational to analyse the attack itself and its legal consequences from the perspective of the EU law. Due to the fact that the bombing was carried out in the departure hall of the airport, in the area that passengers in EU countries normally access freely without prior security checks, our research shall mainly focus on the application of Regulation No. 300/2008 and Directive 2017/541.

Regulation No. 300/2008, whose primary objective is to impose common security measures within the EU, is effective upon the Brussels National Airport, in accordance with Article 2(1) point a), as the facility is not used exclusively for military purposes. Like all airports located in EU countries, it is divided into following areas: landside, airside, security restricted areas and critical parts of the restricted areas (as Article 1.1. paragraph 2 of the Annex to the Regulation stipulates). As we mentioned already, access to the landside part is generally free and open to the public, so all perpetrators (Ibrahim el-Bakraoui and Najim Laachraoui, along with Mohamend Abrini, who later fled) entered it lawfully. However, their activities at the airport's premises were under constant surveillance, which results from Article 1.5. of the Annex.[76] Due to the fact that none of them were passengers (did not have a point of departure at the airport or were in transfer or transit), neither themselves nor their luggage was subjected for screening for the purpose of detection of prohibited items, such as explosives

---

Agenda on Security to fight against terrorism and pave the way towards an effective and genuine Security Union, Brussels, 20.4.2016 COM(2016) 230.

75 To say it more appropriately, Belgium was one of the founding members of European Coal and Steel Community (one of the "predecessors" of the EU) brought to life by the Treaty of Paris in 1951 and establishing a common market of coal and steel. See more: P. Craig, G. de Burca, EU Law, p. 5.

76 All three men were caught on CCTV cameras at the departure hall. Images published by the Belgian Federal Police can be viewed in several online press articles; see e.g.: Yournish K., What Happened at Each Location".

(which arises from Article 4 of the Annex).[77] It is vital to mention here that under Article 4.3 of the Annex, it is mandatory to apply appropriate security measures in regards to "potentially disruptive passengers" who are defined as passengers being either deportees, persons deemed to be inadmissible for immigration reasons, or persons in lawful custody (the definition is stated in Article 3 paragraph 18 of the Regulation). From the wording of the definition itself it can be concluded that any such measure would not be applied against the offenders, as none of them could have been qualified as "a passenger".

To put it briefly, until the perpetrators removed explosives from their luggage in order to detonate themselves, it was difficult to detect that their suitcases contained hazardous materials, as provisions of Regulation No. 300/2008 emphasize securing the airside of airports, obliging the screening of passengers and their baggage upon entering security restricted areas. That served as an advantage for el-Bakraoui and Laachraoui, who did not need to risk detection while having entered only the landside of the terminal. Most probably, regardless of the particular EU airport, the perpetrators could have carried out their attack, and in consequence, cause a great number of victims and massive damage as well. Nevertheless, we have to remember that despite the landside areas being exposed to a higher risk of attack on the grounds of Regulation No. 300/2008 provisions, the act itself contributed to better results in aviation safety across the EU, as since its adoption, offences against civil aviation in EU Member States have been committed only at airport premises (not on board aircraft).

Before presenting the case of the Brussels Airport bombings in the light of Directive 2017/541, we have to point out that at the time when the attack was performed, the Council Framework Decision 2002/475/JHA of 13 June 2002 on combatting terrorism was still in force. However, in 2017, Directive 2017/541 replaced the Framework Decision, and therefore today serves as the basis for juridical analysis of the incident [see sub-chapter 2.4.6. section a)].

First of all, the attack itself matches the definition of a terrorist offence stipulated in Article 3 point d): "causing extensive destruction to a government or public facility, a transport system, an infrastructure facility, […], a public place or private property likely to endanger human life or result in major economic loss".[78] In addition to that, the attack fulfils all criteria of a terrorist act

77 Explosives are listed as articles prohibited to be carried into security restricted areas in Part B of the Annex to Regulation (EC) No 272/2009.

78 Directive 2017/541, Article 3. When the Framework Decision was still in force, it featured the same definition in Article 1 point d). Importantly, the Belgian Penal Code

enumerated in that Article: an intent to commit an offence; causing damage to a country (or international organisation); a particular aim (alternatively):

- serious intimidation of the population;
- undue compelling of a government or an international organisation to perform or abstain from performing any act;
- serious destabilisation or destruction the fundamental political, constitutional, economic or social structures of a country or an international organisation.

Thus, if any similar attack is conducted in any of the EU Member States, it shall be regarded as an offence, and the perpetrators shall bear responsibility of committing a terrorist act. Certainly, the perpetrators of the Brussels bombing, who committed suicide by detonating themselves, cannot incur any penalties, but the text of the Directive enlarges the scope of acts related to terrorism that are criminalised (Articles 5-12). Therefore, any person that intentionally contributed to the commission of the attack by providing training, organising recruitment, or supplying finances is treated as an offender.[79]

But what is most important in the matter is that the Directive by its nature imposes on all Member States an obligation to regard as an offence the act of a terrorist airport bombing (or any offence related thereto), meaning that every Member State is also interested in pursuing the offenders. Article 19 is decisive upon which of the EU members is allowed to establish its jurisdiction, and in the case of the Brussels National Airport bombing, the state with the most solid grounds of to exercise its jurisdiction is obviously the Kingdom of Belgium. Not only was the attack carried out in its territory, but the offenders were also in possession of Belgian-issued passports. Potentially, some other EU Member States whose citizens lost their lives or were injured in the attempt could be allowed to establish their jurisdiction as well (as stipulated in Article 19 paragraph 1 point e). But ultimately, Belgium was the state which decided to proceed with pursuing and prosecuting those involved in the attacks.[80]

---

also practically adopted the same definition in 137§1 point 3 referring to one of the terrorist offences [see section b) of the present sub-chapter].

79 After the attack, the Belgian Police conducted massive raids on homesteads that could have served as a shelter for offenders involved in the Brussels bombing. The arrested persons faced charges of participation in the activities of a terrorist group. See https://www.bbc.com/news/world-europe-35903368 (9 March 2021).

80 Analogical criteria for establishing jurisdiction were provided in the Framework Decision in its Article 9. See more: M. Osiecki, "Zamachy na port", p. 71.

However, if it happens that any person who contributed to the attack (e.g. a person that provided recruitment or financial supplies) is a national of a different Member State, and in consequence, that state considers establishing its own jurisdiction over the case, then under Article 19(2), it should engage in cooperation with other interested states and cooperatively decide which one of them should prosecute the offender and where the proceedings should be centralise. To facilitate achieving an eventual consensus, both parties may resort to Eurojust for providing assistance in coordinating their juridical authorities.

Directive 2017/541 focuses on another important aspect relevant for the Brussels bombing: responsibility of a terrorist group. As the Islamic State has been officially recognised as the organisation in charge of preparing and conducting the attempt, any person leading its local cell or being engaged in the organisation's activities in an EU Member State may incur criminal liability on the basis of Article 4.

If one compares the juridical context of the attacks at the Brussels National Airport under the Framework Decision and Directive 2017/541 respectively, it the Directive's provisions are mostly applied, as they are analogical to those that functioned within the Framework Decision. But the latter document lacked provisions that regulated the responsibility for offences related to terrorism which were later introduced by the Directive. That makes Directive 2017/541 a more complete legal instrument, better adapted to the present conditions of the fight against terrorism across the EU.

We shall also address a few words about the PNR Directive in the light of the Brussels bombings. Although that Directive came into force a month after the attack occurred, the anti-terrorist context of the instrument justifies such an analysis.

The most important point here is a fact that in case of attacks targeting civil airports and their facilities, PNR Directive has a little effectiveness, as the instrument was drafted in aim of transferring data passengers of flights to Member States and their processing for the purpose of preventing, detecting, investigating and prosecuting terrorist offences and serious crimes (as provided in Article 1 of the Directive). As the wording of the Article suggests, a person has to be an air passenger holding an airline ticket if his data is to be transferred to Member States. Neither el-Bakraoui nor Laachraoui had booked air tickets for a flight originating in Brussels before having committed the offence. And of course, from their perspective as perpetrators it was completely unnecessary. As we denoted already, access to landside of airport premises (like departure hall area before security check) is generally open to public. An offender planning to commit a terrorist attack takes much lower risk of being seized if he enters an airport and blows up the charge, than when he decides to book a ticket and therefore makes his personal data available for processing.

c) Provisions of sector Conventions

In similarity with other attacks committed against civil aviation, the Brussels Airport bombing is considered an offence under international law, or, more precisely, the Montreal Convention, Montreal Protocol and Beijing Convention. In the present section, we shall discuss the legal background of the attempt with focus on the mentioned treaties, taking into account that the Beijing Convention was not in force at the time of the attack and then interpreting its applicability in a hypothetical way.[81] As under Article I of the Montreal Protocol, both that instrument and the Montreal Convention shall be read and interpreted as one single document, in this section we shall use the term "Montreal Convention" for both documents jointly.

Without any doubt, we can affirm that the bombing at Brussels Airport fulfilled the conditions of an offence under Article 1 *bis* point a) of the Montreal Convention that reads as follows: "[a]ny person commits an offence if he unlawfully and intentionally, using any device, substance or weapon:

> (a) performs an act of violence against a person at an airport serving international civil aviation which causes or is likely to cause serious injury or death; […]".[82]

Of course, neither el-Bakraoui nor Laachraoui could incur criminal responsibility under that provision, because both of them were killed in the explosions. But that does not mean that the list of suspects is closed. Article 2 of the Convention also introduces the criminalisation of accomplices involved in the offence, which permits the formation of allegations against Mohamend Abrini – the third member of the group who ultimately fled the airport premises after the explosions, or any other person involved in preparation of the bombing. Given the nature of the offence (which does not involve an aircraft), Article 5(1) entitles only the state in whose territory the attempt was committed, so the Kingdom of Belgium, to establish its jurisdiction. However, paragraph 2 of the Article obliges the state in whose territory an alleged offender remains to establish its jurisdiction, if

---

81 At the time of the attack, the Kingdom of Belgium was party to both treaties. It ratified the Montreal Convention on 13 August 1976 (see https://www.icao.int/secretariat/legal/List%20of%20Parties/Mtl71_EN.pdf) and Montreal Protocol on 20 April 1999 (see https://www.icao.int/secretariat/legal/List%20of%20Parties/VIA_EN.pdf).

82 Montreal Protocol, art. II.

it does not extradite him. It theoretically means that if Abrini or another person regarded as an offender had been found in a territory of a state being party to the Montreal Protocol[83], they would have not evaded punishment.[84]

Analogically to the other offences covered by the Montreal Convention, the destruction of airport infrastructure should also be considered an extraditable one in any extradition treaty concluded between state parties to the Convention. Alternatively, the Convention itself might be recognised as a basis for extradition in the absence of a particular bilateral treaty (which is stipulated in Article 8). Extradition itself is of course not required, as the state of the offender's stay decides alone whether they are to be extradited or conducts criminal proceedings against them on its own. That arises from Article 7 of the Convention.

Similarly with the previously analysed cases [see sub-chapters 3.2.2. and 3.2.3.], here, a significant role is played by the current political conditions. If a state in whose territory an offender is present does not have an extradition treaty signed with Belgium and decides ultimately to establish its own jurisdiction, much time may pass until the offender stands trial. Moreover, if the state where an offender stays supports terrorism, then it may simply refuse to extradite such a person due to "political grounds", especially as the Montreal Convention does not oblige to exclude crimes against civil aviation from those of a "political character".[85] In addition to that, many states generally observe the rule of non-extraditing offenders that seek territorial asylum.[86] So, if an offender carefully chooses their place of stay and flees to a country that follows such policy, he may eventually avoid jurisdiction of the state interested in punishing them.

---

83 Currently there are 176 state parties to the Protocol; https://www.icao.int/secretariat/legal/List%20of%20Parties/VIA_EN.pdf (9 March 2021).

84 Mohamed Abrini was in fact arrested shortly after the bombing by Belgian police officers in Anderlecht, Brussels Capital Region. See R.-J. Bartunek, A. Macdonald, "Belgians seize key suspects in Paris, Brussels attacks", Reuters, 8 April 2016. (9 March 2021) https://www.reuters.com/article/us-france-shooting-abrini-arrest/belgians-seize-key-suspects-in-paris-brussels-attacks-idUSKCN0X51QK

85 M. Osiecki, "Terrorism vs. International Law – Case of Attacks in Brussels", in: 5th International Conference of PhD Students and Young Researchers How Deep is Your Law? Brexit. Technologies. Modern Conflicts. Conference Papers, Vilnius University 2017, p. 28, after: R. Abeyratne, "Terror In the Skies: Approaches to Controlling Unlawful Interference with Civil Aviation", International Journal of Politics, Culture and Society, Vol. 2(2) 1997, p. 247.

86 M. Osiecki, "Terrorism vs. International Law" after: B. Ziemblicki, "Wprowadzenie do problematyki ekstradycji", Wrocławskie Studia Erazmiańskie 5/2010, p. 247.

Now we shall examine how the provisions of the Beijing Convention could have influenced the juridical situation of the persons involved in the Brussels bombing, if at the time of the incident, the treaty had been in force.[87]

Significant changes would concern the circle of offenders under Articles 4 and 5 of the Beijing Convention. Article 4 requires the criminalisation of organising and directing others to commit offences against civil aviation (including the destruction of airport infrastructure). Due to the fact, that the Islamic State is an organisation that claimed responsibility for the attack, allegations for the direction and organisation of the attempt would have been formed against the leaders of ISIS cells in Europe, and not only those particular members who assisted the attackers at airport facilities. As for Article 5, the provision opens a way for criminalising the behaviour of all who actually agreed to attack Brussels Airport (point a) and those who contributed in any way to the attack (point b). As it stems from the wording of both Articles, their application would have weakened ISIS as a whole, not just the particular perpetrators.

The question of jurisdiction does not differ much in comparison with the Montreal Convention. Under the Beijing Convention Article 8(2), the states whose nationals died or were injured in the bombing, meaning the United States, Sweden, China, Morocco and several others, would have been entitled to establish their jurisdiction. However, an important issue which we already discussed in previous sub-chapters constitutes the prohibition in Article 13 to treat the destruction of airport infrastructure as a political offence or an offence inspired by political motives. In accordance with it, one state requesting another to extradite an offender or alleged offender has a guarantee that its partner shall not reject the request on the basis of political motives. That solution would reduce the possibility that a perpetrator evades punishment if they flee to a country that supports terrorism.

3.5. Air France 8969: A hijacking that could have ended in tragedy

The history of Air France flight 8969 is a grim example of a terrorist hijacking that, without a clever and well-planned operation prepared by the French government, could have ended in a catastrophe and brought an end to hundreds of lives. In the present sub-chapter, we shall present the history of the flight and its legal background, especially the Tokyo-Hague-Montreal-Beijing system

87 As for March 2021, Belgium has not even signed the Convention.

Conventions, emphasising that the attack against it could be regarded not only as a hijacking, but also other type of offence.

3.5.1. History of the flight

On 24 December 1994, an Air France airliner, an Airbus A300 jet, registered F-GBEC departed, its base at Paris-Orly Airport for a scheduled flight to Houari Boumediene Airport in Algiers. Upon landing, it was bound to fly back to Orly under number 8969 (AF 8969). The crew for the journey were captain Bernard Dhelemme, first officer Jean-Paul Borderie and flight engineer Alain Bossuat.[88] All three were volunteers, much like other pilots flying that route. At that time Algeria, was in the middle of a civil war. In January 1992, during the second round of legislative elections, a military coup was organised against then-president Chadli Benjedid, who did not have enough power to stop the Islamic Salvation Front, a party that won the first round of the elections and aimed to transform Algeria into a strict Islamic Republic. The generals of the army forced the president to step down, and seized the power.[89] The harsh fight between supporters of both sides emerged, and the risk of being hit by a missile or getting the plane hijacked was at the time so high that Air France officially asked the government (owner of the airline) if there was a real need to continue the route. No reply was given.

The plane was about to idle on the tarmac at Boumediene Airport for refuelling, cleaning, and embarking of passengers. In total, 209 persons boarded the aircraft; most were of Algerian or French citizenship, others were German, Irish, Dutch, Norwegian, British, American, and one person was Vietnamese. Together with the crew, 221 people were on board the flight. The plane was nearly ready to move, when suddenly, at 11:15 am, four armed men holding Air Algerie badges entered the cabin to perform, as they claimed, security passport checks. An unscheduled delay alarmed Algerian special forces officers (commonly known as "ninjas") stationing at the airport, who decided to gather around the

---

88 In older types of aircraft, like the Airbus A300, the crew consisted of three members instead of two. Some eastern-built airliners, like those manufactured in former Soviet republics, even required 5 flight crew members to operate.

89 M. Shabafrouz, "Oil and the Eruption of the Algerian Civil War: A Context-sensitive Analysis of the Ambivalent Impact of Resource Abundance", German Institute of Global and Area Studies Working Papers 118/2010, pp. 9-10.
A minor notice on the article: the author mistakenly dated the hijacking of Air France flight 8969 as December 1995 instead of 1994.

Airbus to have it closely watched. Suddenly, all four gunmen shouted *Allah is great!* and revealed their true identity to the crew. They were members of the *Groupe Islamique Armé* (or "GIA", English: "Armed Islamic Group"), a terrorist organisation sympathising with the Islamic Salvation Front that also desired to install an Islamic Republic in Algeria. Their leader was Abdul Abdullah Yahia, aka "Emir", a notorious extremist previously serving as one of GIA's lieutenants.[90] The hijacking of AF 8969 served as part of a plan to expand the war over French territory that was supporting the Algerian regime in the conflict.

The hijackers ordered the crew to first fly to Paris so that they would be able to hold a press conference there. The captain wanted to ask for clearance for taxiing to departure, but moving the plane was impossible. Air stairs were still attached to the machine and in addition to that, Algerian military vehicles were obstructing the runway in accordance with the order issued by the Algerian government. Its will was to keep the aircraft with terrorists on board on the tarmac at all costs to deal with them later. The ongoing delay was frustrating for the hijackers. Yahia ordered one of the passengers, who during the passport check identified himself as a police officer, to disembark and deliver a message to the government. Shortly after leaving the plane, he was shot to death.

Meanwhile, the "ninja" forces were preparing an operation of storming the aeroplane and arresting the hijackers. The plan was consulted with France and caused some tensions. The then-French Minister of Interior, Charles Pasqua, strongly discouraged the Algerians to proceed with the plan. He knew that the "ninjas", known for their exceptional skills and brutality in fights, would definitely eliminate the hijackers, but at the high risk of a bloodbath among innocent passengers. On the other hand, the Algerian government still opted for their plan of keeping the Airbus on their soil and allow the "ninjas" to siege. The Government of France tried to convince their Algerian allies that it would have been safer to let the plane fly to France, where the French armed corps would have seized it without putting the lives of passengers in danger.

The delay was getting longer and longer as AF 8969 still did not receive permission for take-off. Yahia became upset and selected another passenger to be murdered, this time a Vietnamese diplomat was the target. One of the gunmen ordered him to disembark. Upon leaving, he was shot to death. In the meantime, the flight crew was trying their best to calm down the hijackers by explaining to

90 See more: F. Shanty, Countetterrorism: From the Cold War to the War on Terror. Volume 1: Combating Modern Terrorism (1968-2011) (Praeger Security International: Santa Barbara, 2012), p. 135.

them how the aircraft instruments worked. Aside from that, two stewardesses began feigning a conversion to Islamism in front of another hijacker. Several hours passed and negotiators arrived at the airport to convince the GIA members to free at least some hostages. The negotiations resulted in the release of 63 women and children. But the Algerian authorities were still reluctant to allow the plane to fly.

The stalemate continuing until the next day. The French Prime Minister, Edouard Balladur, pressed the Algerian side to let the French special forces siege the crippled jet on the basis that France was entitled to exercise its jurisdiction as the state of the aircraft's registry, and the country where Air France operates. During the discussion between both states, the French government decided to make the first move. They sent a special forces regiment to the proximity of the island of Majorca, the closest point to Algeria within their jurisdiction. The division of GIGN (*Groupe d'Intervention de la Gendarmerie Nationale*) was led by major Denis Favier and during the time of transfer from France to Majorca, all of its members studied the plans of Airbus A300 deeply to prepare for the assault and avoid any mistake in its occurrence.

The ambiance on board AF 8969 became more tense than before. Algerian officials brought Yahia's mother on the tarmac and asked her to convince her son to free the captives. That only made the captors more furious, and resulted in grim consequences, as Yahia requested one of the passengers, a French embassy worker, to speak to air traffic control and inform them that if the aeroplane was not allowed to depart, everybody would be killed. Soon after making the announcement, he was murdered by one of the hijackers. Prime Minister Balladur, at his tolerance limits, warned the Algerian government that he would publicly blame them for the whole situation, which would have seriously affected the reputation of Algeria. That decision paid off, and AF 8969 was allowed to take off from Boumediene Airport for its flight back to France. But apparently, the jet was only able to reach the southern part of the country, and then had to refuel for to continue its journey, as during the stalemate on the tarmac, captain Dhellemme kept the APU[91] running. It had consumed so much fuel during their

91 An APU (or "auxiliary power unit") is a small device installed on most civil aircraft that provides a source of electrical power and compressed air to operate some basic on-board instruments and the air conditioning system, or to start the engines. It is normally online when a plane is parked and sometimes during taxiing.
See J. Kinsey, M. Timko, S. Herndon, Ezra Wood, Z. Yu, R. Miake-Lye, P. Lobo, P. Whitefield, D. Hagen, C. Wey, B. Anderson, A. Beyersdorf, C. Hudgins, K. Thornhill, E. Winstead, R. Howard, D. Bulzan, K. Tacina & W. Knighton, "Determination of the

39-hour-long stay at the airport that the A300 had enough to only reach as far as Marseilles.

The aircraft landed at Marseilles-Provence Airport on 26 December at 3.30 am, while the team of GIGN commandos led by major Favier was already en route from Majorca and well prepared for an eventual siege. To enable the commandos to perform an effective assault, the plane was parked at a remote point of the airport. Meanwhile, French authorities received information that the true aim of the terrorists was to seize the plane while airborne and use it as a fire bomb to crash on the Eiffel Tower in Paris instead of holding a press conference.[92] Those suspicions became even clearer when Yahia ordered the captain to request 27 tonnes of fuel instead of the normal 9 to be loaded into the plane, enough to reach Paris. Marseilles Airport ATC in turn asked captain Dhellemme to convince the captors to accept the organisation of a press conference on board the A300 itself. Yahia agreed, only under the condition that CNN reporters would be present. He was not aware that all of this was part of major Favier's tactical plan, as his aim was to strike from the front of the plane, while the passengers would be moved to the rear. The situation later became complicated as Yahia heard from the captain's conversation with the control tower that the conference was not ready at the moment. The hijackers were frustrated and ordered the captain to get the plane closer to the terminal and then depart for Paris. Tactically, this move was highly inconvenient for Favier; he needed to quickly relocate his men and organise snipers on the roofs of the terminal for the assault.

At 7.00 am, AF 8969 was still not refuelled. Major Favier slightly changed his tactical plan and ordered three squads of commandos to approach the plane using air stairs. Two would enter the machine from the rear, while the last one would go through the front door and cut off the cockpit where Yahia was seated from the rest of the plane. The hijackers spotted the armed group and started firing at them from the cockpit windows. At that moment, Favier's regiment reacted. In accordance with the plan, two squads stormed the plane from behind and one from the front to kill two of the captors. Yahia, accompanied by another captor, was still inside the flight deck, but were quickly shot by one of the snipers. Just several minutes after the start of the siege, nearly all passengers were evacuated from the A300. One last hijacker hid in the cockpit, but was later killed

---

emissions from an aircraft auxiliary power unit (APU) during the Alternative Aviation Fuel Experiment (AAFEX)", Journal of the Air & Waste Management Association, Vol. 62(4) 2012, p. 421.

92 F. Shanty, Counterterrorism, p. 135.

by one of the squad members. As a result of Favier's operation, all remaining passengers and crew of AF 8969 survived and all four offenders were killed. The operation was claimed to be one of the most successful anti-terrorist actions ever carried out.[93]

Since the attack, Air France no longer marks any of its flights as 8969 (excluding those operated on code share basis by other carriers[94]).

3.5.2. Presence of a terrorist factor

Flight AF 8969 was one of those that *prima facie* could be associated with terrorism. A brutal hijacking performed by an extremist group, political background, visible use of violence are factors that would convince an average observer that they were witnesses to a terrorist attack. However, to precisely assess whether we really dealt with terrorism in the case of AF 8969 it is necessary to analyse it on the basis of the definition of terrorism itself.

Like in the previously studied cases in the present monograph, we shall indicate whether all elements of a "terrorist offence" are featured:

1) Intentional use of violence or threat thereof,
2) Conduct against the law,
3) Realisation of particular ideological or political goals,
4) The aim to spread fear or danger throughout society,
5) Affecting entities such as states or international organisations.

Intentional use of violence or threat thereof.

It is not too complicated to prove that the behaviour of the GIA members in that case involved the use of violence. Yahia and his companions seized control of AF 8969 by force, having threatened those on board with weapons. And above all, they killed two passengers in an act of protest against the Algerian government's

---

93 Facts of the attack can be read inter alia in the following articles:
A. Riding, Hijacked Airliner forced to France, "The New York Times", 26 December 1994. (9 March 2021) https://www.nytimes.com/1994/12/26/world/hijacked-airliner-forced-to-france.html
T. Sancton, "Anatomy of a Hijack", Time, 24 June 2001. (9 March 2021) http://content.time.com/time/magazine/article/0,9171,163487,00.html

94 Code-share is a common practice in civil aviation that concerns the usage of a flight designator by one flight carrier on a service performed by another carrier (e.g. an Air France uses its designator "AF" and sells tickets on a flight that is performed by Delta Air Lines), normally based on a common agreement. See ICAO, Glossary.

decision to deny take-off. The losses could have been much greater had the realised their plan of crashing the plane into the Eiffel Tower in Paris. Such an act would have resulted in extensive damage to property and probably the death of many innocent people.

Conduct against the law.

The hijacking of AF 8969, as well as many other related acts performed by the GIA members are considered crimes in the legal systems of most states, including those that were involved in the case. The French Penal Code criminalises unlawful aircraft seizure in Article 224-6 which reads as follows: "[t]he seizure or taking over by violence or threat of violence of a plane, ship or any other means of transport on board which persons have taken their places, or of any permanent platform situated on the continental shelf, is punished by twenty years of criminal imprisonment".[95] Along lines of the French regulation, the Algerian Penal Code also introduces criminalisation of that act in Article 417 *bis*: "Any person that by force or threat thereof, seizes or exercises control of aircraft on board which persons have taken their places is punished by the death penalty [...]".[96]

What is even more important, both the Penal Code of France and of Algeria introduce a division between terrorist crimes and non-terrorist crimes, and that division influences the severity of punishment incurred by an offender, which is normally increased in case of terrorist crimes. Like the criminal law acts of other states, both codes explain how to understand the term "terrorist offences". The French Penal Code features the following definition in Article 421-1: "[c] onstitute acts of terrorism [an offence] committed intentionally in connection with an individual or collective undertaking, the purpose of which is to seriously disturb public order through intimidation or terror".[97] In the listed points offences regarded as terrorist are described, with hijacking of aircraft being one of them (point 1).

The Algerian Penal Code establishes the following definition of terrorism: "considered is as an act of terrorism [...] any act endangering safety of the state, territorial integrity, stability and normal functioning of [state] institutions

95 Code pénal, Legifrance art. 224-6 (official translation of the text into English).

96 Ordonnance n° 66-156 du 8 juin 1966 portant code pénal, modifiée et complété, art. 417 bis (author's personal translation from French in absence of official translation into English).

97 Code pénal, Legifrance, Art. 421-1 (official translation into English).

[…]".[98] Similarly to the French act, the hijacking of aircraft is also enumerated as a terrorist offence.

The acts of the GIA members are also regarded as offences under the Tokyo-Hague-Montreal-Beijing system conventions, which shall be discussed in subsequent sections of this sub-chapter.

Realisation of particular ideological or political goals.

The Armed Islamic Group, in which Yahia and other captors were actively involved, supported the ISF, whose main political goal was the transformation of Algeria into an Islamic republic. The act of hijacking AF 8969 was a part of that campaign and had a symbolic meaning – to strike at the Republic of France, one of the states of western civilisation regarded by Islamic extremists as an enemy [see above]. Then, there is no doubt that capturing the Airbus by GIA fighters had a very strong political and religious tone.

The aim to spread fear or danger throughout society.

It is difficult to refute the argument that the aim the of GIA members was to spread fear throughout society. Yahia's original plan of crashing the A300 into the Eiffel Tower, if realised, would have probably caused massive panic among Parisians and other French nationals, and attract media attention. As passengers on board the hijacked plane represented multiple nationalities and were held captive for several days, the fear for their fate probably spread extensively.

Affecting entities such as states or international organisations.

The fact that hijacking AF 8969 strongly affected several states was clear from the very first minutes. The act itself was a manifestation of political ambitions of the GIA that were directed against the Algerian government and provoked the latter to organise an assault to free all the captive passengers, ultimately blocked by France, who decided to carry out an its own operation. As a result of the hijacking, both countries also engaged in a dispute that later became very tense and would have damaged Algeria's reputation. The influence of the event on the behaviour of the states would have been even stronger if the Airbus had been destroyed in a collision with the Eiffel Tower.

98 Ordonnance n° 66-156 du 8 juin 1966 portant code pénal, modifiée et complété, Art. 87 bis (author's personal translation in the absence of official translation into English).

To conclude, we can clearly determine that the attack by the GIA members on AF 8969 had all the traits of terrorism. Thus, media reports openly calling it "a terrorist attempt" where not by any means exaggerated.

3.5.3. Classifying the offence as hijacking

a) *The Tokyo Convention perspective*

The act of the GIA fighters against AF 8969 could *prima facie* be classified as a typical skyjacking. The attackers seized control over the aeroplane and ordered the crew to fly in a different direction than originally scheduled (see sub-chapter 1.3.3. section b). But how is (or would be) the legal situation of the flight shaped on the basis of Conventions that deal with the unlawful seizure of aircraft? That question shall be answered in the present section.

Before we concentrate on a particular treaty's provisions, we have to point out that, interestingly enough, at the time of the attack, only the Republic of France was a party to both the Tokyo and Hague Conventions (since 11 September, 1970 and September 18th, 1972 respectively). In turn, Algeria entered into both acts in October 1995.[99] It is then quite probable that the hijacking of AF 8969 acted as an impulse for the country to ratify the treaties and in consequence, assure better security of civil aircraft in its territory.

First and foremost, we should turn our attention to Article 11 of the Tokyo Convention that obliges state parties to apply measures that would restore control of the aircraft to its lawful commander, in case the plane is subject to unlawful interference or forceful seizure (or by threat of using the force) during the flight. From the wording of the provision, we can affirm that its application would have been of concern in the case of AF 8969, if the People's Democratic Republic of Algeria had been a party to it. It is true that aircraft was seized. The GIA fighters boarded the Airbus using fake identity cards and shouted several times that they were mujahideens and would blow up the plane if their orders were not followed. Therefore, there were threats to use physical force. As all four hijackers were armed with guns and from their behaviour, passengers could have claimed that they would have really been members of the GIA, the threat should be treated as real or at least convincing to be real.

Now a key question arises if, at the moment the seizure occurred, the aircraft could have been qualified as being "in flight". According to Article 1(3) of the

99 http://www.icao.int/secretariat/legal/List%20of%20Parties/Tokyo_EN.pdf; https://www.icao.int/secretariat/legal/List%20of%20Parties/Hague_EN.pdf.

Convention, once power is turned on for the purpose of take-off, the plane starts being regarded as "in flight". As we mentioned previously, after R. Abeyratne [see sub-chapter 2.2.2., section b)], the running of an APU that delivers basic power to the aeroplane for taxi and take-off is sufficient to regard it as "in flight". The A300 was standing on the tarmac while the offenders were boarding it and had its APU online, until the machine finally started taxiing. Therefore, the case of AF 8969 under the Tokyo Convention might be regarded as an unlawful aircraft seizure since the GIA members took control of the aircraft. Nevertheless, Algeria, although not a party to the Convention in 1994, attempted to take action and restore control to the cabin crew by ordering the "ninjas" to storm the plane, but the operation did not materialise due to the strong opposition from France [see above].

As it was already mentioned, the importance of the AF 8969 case is marked also by the jurisdictional dispute that arose between political partners: France and Algeria. From the very beginning of the crisis, both states struggled to convince one another about their appropriateness of exercising jurisdiction over the act. Pursuant to the Tokyo Convention, the factor determining which state is entitled in the matter is the aircraft's registration. Certainly, in the discussed case, France was the one entitled to its jurisdiction, as the A300 involved carried the registration markings of F-GBEC, "F" being assigned to France, according to Annex 7 to the Chicago Convention and ICAO documents.[100] As a result, France had full right under Article 3(2) of the Tokyo Convention to take all necessary steps to exercise its jurisdiction over AF 8969. Algeria in reality (if at the time of the event had been a signatory of the legal act) would have had only the right to exercise its criminal jurisdiction (typically initiation of pursuit against offenders) if the jet had been in flight. On the other hand, when taking into account the wording of Article 4, its grounds for jurisdiction would be strong, because of the prominent weight of the offenders' nationality. As all hijackers were of Algerian origin, Article 4(b) permits Algeria to claim its jurisdiction.

When speaking about Tokyo Convention provisions, it is necessary to mention the powers of the aircraft commander discussed in Chapter III of the Convention. According to that provision, captain Dhellemme would have been eligible to take appropriate measures against the hijackers from the moment of all external doors of the aeroplane closing (Article 5 paragraph 2). Also, Article 5(1) stipulates that provisions of Chapter III are not applicable when an offence is committed or is about to be committed on board an aircraft being either in

100 ICAO, Aircraft nationality marks and common marks, p. 1.

flight in the airspace of the state of registration, or over the high seas, or an area not belonging to any state. Exemptions to that rule are situations when an aircraft's last place of take-off or its next point of intended landing is situated in a state that is not the one of registry, or that aircraft subsequently flies in the airspace of a state other than that of its registration with an offender still on board. From the perspective of the said provision, the A300 was all the time (during the hijack) covered by Chapter III applicability. When the hijackers boarded the plane, it was located in the territory of Algeria, and continued to be there until take-off for Marseilles. Even when it was flying over the Mediterranean, and then subsequently in the skies of France, Chapter III was in force, as the last point of A300 take-off was Algiers located outside the territory of the jet's state of registry. However, despite the fact that under Chapter III, Dhellemme had the full right to execute appropriate measures of restraint against the hijackers, he decided not to use any of them. Neither did he request any help in that matter from the crew members or passengers, on the basis of Article 6.

As the dispute on which country's special forces should storm the Airbus A300 was finally settled in favour of France which at that time was a party to the Tokyo Convention, the state engaged all available measures to rescue passengers of the doomed flight that were eligible pursuant to the Convention. The deployment of special forces from GIGN led by major Denis Favier, was organised in accordance with French domestic law that, following the provisions of the Criminal Procedure Code (*Code de procédure pénale*), namely its Articles from R15 to R26, entitles both the national police and the gendarmerie to safeguard and execute public order. That is why none of the offenders were taken into custody or extradited. Therefore, the provisions of Chapter V in relation to AF 8969 have basically no applicability.

b) *The Hague Convention regulations*

Interpreting the case of AF 8969 from the perspective of The Hague Convention seems to be the most adequate, as among all treaties on aircraft hijacking, that Convention had been introduced most recently at the time. We just have to remind here that in 1994, France was a single state party to the Convention. The Hague Convention's provisions are also applicable in the AF 8969 case.

Already in Article 1(1) of the Convention one can see that its wording nearly equals the formulation used in Article 224-6 of the French Penal Code that defines aircraft hijacking [see above section]. Therefore, under The Hague Convention and its internal law, France had the obligation to pursue hijackers as those who had committed criminal offence. As for Algeria that was not a party to the treaty at that time, its authorities planned to deploy the "ninjas" armed corps to eliminate the captors, probably on the basis of other provisions of its domestic criminal law in force at the time.[101]

The Hague Convention, in opposition to the Tokyo Convention, establishes the criminalisation of the offence of unlawful aircraft seizure, but on the other hand shrinks the time criterion for that offence by shortening the period "in flight" [see sub-chapter 2.2.2. section b)]. France had full authorisation to regard the act of Yahia and his comrades as crimes no sooner than after closing the aircraft's door following embarkation. Certainly, the criterion of location is fulfilled – in the light of the Article 3(3) the Convention is applicable, as the place of take-off of AF 8969 was in Algiers, and not in the aircraft's state of registry, France.

Just like the Tokyo Convention, The Hague Convention's provisions are formulated in a way permitting France to exercise its jurisdiction over the case of AF 8969. Although Article 4 of The Hague Convention does not expressly determine which state has a priority in exercising its jurisdiction, the analysis of said provision results in the conclusion that France was the one and only entity able to claim its jurisdiction. First and foremost, France was the state of the A300 jet's registry and thus is empowered with that right under paragraph 1(a). Secondly, after the hijacking, AF 8969 was flown to France where it actually landed with all of the offenders still on board, which strengthened its claims on the basis of paragraph 1(b). Taking into account that the A300 was fully owned by Air France on the basis of purchase (the machine was not the subject of a contract of lease), sub-paragraph (c) has no applicability here.[102] On the side of Algeria, an argument of exercising jurisdiction could have arisen if the state had been a party to the Convention. As the Article 4(2) entitles the state in whose territory an offender is present to establish jurisdiction over the offence if the offender is not extradited, Algeria would have had full right to cover the act by its own jurisdiction. It should be noted that all bases of jurisdiction enumerated in Article 4 are of equal value. Therefore, if at the time of the AF 8969 hijacking, Algeria had

101 It is worth mentioning that both states have, in accordance with Article 2, introduced severe penalties against aircraft hijackers. Under Article 224-6 of the French Penal Code the penalty for the offence is twenty years of imprisonment, whereas Article 417 bis of the Algerian Penal Code punishes aircraft hijackers by capital punishment. See Ordonnance n° 66-156 du 8 juin 1966 portant code pénal, modifiée et complété, Art. 417 bis, Code pénal, Legifrance, art. 224-6.

102 http://www.airfleets.net/ficheapp/plane-a300-104.htm.

been a party to The Hague Convention, the outcome of the dispute between the two states might have been different.

Neither Algeria nor France were eager to let the hijackers leave their territories and took actions to keep them under control until a rescue siege was launched. As none of the hijackers were taken into custody by either state, provisions of Article 6(2) and onward do not apply in the case of AF 8969. However, according to Article 7, which obliges states to submit the case to the competent authorities for the purpose of prosecution, the French authorities enabled the Minister of the Interior, Charles Pasqua, to take appropriate decisions in relation to the case. As, officially, GIGN forces are supervised by the Ministry of Interior of France, and, according to French law, are the relevant forces to counter terrorist threats, Pasqua's decision to engage them was genuine.[103]

Algeria is one of the states with which France has a bilateral extradition treaty signed. The first one was concluded in 1964, long before The Hague Convention came into force.[104] As both states are parties to the Convention (Algeria since 1996), pursuant to its Article 8, unlawful aircraft seizure should be regarded as an extraditable offence between them. However, both states aimed at eliminating the hijackers using their special forces, so in reality no talks about the extradition of offenders could take place. Theoretically, the submission of an extradition request would have been possible if the offenders had been arrested and detained by the requested state. In accordance with Article 8(4) in conjunction with Article 4(1) of the Convention, the offence would have been treated as committed both on the territory of France (being the state of the aircraft's registry and of last landing), and Algeria (being the state where the offence was committed).

103 In France, like in many other states, the gendarmerie nationale functions as a body supervised by the Ministry of the Interior. See more: http://www.interieur.gouv.fr/Le-ministere/Gendarmerie-nationale (9 March 2021).

104 The Convention on Exequatur and Extradition was signed in Algiers on 27 August 1964 and entered into force one year later, on August 8 1965. See Convention entre la France et l'Algérie relative à l'exequatur et à l'extradition, JORF, 17 August 1965, pp. 7269-7272.
The new bilateral agreement on extradition between both states was signed on 27 January 2019.

c) *Hypothetical application of the Beijing Protocol*

Our final stage of analysis of the hijacking of AF 8969 shall be devoted to the hypothetical application of the Beijing Protocol that, naturally, was not even at its preparatory draft stage when the event took place.

First of all, pursuant to the Protocol's provisions, the criterion of time in relation to the offence is extended and applies from the moment of beginning preflight preparations of the aircraft by ground personnel or crew for a particular flight until twenty-four hours after landing (Article V amending Article 3 of The Hague Convention). Therefore, the actions of Yahia and his companions would have been regarded as an offence once the crew or ground staff started preparing the jet for its flight to Paris. Apart from that, the liability for the hijacking would have been also probably extended to the leadership of the GIA as those who organised the hijacking. This stems from Article II supplementing The Hague Convention by Article 1 paragraph 3 point b). What is more, under the subsequent paragraph, the liability would also be incurred by those participating as accomplices with Yahia's group. Potentially, those would have been the people who provided them with guns or fake police identity cards.

Importantly, France belongs to a narrow circle of states that have ratified the Beijing Protocol (the act of ratification is dated 15 December 2016).[105] Even before the state signed the treaty on 15 April 2011, Article 224-6-1 was implemented into its Penal Code and contains the following wording: "If an offence [of unlawful aircraft seizure] is committed in an organised band, the penalty is increased to thirty years of imprisonment".[106] It strongly refers to Article II supplementing The Hague Convention by Article 1 paragraph 4 on the commission of an offence by a group of persons acting with a common purpose. In contrast, the Algerian Penal Code does not provide any solution to establish the liability of a group that commits an offence. But certainly, these shall be introduced if the People's Democratic Republic of Algeria ratifies the Protocol. If it had been applicable at the time of the AF 8969 hijack, the offence would have been thus regarded as furthering the general criminal purpose of the GIA on the basis of Article II supplementing The Hague Convention by Article 1 paragraph 4 subparagraph (b), points (I) and (ii).

---

105 https://www.icao.int/secretariat/legal/List%20of%20Parties/Beijing_Prot_EN.pdf (9 March 2021).

106 Code pénal, Legifrance, Art. 224-6-1 (official translation into English).

Highly important, particularly in the case of AF 8969, are the provisions of Article VI supplementing The Hague Convention by Article 3 *bis*. Multiple international law instruments deal exclusively with the commission of certain offences in conditions of war. Paragraph 2 of the said article *expressis verbis* excludes the Protocol's applicability from activities of armed forces during armed conflict, leaving that to be regulated by separate humanitarian law acts. However, in the subsequent paragraph, the Protocol states that it should not be interpreted as condoning or making lawful otherwise unlawful acts, or precluding the offenders' prosecution. In consequence, the conditions of civil war, in which Algeria was engulfed at that time, would have had no influence on the justification of hijacking AF 8969, even on behalf of the emerging new political system, the Islamic Republic.

In comparison with the previously discussed instruments, the Algeria's rights to exercise its jurisdiction over the offence under the Beijing Protocol are considerably extended. Pursuant to Article VII amending Article 4 of The Hague Convention, Algeria would be entitled to pursue offenders as the state of occurrence (amended paragraph 1 point a), and the state of nationality of the perpetrators (amended paragraph 1 point e). Therefore, Algeria would have had very strong arguments against France in their dispute concerning their relevance of jurisdiction over the case. Problems arise when interpreting paragraph 2 sub-paragraph a) of amended Article 4. It stipulates that a state has a right to exercise its jurisdiction if an offence was committed against one of their nationals. Taking into account that most of the AF 8969 passengers were either of French or Algerian nationality, both states would have had equal powers to cover the case by their jurisdiction. On the other hand, as it was mentioned in the beginning of the present sub-chapter, the plane was filled with passengers of multiple nationalities, including British, Norwegian and even one Vietnamese then killed by one of Yahia's men. As a result, if according to the interpretation of the said provision, every single passenger of AF 8969 is the one against whom the offence is committed, significantly more states would have had the right to exercise their jurisdiction over the case.

As none of the hijackers were taken into custody by either of states' security forces, the discussion of the potential applicability of Article IX amending Article 6 paragraph 4 of The Hague Convention is not essential in the case. It also concerns Article X adding Article 7 *bis*.

Extradition matters related to AF 8969 have already been discussed in the present chapter. The single *novum* in relation to The Hague Convention that deserves attention is the wording of Articles XII and XIII adding Articles 8 *bis* and 8 *ter* respectively. As it was already mentioned, the former one deals with interdiction of refusing extraditing an offender on the grounds of claiming that the offence has a political character. Taking into account that the impulse for the international community to delegitimize the crime having a purely political nature as grounds for refusing the extradition of offenders was the 11 September, 2001 terrorist attack, it is uncertain if Algeria or France would have refused the extradition of hijackers in case of their detention. Similarly, an extradition refusal on the basis of ethical, religious or racial reasons would have been possible.

3.5.4. The attempt to use A300 as a weapon: A brief analysis

We have already admitted that the AF 8969 was recognised as probably the first ever attempt to use a civil aircraft as a weapon in history [see sub-chapter 1.3.3. section c)]. The members of the GIA under Yahia's leadership who captured the plane were planning to crash it into the Eiffel Tower, causing extensive damage to and destruction of high-cultural-value property and the deaths of many people [see sub-chapter 2.2.5., section b)].

The Beijing Convention is the first treaty that contains provisions *expressis verbis* requiring the criminalisation of the use of an aircraft as a weapon. The relevant provision in question is Article 1 sub-paragraph 1 point f) which prohibits the usage of an aircraft in service for the purpose of causing serious bodily injury or serious damage to property or the environment. Much like the Protocol, the Beijing Convention establishes that the time "in service" is regarded as the period from the start of pre-flight preparation of the aircraft by ground personnel or crew for a particular flight until twenty-four hours after landing (so when the aircraft is "in service" according to Article 2, point b)). Thus, crashing the plane into the Tower would have been regarded as an offence.

Currently, France is one of very few states that have ratified the Convention (the country became a party to the treaty on 15 December 2016). Its Penal Code does not feature a separate provision repeating the wording of Article 1(1), point f) of the Convention so far. However, the impact study related to drafting the bill of ratification of the Convention shows that France seriously considers implementing such an offence into the Code.[107]

107 Ministry for Europe and Foreign Affairs of the Republic of France, Projet de loi autorisant la ratification de la convention sur la répression des actes illicites dirigés contre l'aviation civile internationale et du protocole complémentaire à la convention pour la répression de la capture illicite d'aéronefs, p. 2.

Due to the fact that the Beijing Convention features fairly similar provisions on the jurisdiction and extradition as the Protocol, their applicability shall be analogical in relation to what was described in the previous section.

Concluding remarks

Though "the global war on terror", hailed by the United States and its allies after the attacks of 11th September 2001, borne some desired fruit and acted as an impulse for states of the world to tackle the terrorist threat, it remains far from over. Additionally, civil aviation is still perceived by terrorist networks as an "attractive target". In that area, only the *modus operandi* of the offenders has slightly changed. In the second half of the twentieth century, the attackers' preferred methods of realisation of their goals were the hijacking aircraft, whereas nowadays they reach for other forms of attack, like bombing airports, blowing up aeroplanes, etc.

In this context, the fight against aerial terrorism resembles a never-ending race between the international community and terrorists, where at the start, the terrorists were winning. Arguments supporting that claim are numerous; in the 1960s and early 1970s, those that today are considered "terrorists" were called "freedom fighters" by the United Nations in their organs' resolutions and, in consequence, perceived more so as victims of state cruelty rather than those who unlawfully bring death. What is more, the Tokyo Convention, being a first-of-its-kind instrument dealing with aviation security, did not even provide for the criminalisation of aircraft hijackings, which at the time were very frequent on both sides of the Atlantic.

Since we mentioned the Tokyo Convention, that particular treaty and others from the Tokyo-Hague-Montreal-Beijing system are those that commonly form a basic framework for pursuing and judging air terrorists, but in spite of that, states are reluctant to become parties thereto. Many countries ratified The Hague Convention, Montreal Convention or Montreal Protocol three or more decades after their signature (*sic!*). As for the Beijing instruments, they both entered into force in 2018, so nearly 8 years after their adoption, and the number of parties currently amounts to 33 for the Convention and 34 for the Protocol (as of May 2020), including states that are less involved in the global campaign against terrorism (mostly African countries). That only shows that states of the world are often unable to have one common voice even on a matter as important as aerial terrorism.

Nevertheless, the overall activity of the international community undertaken to make the skies safer and protect air passengers from terrorists should be rated positively. Governments were able to respond accurately to newly emerging threats and draft new legislation on that basis. Both the Security Council and the

General Assembly of the United Nations frequently adopted appropriate Resolutions in response to brutal terrorist attempts, showing their interest in shaping global policy on the problem. It especially concerns Resolutions 1368, 1373 and 1377 issued after the 11 September attacks. Those documents contributed significantly to the concept of the war on terror as we know it today. Another great example is Resolution 2309, the first one devoted totally to addressing key issues on the protection of civil aviation on UN Member States' level. It all proves that the United Nations treat the elimination of aerial terrorism with high priority.

The ICAO as the primary body regulating international civil aviation has made great efforts to improve the general level of aviation security. Every single treaty from the Tokyo-Hague-Montreal-Beijing system drafted under its auspices was implemented as a response to a growing threat from aerial terrorism in particular areas (hijackings, attacks at international airports, etc.). But the Beijing instruments are the first ones of their kind to provide juridical solutions for the problems that might arise in the future, like cyberterrorism, or wider usage of BCN weapons. That idea deserves approval, as it appears to be "a step ahead of terrorists", before they would actually apply new technologies in weapons in aerial terrorism, the international community is already equipped with tools to criminalise it (but only if the Beijing instruments are more widely ratified; see above). That gives a strong impression that states adopted a more forward-thinking approach in regard to passengers' security, and states themselves are now able to take more a "courageous" stance toward fight against terrorism than in the mid-twentieth century.

The European Union also brought assumed a hard stance towards aerial terrorism, especially in recent years. A system of the regulations on common basic standards on civil aviation security adopted between 2010 and 2013 was a response to the intensification of terrorist attacks on the continent and attempts to blow up planes crossing the Atlantic with liquid explosives. The Community also took the wise decision of replacing the ageing Framework Decision 2002/475/JHA with Directive (EU) 2017/541 that established a uniform system of rules of combatting terrorism within the EU, including the attacks on civil aviation. Only the PNR Directive seems to provide measures that are too intrusive in regards to the right of data protection if compared to the level of security it provides. Overall, an advantage the EU system of norms has is its mandatory applicability by Member States, in contrast to international conventions whose geographical scope of application is dependent on individual parties. In consequence, the juridical system of protecting civil aviation from terrorism becomes more uniform, especially in Europe, thus assuring common standards in that area.

And finally, the mechanisms set both by international legal measures and European law might be perfectly applicable in practice, which was proven in the last chapter. All those provisions that constitute air security law cannot work in a vacuum, as otherwise it would depend upon their failure to meet pre-set goals. Instead, we can clearly see that the system of norms produced under auspices of the international community can perfectly "work" and contribute to the "global war on terror".

Briefly speaking, the international community has undertaken reasonable juridical solutions to protect us, aerial passengers, from terrorism, especially in recent years. The growing interest of states of the world in an aviation security system that results in the adoption of legal measures that better reflect current trends in the fight against terrorism is worth approval. Nevertheless, due to the contradictory political interests of states and a lack of unanimity in the concept of that fight, the system is still imperfect. The international community must not stop working on improving it and strive to unite in this campaign against aerial terrorism in which the safety of people is far more important than political interests.

Bibliography

Articles and chapters:

R. Abeyratne, "Beijing Convention of 2010 on the suppression of unlawful acts relating to international civil aviation—an interpretative study," *Journal of Transportation Security*, 4/2011

R. Abeyratne, "Cyber terrorism and aviation – national and international responses," *Journal of Transportation Security*, Vol. 4(4) 2011

R. Abeyratne, "Ethiopian airlines hijacking – the international perspective," *Journal of Transportation Security*, 7/2014

R. Abeyratne, "Flight MH 17 and state responsibility for ensuring safety and security of air transport," *Journal of Transportation Security* 7/2014

R. Abeyratne, "Terror In the Skies: Approaches to Controlling Unlawful Interference with Civil Aviation," International Journal of Politics, *Culture and Society*, Vol. 2(2) 1997

T. Aleksandrowicz, "Krótki film o ścinaniu głowy. O symbiozie między terrorystami i mediami," *Wszystko co najważniejsze*, 9 May 2015. (9 March 2021) https://wszystkoconajwazniejsze.pl/tomasz-aleksandrowicz-krotki-film-o-scinaniu-glowy/.

S.-D. Bachmann, "Malaysia Airlines flight MH17: the day Russia became a state sponsor of terrorism," *Amicus Curiae*, 97/2014

A. H. Barrientosa, P. P. Longoria, "Understanding the Interrelationship Between Global Terrorist Attacks and the Citizen's Wellbeing: The Complexity of Terrorism," *Sociology Study*, Vol. 6(5) 2016

S. Bennett, "Commercial Aircraft Bomb-Proofing Technologies: A Social Science Critique," *Risk Management*, Vol. 1(3) 1999

A. Cassese, "Terrorism is also Disrupting Some Crucial Legal Categories of International Law," *European Journal of International Law*, Vol. 12(5) 2001

L. Condorelli, "Les Attentats du 11 Septembre et Leurs Suites: Où Va le Droit International?," *RGDIP*, Vol. 105/2001

H. G. Dawson, "Civil Aviation, Hijacking and International Terrorism – An Historical and Legal Review," *International Business Lawyer*, Vol. 15(57) 1987

P. Dempsey, "Aviation Security: The Role of Law in the War against Terrorism," *Columbia Journal of Transnational Law*, Vol. 41(3) 2003

M. Dupont-Elleray, "Géopolitique du terrorisme aérien: de l'évolution de la menace à la diversité de la riposte," *Stratégique*, nr 1(85) 2005

G. F. Fitzgerald, "Aviation Terrorism and the International Civil Aviation Organization," 25 *Canadian Yearbook of International Law*, (1987)

J. Gierszewski, "Unia Europejska w walce z terroryzmem międzynarodowym," *Acta Pomerania*, Vol. 2 2009

C. Greenwood, "International law and the 'war against terrorism'," *International Affairs*, Vol. 78(2) 2002

E. A. Heinze, "The evolution of international law in light of the 'global War on Terror'," *Review of International Studies*, Vol. 37 2010

T. Lachowski, "Kto strzelał – kto odpowie? Kwalifikacja prawna tragedii MH17," *Studia Prawnicze KUL*, Vol. 62 (2) 2015

A. Lekas, "ISIS: The Largest Threat to World Peace Trending Now", *Emory International Law Review*, Vol. 30(2) 2015

L. Łukasik, „Prawnomiędzynarodowe środki zwalczania terroryzmu powietrznego," *Sprawy Międzynarodowe*, (1973)

A. Jakab, "Breaching constitutional law on moral grounds in the fight against terrorism: Implied presuppositions and proposed solutions in the discourse on 'the Rule of Law vs. Terrorism," *International Journal of Constitutional Law*, Vol. 1 (9) 2011

J. Kinsey, M. Timko, S. Herndon, ezra Wood, Z. Yu, R. Miake-Lye, P. Lobo, P. Whitefield, D. Hagen, C. Wey, B. Anderson, A. Beyersdorf, C. Hudgins, K. Thornhill, E. Winstead, R. Howard, D. Bulzan, K. Tacina & W. Knighton, "Determination of the emissions from an aircraft auxiliary power unit (APU) during the Alternative Aviation Fuel Experiment (AAFEX)," *Journal of the Air & Waste Management Association*, Vol. 62(4) 2012

A. Knauth, "The Aircraft Commander in International Law," *Journal of Air Law and Commerce*, Vol. 14(157) 1947

K. Kowalczewska, "Humanity in modern warfare, empathy and jus in bello," *Security Dimensions. International & National Studies*, No. 2 (12) 2014

A. Meyer, Les infractions à bord des aéronefs. Examinées à la lumière du rapport du sous-comité du comité juridique de l'O.A.C.I., *Revue Française du Droit Aérien*, Vol. 4/1957

R. H. Mankiewicz, "La Convention de Montréal (1971) pour la répression d'actes illicites dirigés contre la sécurité de l'aviation civile," *Annuaire français de droit international*, Vol. 17/1971

R. H. Mankiewicz, "Le détournement d'avions," *Revue français de droit aérien* (1971)

C. Martin, "Challenging and Refining the "Unwilling or Unable" Doctrine," *Vanderbilt Journal of Transnational Law*, Vol. 52 (387) 2019

C. Michaelsen, "The Proportionality Principle in the Context of Anti-Terrorism Laws: An Inquiry into the Boundaries between Human Rights Law and Public Policy," in: *Fresh Perspectives on the 'War on Terror,'* eds. M. Gani, P. Mathew (ANU E Press: Canberra, 2008)

J. Monar, "The EU's approach post-September 11: global terrorism as a multidimensional law enforcement challenge," *Cambridge Review of International Affairs*, Vol. 20(2)

B. Nowak, "Akty terroryzmu w lotnictwie cywilnym a tokijsko-hasko-montrealski system międzynarodowego lotniczego prawa karnego," *Studia Europejskie*, 3/2003

B. Nowak, "Problemy bezpieczeństwa w międzynarodowym lotnictwie cywilnym w świetle Konwencji Haskiej z 1970 r.," *Studia Europejskie*, 3/2001

M. Osiecki, "ISIS vs. the World – the Combat from the Perspective of International Law," in: *Світ очима молодих. Orbis terrarum oculis iuvenibus* (Прикарпатський національний університет імені Василя Стефаника: Ivano-Frankivsk, 2016)

M. Osiecki, "Shooting down civil aircraft in the light of Sovereignty in the Airspace," *Sociology Study*, Vol. 6(6) 2016

M. Osiecki, "Terrorism vs. International Law – Case of Attacks in Brussels," in: *5th International Conference of PhD Students and Young Researchers How Deep is Your Law? Brexit. Technologies. Modern Conflicts. Conference Papers*, Vilnius University 2017, p. 28, after: R. Abeyratne, "Terror In the Skies: Approaches to Controlling Unlawful Interference with Civil Aviation," *International Journal of Politics, Culture and Society*, Vol. 2(2) 1997

M. Osiecki, "Zamachy na port lotniczy w Brukseli – prawo międzynarodowe i europejskie wobec zdarzenia," *Internetowy Kwartalnik Monopolowy i Regulacyjny*, Vol 2(6) 2016

M. Osiecki, "Zestrzelenie samolotu a zasada zwierzchnictwa powietrznego," *Studia Prawno-Ekonomiczne*, Vol. 101

N. M. Poulantzas, "Convention for the Suppression of Unlawful Seizure of Aircraft," *World Peace through Law Center Pamphlet Series*, No. 18/1971

I. Primoratz, *State terrorism and Counterterrorism*, Centre for Applied Philosophy and Public Ethics Working Paper 2002/3 (University of Melbourne: Melbourne, 2002)

P. Rembauville-Nicole, "L'effectivité du droit de la securité aérienne," in: ed. X. Latour, *La securité et la sûreté des transports aériens* (L'Harmattan: Paris, 2005)

K. Rękawek, D. Cristiani, "Al Qaeda at 25: No Point in Fighting Them Since They Themselves are Fighting Each Other?," *The Polish Institute of International Affairs Policy Paper*, Vol. 26 (74) 2013

K. B. Sælebakke, *Into the Quagmire? Explaining Russia's Military Intervention in Syria*, University of Oslo, Oslo 2016

M. P. Scharf, "How the War Against ISIS Changed International Law," *Case Western Reserve Journal of International Law*, Vol. 48 2016

M. Shabafrouz, "Oil and the Eruption of the Algerian Civil War: A Context-sensitive Analysis of the Ambivalent Impact of Resource Abundance," *German Institute of Global and Area Studies Working Papers* 118/2010

M. J. Stephan, "Civil Resistance vs. ISIS," *Journal of Resistance Studies*, Vol. 1(2) 2015

J. E. Stromseth, "An Imperial Security Council? Implementing Security Council Resolutions 1373 and 1390," *American Society of International Law Proceedings*, Vol. 97 (2003)

S. Talmon, "The Security Council as World Legislature," *American Journal of International Law*, Vol. 99 (2005)

C. Tams, "The Use of Force against Terrorists," *The European Journal of International Law*, Vol. 20 (2)

B. ter Haar, "Lessons from the MH17 Disaster," *Security and Human Rights* 25/2014

J. D. van der Vyver, "The ISIS Crisis and the Development of International Humanitarian Law," *Emory International Law Review*. 2016, Vol. 30 (4)

J. A. Urban, "The Protocol to Amend the Convention on Offences and Certain Acts Committed on Board Aircraft: A Missed Opportunity or a Sufficient Modernization?," *Indiana Law Review*, Vol. 49(713) 2016

S. Villani, "Some Further Reflections on the Directive (EU) 2016/681 on PNR Data in the Light of the CJEU Opinion 1/15 of 26 July 2017," *Revista de Derecho Politico*, No 101 2018

M. Wade, "The European union as a counter–terrorism actor: right path, wrong direction?," *Crime, Law and Social Change*, Vol. 62 (2014)

J. Walulik, "Pekińska reforma lotniczego prawa karnego – geneza, istota, rekomendacje," *Ruch Prawniczy, Ekonomiczny i Socjologiczny*, Vol. 3/2013

C. Warbrick, "The European Response to Terrorism in the Age of Human Rights," *The European Journal of International Law*, Vol. 15(5) 2004

P. Wilkinson, "Weaknesses in Airport Security Must be Fixed," *The Scotsman* (8 February 2000)

A. S. Williams, "The Interception of Civil Aircraft over the High Seas in the Global War on Terror," *Air Force Law Review*, Vol. 59(73) 2007

R. Wolfrum, C. E. Philipp, "The Status of the Taliban: Their Obligations and Rights under International Law," *Max Planck Yearbook of United Nations Law*, Vol. 6 (2002)

G. Zając, "Prawnomiędzynarodowe regulacje dotyczące zwalczania terroryzmu w lotnictwie cywilnym," *Stosunki Międzynarodowe – International Relations*, Vol. 1/2 (43) 2011

B. Ziemblicki, "Wprowadzenie do problematyki ekstradycji," *Wrocławskie Studia Erazmiańskie* 5/2010

M. Żylicz, "Terroryzm lotniczy," Palestra 49/3-4 (2004)

Books:

Encyklopedia prawa międzynarodowego i stosunków międzynarodowych, Wiedza Powszechna, Warsaw 1976

Encyklopedia terroryzmu, Muza, Warszawa 2004

D. M. Adeniji, *Nigeria: Boko Haram and National Security* (Garamond Projects Ltd.: Abuja, 2015)

T. Aleksandrowicz, *Terroryzm międzynarodowy* (Wydawnictwa Akademickie i Profesjonalne: Warsaw, 2008)

T. Aleksandrowicz, K. Liedel, *Zwalczanie terroryzmu lotniczego* (Wydawnictwo Wyższej Szkoły Policji: Szczytno, 2010)

W. Anderson, *The ETA. Spain Basque's Terrorists* (The Rosen Publishing: New York, 2003)

A. Aust, *Handbook of International Law* (Cambridge University Press: Cambridge, 2010)

J. Barcz, *Źródła prawa Unii Europejskiej* (Instytut Wydawniczy EuroPrawo: Warsaw, 2012)

R. Barrett, *The Islamic State* (The Soufan Group: New York, 2014)

S. Bazin, *Le droit pénal de l'aviation civile* (Atelier National de Reproduction de Thèses: Lille, 2002)

A. Bieńczyk-Missala, S. Dębski, ed. *Rafał Lemkin: A Hero of Humankind* (The Polish Institute of International Affairs: Warsaw, 2010)

R. Bierzanek, J. Symonides, *Prawo międzynarodowe publiczne* (LexisNexis: Warsaw, 2005)

B. Cheng, *The Law of International Air Transport* (Stevens: London, 1962)

V. P. Cogliati-Bantz, *Means of Transportation and Registration of Nationality: Transportation Registered by International Organizations* (Routledge: London/New York, 2015)

P. Craig, G. de Burca, *EU Law. Text, Cases and Materials* (Oxford University Press: New York, 2011)

Y. Dinstein, *War, Aggression and Self-Defence*, Cambridge University Press, Cambridge 2001

O. Elagab, *International law Documents relating to Terrorism* (Routledge: London/ Sydney, 1997)

C. Emanuelli, *Les moyens de prévention et de sanction en cas d'action illicite contre l'aviation civile internationale* (Editions A. Pedone: Paris, 1974)

C. Fijnaut, J. Wouters, F. Naert, *Legal instruments in the Fight against International Terrorism. A Transatlantic Dialogue* (Martinus Nijhoff Publishers: Leiden/ Boston, 2004)

D. French, *Fighting EOKA: The British Counter-Insurgency Campaign on Cyprus, 1955–1959* (Oxford University Press: Oxford, 2015)

Z. Galicki, *Terroryzm lotniczy w świetle prawa międzynarodowego* (Wydawnictwo Uniwersytetu Warszawskiego: Warsaw, 1981)

eds. M. Gani, P. Mathew, *Fresh Perspectives on the 'War on Terror,* (ANU E Press: Canberra, 2008)

C. Gray, *International Law and the Use of Force* (Oxford University Press: Oxford, 2000)

G. Guillaume, G. Levasseur, *Terrorisme international* (Pédone: Paris, 1976)

J. Huang, *Aviation Safety and ICAO* (Kluwer Law International: Alphen aan den Rijn,2009)

B. Hołyst, *Terroryzm, t.1* (LexisNexis: Warsaw, 2011)

L. Hoppe, *Le statut juridique des drones aéronefs non habités* (Presses Universitaires d'Aix-Marseille: Aix-en-Provence, 2008)

K. Indecki, *Prawo karne wobec terroryzmu i aktu terrorystycznego* (Wydawnictwo Uniwersytetu Łódzkiego: Łódź, 1998)

K. Jałoszyński, *Współczesny wymiar antyterroryzmu*, (Trio: Warsaw, 2008

B. I. Koerner, *Niebo jest nasze. Miłość i terror w złotym wieku piractwa powietrznego* (Wydawnictwo Czarne: Wołowiec, 2017)

J. Kranz, *Wojna, pokój czy uspokajanie? współczesne dylematy użycia siły zbrojnej* (Fundacja Centrum Stosunków Międzynarodowych: Warsaw, 2006)

D. Kretzmer, "The Inherent Right to Self-Defence and Proportionality in Jus Ad Bellum," *The European Journal of International Law*, Vol. 24 (1) 2013

J. J. Lambert, *Terrorism and Hostages in International Law* (Grotius Publications Ltd.: Cambridge, 1992)

M. Lech, *Ochrona prawna społeczności międzynarodowej wobec zagrożenia terroryzmem* (Wydawnictwo Uniwersytetu Gdanskiego: Gdansk, 2014)

A. Lele, A. Mishra, "Aerial Terrorism and the Threat from Unmanned Aerial Vehicles," *Journal of Defence Studies*, Vol. 3(3) 2009

K. Liedel, *Zwalczanie terroryzmu lotniczego. Aspekty prawnomiędzynarodowe* (Jurysta: Warsaw, 2003)

eds. K. Liedel, J. Szafrański, *Problemy prawno-organizacyjne zwalczania terroryzmu w Polsce* (Wydawnictwo Wyższej Szkoły Policji: Szczytno, 2011)

M. Madej, *Zagrożenia asymetryczne bezpieczeństwa państw obszaru transatlantyckiego*, (PISM: Warsaw, 2007)

M. Marcinko, *ONZ wobec terroryzmu międzynarodowego* (Fundacja Instytut Studiów Strategicznych: Kraków, 2008)

P. Mendes de Leon, *Introduction to Air Law* (Kluwer Law International: Alphen aan den Rijn, 2017)

J. Menkes, A. Wasilkowski, *Organizacje międzynarodowe. Prawo instytucjonalne* (Wolters Kluwer Polska: Warszawa, 2010)

E. McWhinney, *Aerial Piracy and International Terrorism* (Martinus Nijhoff Publishers: Dordrecht 1987)

eds. E. Mikos-Skuza, K. Myszona-Kostrzewa, J. Poczobut, *Prawo międzynarodowe – teraźniejszość, perspektywy, dylematy. Księga jubileuszowa Profesora Zdzisława Galickiego* (Lex: Warsaw, 2013)

T. R. Mockaitis, *The "New" Terrorism: Myths and Reality* (Stanford Security Studies: Stanford, 2008)

C. Murphy, *EU Counter-Terrorism Law. Pre-Emption and the Rule of Law* (Hart Publishing: Oxford/Portland, 2012)

C. Naudin, *Sûrete aérienne. La grande illusion* (La Table Ronde: Paris, 2007)

A. Oehmichen, *Terrorism and Anti-Terror Legislation: The Terrorised Legislator?A Comparison of Counter-Terror Legislation and Its Implications on Human Rights in the Legal Systems of the United Kingdom, Spain, Germany and France* (Intersentia: Antwerp-Oxford-Portland, 2009)

T. Ostropolski, *Zasada jurysdykcji uniwersalnej w prawie międzynarodowym* (Instytut Wydawniczy EuroPrawo: Warsaw, 2008)

M. L. O'Sullivan, *Shrewd Sanctions: Statecraft and State Sponsors of Terrorism* (Brookings Institution Press: Washington D. C., 2003)

V.-J. Proulx, *Transnational Terrorism and State Accountability. A New Theory of Prevention* (Hart Publishing: Oxford-Portland, 2012)

M. Sczaniecki, *Powszechna historia państwa i prawa* (LexisNexis: Warsaw, 2009)

F. Shanty, *Countetterrorism: From the Cold War to the War on Terror. Volume 1: Combating Modern Terrorism (1968–2011)* (Praeger Security International: Santa Barbara, 2012)

M. N. Shaw, *International Law* (Cambridge University Press: Cambridge, 2014)

S. Schubber, *Jurisdiction over Crimes on Board Aircraft* (Martinus Nijhoff: The Hague, 1973)

A. Szpak, *Międzynarodowe prawo humanitarne* (Wydawnictwo Naukowe Uniwersytetu Mikołaja Kopernika: Toruń, 2014)

C. Townshend, *Terroryzm* (Wydawnictwo Uniwersytetu Łódzkiego: Lodz, 2017)

P. Van Krieken, *Terrorism and the International Legal Order: With Special Reference to the UN, the EU and Cross-Border Aspects* (T. M. C. Asser Press: The Hague, 2002)

G. Verhofstadt, *Europe's Last Chance. Why the European States Must Form a More Perfect Union* (Basic Books: New York, 2017)

A. Wejkszner, *Globalna sieć Al-Kaidy. Nowe Państwo Islamskie?* (Difin: Warsaw, 2017)

L. Wright, *Wyniosłe wieże. Al-Kaida i atak na Amerykę* (Wydawnictwo Czarne: Wołowiec 2018)

M. Zimny, *Terroryzm samobójczy* (Difin: Warsaw, 2017)

A. Zoll, W. Wróbel, *Polskie prawo karne. Część ogólna* (Wydawnictwo Znak: Kraków, 2010)

M. Żylicz, *Prawo lotnicze międzynarodowe, europejskie i krajowe* (Wydawnictwo LexisNexis: Warsaw, 2011)

Press articles:

S. Al-Atrush, M. Antonova, "Experts explain why it's 'unlikely' that ISIS is responsible for the Russian plane crash," *Business Insider*, 1 November 2015. (9 March 2021) https://www.businessinsider.com/afp-russia-holds-day-of-mourning-after-224-die-in-sinai-plane-crash-2015-11?IR=T.

R.-J. Bartunek, A. Macdonald, "Belgians seize key suspects in Paris, Brussels attacks," *Reuters*, 8 April 2016. (9 March 2021) https://www.reuters.com/article/us-france-shooting-abrini-arrest/belgians-seize-key-suspects-in-paris-brussels-attacks-idUSKCN0X51QK.

L. Dearden, "Isis supporters claim group responsible for Brussels attacks: 'We have come to you with slaughter'," *The Independent*, 22 March 2016. (9 March 2021) https://www.independent.co.uk/news/world/europe/isis-supporters-claim-responsibility-for-brussels-attacks-bombings-belgium-airport-maalbeek-metro-we-a6945886.html.

T. Dunning, "Politics, economics and security: Implications of Metrojet Flight 9268," *Daily Sabah*, 21 November 2015. (9 March 2021) https://www.dailysabah.com/op-ed/2015/11/21/politics-economics-and-security-implications-of-metrojet-flight-9268.

J. E. Dyer, "Newly declared caliphate: Why it's 'ISIS' (not ISIL) – 'Iraq and al-Sham' (not Syria)," *Liberty Unyielding*, 30 June 2014. (9 March 2021) https://libertyunyielding.com/2014/06/30/newly-declared-caliphate-isis-isil-iraq-al-sham-syria/.

L.-M. Eleftheriou-Smith, "Brussels Metro system shut down after station explosion as Belgium terror alert raised to maximum," *The Independent*, 22 March 2016. (9 March 2021) https://www.independent.co.uk/news/world/europe/brussels-metro-system-shut-down-following-explosion-at-station-near-eu-institutions-leaving-several-a6945431.html.

J. Fioretti, "Brussels Attacks Death Toll Lowered To 32," *Huffington Post,* 29 March 2016. (9 March 2021) https://www.huffingtonpost.com/entry/brussels-attacks-death-toll-lowered_us_56facaa4e4b0a372181b27ed.

P. Graff, "Exclusive: EgyptAir mechanic suspected in Russian plane crash," *Reuters*, 29 January 2016. (9 March 2021) https://www.reuters.com/article/us-egypt-crash-suspects/exclusive-egyptair-mechanic-suspected-in-russian-plane-crash-idUSKCN0V712V.

A. S. Hashim, "The Islamic State: from Al-Qaeda affiliate to caliphate," *Middle East Policy Council Journal*, Winter 2014, Vol. XXI (4), p. 1. (9 March 2021) http://www.mepc.org/islamic-state-al-qaeda-affiliate-caliphate.

J. Ireland, "MH17: Abbott government may declare downing of plane a terrorist attack, triggering payments to families," *The Sydney Morning Herald*, 21 July 2014. (9 March 2021) https://www.smh.com.au/politics/federal/mh17-abbott-government-may-declare-downing-of-plane-a-terrorist-attack-triggering-payments-to-families-20140721-3cajb.html.

E. Magdelaine, "Attentats à Bruxelles: contrôles renforcés à la frontière franco-belge," *Franceinfo*, 22 March 2016. (9 March 2021) https://france3-regions.francetvinfo.fr/hauts-de-france/explosions-bruxelles-controles-renforces-la-frontiere-franco-belge-957629.html.

C. Mitchell, "Mercenaries to stand trial on coup attempt," *UPI Archives*, 14 June 1981. (9 March 2021) https://www.upi.com/Archives/1982/06/14/Mercenaries-to-stand-trial-on-coup-attempt/4805392875200/.

J. Neriah, "The Structure of the Islamic State (ISIS)," *Jerusalem Center for Public Affairs*, 8 September 2014. (9 March 2021) http://jcpa.org/structure-of-the-islamic-state/.

J. Nicas, R. Wall, "Height of Ukraine No-Fly Zone Faces Scrutiny," *The Wall Street Journal*, 17 July 2014. (9 March 2021) https://www.wsj.com/articles/height-of-ukraine-no-fly-zone-faces-scrutiny-1405639624.

P. Paganini, "DHS – Tests demonstrate Boeing 757 airplanes vulnerable to hacking," *Security Affairs*, 13 November 2017; (9 December 2020) https://securityaffairs.co/wordpress/65463/hacking/dhs-boeing-757-hacking.html

R. Rabil, "The ISIS chronicles: A History," *The National Interest*, 17 July 2014. (9 March 2021) http://nationalinterest.org/feature/the-isis-chronicles-history-10895.

T. Reals, "Deadly explosions rock Brussels airport, subway," *CBS News*, 22 March 2016. (25 May 2020) https://www.cbsnews.com/news/reported-explosions-at-brussels-airport-in-belgium/.

A. Riding, Hijacked Airliner forced to France, "The New York Times," 26 December 1994. (9 March 2021) https://www.nytimes.com/1994/12/26/world/hijacked-airliner-forced-to-france.html.

T. Sancton, "Anatomy of a Hijack," *Time*, 24 June 2001. (9 March 2021) http://content.time.com/time/magazine/article/0,9171,163487,00.html.

T. Smith, "Israeli Jets Over Lebanon Force Down Arab Airliner," *The New York Times*, 11 August 1973 (9 March 2021) https://www.nytimes.com/1973/08/11/archives/israeli-jets-over-lebanon-force-down-arab-airliner-military-says-it.html.

L. Upton, "2017 was the safest year in aviation history; though caution urged on remarkable figures continuing," *Transport Security World* (9 March 2021) http://www.transportsecurityworld.com/2017-was-safest-year-in-aviation-history-though-caution-urged-on-remarkable-figures).

N. Vavoula, "'I Travel, therefore I Am a Suspect:' an overview of the EU PNR Directive," *EU Immigration and Asylum Law and Policy*, 26 October 2016. http://eumigrationlawblog.eu/i-travel-therefore-i-am-a-suspect-an-overview-of-the-eu-pnr-directive/.

N. Waller, "Ex-Separatist Leader Launches Party Aimed at Restoring Russia's Empire," *Georgia Today*, 2 June 2016. (9 March 2021) https://web.archive.org/web/20160602041435/http://georgiatoday.ge/news/3927/Ex-Separatist-Leader-Launches-Party-Aimed-at-Restoring-Russia%E2%80%99s-Empire.

W. Wei, "You Can Hijack Nearly Any Drone Mid-flight Using This Tiny Gadget," *The Hacker News*, 27 October 2016. (9 March 2021) http://thehackernews.com/2016/10/how-to-hack-drone.html. The author reports about a device designed by J. Andersson able to hack drones and control them remotely.

K. Wilsher, "France in shock again after Isis murder of priest in Normandy," *The Guardian*, 26 July 2016. (9 March 2021) https://www.theguardian.com/world/2016/jul/26/france-shock-second-isis-attack-12-days.

K. Yournish, et al., "What Happened at Each Location in the Brussels Attacks," *The New York Times*, 22 March 2016. (9 March 2021) https://www.nytimes.com/interactive/2016/03/22/world/europe/brussels-attacks-graphic.html?_r=1.

Official reports and other non-legal documents:

Asia-Pacific Center for Security Studies, *Uyghur Muslim Ethnic Separatism in Xinjiang, China*, January 2008.

Council of Europe/European Court of Human Rights, *National security and European case-law*, 2013.

Dutch Public Prosecution Service, *JIT: Flight MH17 was shot down by a BUK missile from a farmland near Pervomaiskyi,* 28 September 2016.

Dutch Public Prosecution Service, *Joint investigation into Flight MH17,* 29 August 2014.

Dutch Public Prosecution Service, *Radar experts confirm previous conclusion of the JIT,* 3 April 2018.

Dutch Public Prosecution Service, *Update in criminal investigation MH17 disaster*, 24 May 2018.

Dutch Safety Board, *Crash of Malaysia Airlines flight 17.*

Dutch Safety Board, *Preliminary report. Crash involving Malaysia Airlines Boeing 777–200 flight 17.*

EUROCONTROL, *Definition of State Aircraft*, Decision of the Provisional Council session 11 on 12 July 2001.

European Commission, *Communication from the Commission to the European Parliament, the European Council and the Council delivering on the European Agenda on Security to fight against terrorism and pave the way towards an effective and genuine Security Union*, Brussels, 20 April 2016 COM (2016) 230.

IATA, *Comments on the Issue of State of Operator Jurisdiction*, DCTC Doc. No. 18

ICAO, *Aircraft nationality marks and common marks*

ICAO, *Annual Report of the Council – 2010*

ICAO, *Glossary*

ICAO, *Guidelines on Passenger Name Record (PNR) Data*, ICAO Doc 9944

ICAO, *Supplementary Report on Activities of the Organization in the First Half of 2010*, ICAO Doc 9921 Supplement

Inter-American Commission on Human Rights, *Armando Alejandre Jr., Carlos Costa, Mario de la Pena y Pablo Morales v. Republica de Cuba*, Case 11.589, Report No. 86/99, OEA/Ser.L/V/II.106 Doc. 3 rev. at 586 (1999)

International Civil Aviation Organisation, 9th Session of the Legal Committee, Rio de Janeiro, 25 August to 12 September 1953. ICAO Doc 7450-LC/136, Vol. I

International Law Association, Paris Reunion 1984, *Report*

Ministry of the Russian Federation for Civil Defence, Emergencies and Elimination of Consequences of Natural Disasters, list of passengers and crew of aeroplane Airbus A321 "Kogalymavia" 7K-9268 (Министерство Российской Федерации по делам гражданской обороны, чрезвычайным ситуациям и ликвидации последствий стихийных бедствий, список пассажиров и экипажа самолета Airbus A321 авиакомпании «КогалымАвиа» 7К9268)

Ministry of Civil Aviation of Arabic Republic of Egypt, *Issuance of the Preliminary Report for the Metrojet Russian Airplane accident*

Ministry of Europe and Foreign Affairs of the Republic of France, *Projet de loi autorisant la ratification de la convention sur la répression des actes illicites dirigés contre l'aviation civile internationale et du protocole complémentaire à la convention pour la répression de la capture illicite d'aéronefs*

Report of the Ad Hoc Committee on International Terrorism, United Nations General Assembly Official Records, Thirty-Fourth Session, Supplement No. 37 (A/34/37)

Reporters without Borders, *Anti-terrorism law among targets of Addis Ababa protest*, 1 October 2013

T. S. Huay, *The Montreal Protocol 2014 – What Changes Will It Bring?*, PowerPoint Presentation on *ICAO Legal Seminar, on 28 November 2017, Nairobi, Kenya*

The U.S. Vice President's Task Force on Combatting Terrorism (1988). *Terrorist Group Profiles*

United Nations Office on Drugs and Crime, *Implementation Kits for the International*

Counter-Terrorism Conventions – Chapter 1. Introduction

United Nations Office on Drugs and Crime, *Implementation Kits for the International*

Counter-Terrorism Conventions – Chapter 5. Protocol for the Suppression of Unlawful Acts of Violence at Airports Serving International Civil Aviation 1988 ('Montreal Protocol')

United Nations Office on Drugs and Crime, *Manual on Mutual Legal Assistance and Extradition*, United Nations Office, Vienna 2012

United Nations Security Council Counter-Terrorism Committee Executive Directorate, *Technical guide to the implementation of Security Council Resolution 1373 (2001) and other relevant resolutions*

Domestic legal documents:

Algeria: Ordonnance n° 66–156 du 8 juin 1966 portant code pénal, modifiée et complété

Belgium: Law of 8 June 1867 – Belgian Penal Code, number 1867060850, page 3133

China: Criminal Law of the People's Republic of China

Cuba: Law No. 62 – Penal Code of Cuba

Egypt: Law No. 58 01 The year 1937 Promulgating the Penal Code, Government Bulletin, 1937–08-05, No. 71

France: Code pénal, Legifrance

Iraq: Staute No. (111) 1969 – Penal Code of Iraq

Pakistan: Act XLV of 1860 – Pakistan Penal Code

Poland: Ustawa z dnia 6 czerwca 1997 r. – Kodeks karny. (Dz.U. 1997 nr 88 poz. 553)

United States: United States Code

United States Code of Federal Regulations

International legal documents:

Annex 2 to Convention on International Civil Aviation, done at Chicago, 7 December 1944 – *Rules of the Air*, Tenth Edition 2005

Annex 7 to Convention on International Civil Aviation, done at Chicago, 7 December 1944 – *Aircraft Nationality and Registration Marks*, Sixth Edition 2012

Annex 13 to Convention on International Civil Aviation, done at Chicago, 7 December 1944 – *Aircraft Accident and Incident Investigation*, Eleventh Edition, July 2016

Annex 14 to Convention on International Civil Aviation, done at Chicago, 7 December 1944 – *Aerodromes*, Vol. 1, Fifth edition

Annex 17 to Convention on International Civil Aviation, done at Chicago, 7 December 1944 – *Security*, Tenth Edition, 2017

Charter of the United Nations, *United Nations Treaty Series*

Convention entre la France et l'Algérie relative à l'exequatur et à l'extradition, JORF 17-08-p. 1965 7269-7272

Convention on Offences and Certain Other Acts Committed on Board Aircraft done at Tokyo, 14th September 1963, ICAO Doc 8364

Convention on the Prevention and Punishment of Crimes against Internationally Protected Persons, including Diplomatic Agents, done at New York, 14 December 1973, *United Nations Treaty Series*, Vol. 1035, Re.g. 15410

Convention for the Prevention and Punishment of Terrorism, done at Geneva, 16 November 1937, World Digital Library

Convention for the Protection of Human Rights and Fundamental Freedoms done at Rome, 4th November 1950, *Council of Europe Treaty Series*, No. 005

Convention for the Suppression of Unlawful Acts against the Safety of Civil Aviation, done at Montreal, 23rd September, 1971, *United Nations Treaty Series*, Vol. 974, Re.g. 14118

Convention on the Suppression of Unlawful Acts Relating to International Civil Aviation, done at Beijing, 10th September, 2010, ICAO Doc. 9960

Convention for the Suppression of Unlawful Seizure of Aircraft, done at The Hague, 16 December 1970, *United Nations Treaty Series*, Vol. 860, Re.g. 12325

Convention on the High Seas, done at Geneva, 29 April 1958, *United Nations Treaty Series*, Vol. 450, Re.g. 6465

Convention on International Civil Aviation, done at Chicago, 7 December 1944

Council of Europe Convention on the Prevention of Terrorism done at Warsaw, 16 May 2005, *Council of Europe Treaty Series*, No. 1956

Draft articles on Responsibility of States for Internationally Wrongful Acts, UN Doc A/56/10

Final Act of the International Conference on Air Law (Diplomatic Conference on Aviation Security) held under the auspices of the International Civil Aviation Organization at Beijing from 30 August to 10 September 2010, DCAS Doc Series, No. 17

ICAO, *Unmanned Aircraft Systems*, ICAO Circular No. 328

ICAO Safety Report. 2016 Edition, Montreal 2016

International Convention Against the Taking of Hostages done in New York on 17 December 1979, *United Nations Treaty Series*, Vol. 1316, Re.g. 21931

International Convention for the Suppression of the Financing of Terrorism, done in New York, 9 December 1999, *United Nations Treaty Series*, Vol. 2178, Re.g. 38349

International Covenant on Civil and Political Rights, done at New York, 19 December 1966, *United Nations Treaty Series*, Vol. 999 Re.g. 14668

Protocol to Amend the Convention on Offences and Certain Other Acts Committed on Board Aircraft, done at Montreal on 4 April 2014

Protocol Supplementary to the Convention for the Suppression of Unlawful Seizure of Aircraft done in Beijing, on 10 September 2010, ICAO Doc. 9959

Protocol for the Suppression of Unlawful Acts of Violence at Airports Serving International Civil Aviation, Supplementary to the Convention for the Suppression of Unlawful Acts against the Safety of Civil Aviation, done at Montreal on 23 September 1971, signed at Montreal on 24 February 1988, *United Nations Treaty Series,* Vol. 1589, Re.g. 14118

Treaty on Cooperation among the States Members of the Commonwealth of Independent States in Combating Terrorism, done at Minsk on 4 June 1999

United Nations Convention on the Law of the Seas done at Montego Bay on 10 December 1982, *United Nations Treaty Series*, Vol. 1833, Re.g. 31363

United Nations General Assembly Resolution 41/60, 9 December 1985

United Nations General Assembly Resolution 42/159, 7 December 1987

United Nations General Assembly Resolution 49/60, 17 February 1995, Annex

United Nations General Assembly Resolution 50/210, 16 January 1997

United Nations General Assembly Resolution 51/210, 17 December 1996

United Nations General Assembly Resolution 58/174, 22 December 2003

United Nations General Assembly Resolution 217 A, 10 December 1948

United Nations General Assembly Resolution 3034 (XXVII), 18 December 1972

United Nations General Assembly Resolution 3314, 14 December 1974

United Nations Security Council Resolution 337, 15 August 1973

United Nations Security Council Resolution 496, 15 December 1981

United Nations Security Council Resolution 635, 14 June 1989

United Nations Security Council Resolution 748, 31 March 1992

United Nations Security Council Resolution 883, 11 November 1993

United Nations Security Council Resolution 1067, 26 July 1996

United Nations Security Council Resolution 1368, 12 September 2001

United Nations Security Council Resolution 1373, 28 September 2001

United Nations Security Council Resolution 1377, 12 November 2001

United Nations Security Council Resolution 1450, 13 December 2002

United Nations Security Council Resolution 2166, 21 July 2014

United Nations Security Council Resolution 2309, 22 September 2016

United Nations Security Council Resolution 2395, 21 December 2017

United Nations Security Council Resolution 2396, 21 December, 2017

EU legal documents:

Charter of Fundamental Rights of the European Union (Official Journal of the European Union C 326/391)

Commission Regulation (EC) No. 272/2009 of 2 April 2009 supplementing the common basic standards on civil aviation security laid down in the Annex to Regulation (EC) No. 300/2008 of the European Parliament and of the Council (Official Journal of the European Union L 91/7)

Council of the European Union Act of 26 July 1995 drawing up the Convention based on Article K.3 of the Treaty on European Union, on the establishment of a European Police Office (Official Journal of the European Communities C 316/1)

Council of the European Union, The European Union Counter-Terrorism Strategy (14469/4/05)

Council Common Position 2009/468/CFSP of 15 June 2009 updating Common Position 2001/931/CFSP on the application of specific measures to combat terrorism and repealing Common Position 2009/67/CFSP (Official Journal of the European Union L 151/45)

Directive 2013/40/EU of the European Parliament and of the Council of 12 August 2013 on attacks against information systems and replacing Council Framework Decision 2005/222/JHA (Official Journal of the European Union L 218/8)

Directive (EU) 2016/681 of the European Parliament and of the Council of 27 April 2016 on the use of passenger name record (PNR) data for the prevention, detection, investigation and prosecution of terrorist offences and serious crime (Official Journal of the European Union L 119/132)

Directive (EU) 2017/541 of the European Parliament and of the Council of 15 March 2017 on combating terrorism and replacing Council Framework Decision 2002/475/JHA and amending Council Decision 2005/671/JHA (Official Journal of the European Union L 88/6)

Regulation (EC) No. 300/2008 of the European Parliament and of the Council of 11 March 2008 on common rules in the field of civil aviation security and repealing Regulation (EC) No. 2320/2002 (Official Journal of the European Union L 97/72)

Regulation (EU) 2018/1139 of the European Parliament and of the Council of 4 July 2018 on common rules in the field of civil aviation and establishing a European Union Aviation Safety Agency, and amending Regulations (EC) No 2111/2005, (EC) No 1008/2008, (EU) No 996/2010, (EU) No 376/2014 and Directives 2014/30/EU and 2014/53/EU of the European Parliament and of the Council, and repealing Regulations (EC) No 552/2004 and (EC) No 216/

2008 of the European Parliament and of the Council and Council Regulation (EEC) No 3922/91 (Official Journal of the European Union L 212/1)

Treaty on the Functioning of the European Union (Official Journal of the European Union Official Journal C 326/01)

Judgements:

Case concerning the difference between New Zealand and France concerning the interpretation or application of two agreements, concluded on 9 July 1986 between the two States and which related to the problems arising from the Rainbow Warrior Affair, 30th April 1990, United Nations Reports of International Arbitral Awards, Vol. XX, 1990

Corfu Channel Case, Judgement of 9 April 1949: ICJ Reports 1949

Handyside vs. United Kingdom, European Court of Human Rights, 7 December 1976

Klass vs. Germany Case, European Court of Human Rights, 6 September 1978, Series A, No. 28

Lawless vs. Ireland Case, European Court of Human Rights, 1 July 1961, No. 3

Legal Consequences for States of the Continued Presence of South Africa in Namibia (South West Africa) notwithstanding Security Council Resolution 276 (1970), Advisory Opinion of 21 June 1970: ICJ. Reports 1971

Militarv and Puramilitary Activities in und aguinst Nicaragua (Nicaragua v. United States of America), Judgement of 27 June 1986: ICJ Reports 1986

Trail Smelter Case (US vs. Canada) (1941), Reports of International Arbitral Awards

United States Diplomatic and Consular Staff in Tehran Case, Judgement of 24 May 1980: ICJ Reports 1980

Websites:

http://www.airfleets.net/ficheapp/plane-a300-104.htm.

https://www.airfleets.net/ficheapp/plane-a321-663.htm.

http://alphahistory.com/northernireland/ira-1919-1968/.

http://avalon.law.yale.edu/20th_century/hamas.asp.

https://aviation-safety.net/database/record.php?id=19310221-0.

https://aviation-safety.net/database/record.php?id=19680723-0.

https://aviation-safety.net/database/record.php?id=19490507-0.

https://aviation-safety.net/database/record.php?id=19731217-3.

https://aviation-safety.net/database/record.php?id=19850623-2.

https://aviation-safety.net/database/record.php?id=19851124-0.

https://aviation-safety.net/database/record.php?id=19880703-0.

https://aviation-safety.net/database/record.php?id=19890919-1.

https://aviation-safety.net/database/record.php?id=20021128-1.

https://aviation-safety.net/database/record.php?id=20140717-0.

http://aviation-safety.net/database/record.php?id=20151031-0.

https://aviation-safety.net/database/dblist.php?Event=SEB.

http://aviation-safety.net/photos/displayphoto.php?id=20151031-0&vnr=1&kind=G.

https://www.bbc.com/news/world-europe-35903368.

https://www.brusselsairport.be/pressroom/brussels-airport-welcomed-21-8-million-passengers-in-2016/.

https://www.cbc.ca/news/world/montreal-toronto-flights-targeted-in-alleged-british-bomb-plot-1.747225.

https://www.consilium.europa.eu/en/policies/fight-against-terrorism/.

https://www.courtmh17.com/en/timeline/timeline-mh17-trial.

https://www.courtmh17.com/en/timeline/timeline-articles/first-hearing?referrer=3f920eb7-ba11-443e-8836-29d596ba61b0.

http://www.crime-research.org/Cyber_Terrorism_new_kind_Terrorism.

https://www.datagraver.com/case/people-killed-by-terrorism-per-year-in-western-europe-1970-2015.

https://ec.europa.eu/home-affairs/news/list-member-states-applying-pnr-directive-intra-eu-flights_en.

https://ec.europa.eu/eurostat/statistics-explained/index.php/Air_transport_statistics.

https://ec.europa.eu/transport/modes/air/security/aviation-security-policy/lags_en.

https://edri.org/cjeu-to-decide-on-processing-of-passenger-data-under-pnr-directive/.

https://eur-lex.europa.eu/legal-content/EN/TXT/?uri=celex: 32002F0475.

https://www.france24.com/en/20151101-russian-plane-crash-sinai-egypt-broke-air-says-aviation-official.

https://www.icao.int/Newsroom/Pages/Beijing-Protocol-to-enter-into-force-following-Ugandas-ratification.aspx.

https://www.icao.int/Newsroom/Pages/Ukraine-requests-ICAO-assistance-in-MH17-accident-investigation.aspx.

https://www.icao.int/publications/pages/doc7300.aspx.

https://www.icao.int/secretariat/legal/List%20of%20Parties/Hague_EN.pdf.

https://www.icao.int/secretariat/legal/List%20of%20Parties/MEX_EN.pdf.

https://www.icao.int/secretariat/legal/list%20of%20parties/montreal_prot_2014_en.pdf.

https://www.icao.int/secretariat/legal/List%20of%20Parties/Mtl71_EN.pdf.

https://www.icao.int/secretariat/legal/List%20of%20Parties/Tokyo_EN.pdf.

https://www.icao.int/secretariat/legal/List%20of%20Parties/VIA_EN.pdf.

https://www.icao.int/secretariat/PostalHistory/legal_instruments_related_to_aviation_security.htm.

http://www.interieur.gouv.fr/Le-ministere/Gendarmerie-nationale.

https://ijrcenter.org/european-court-of-human-rights/.

https://isis.liveuamap.com/.

http://www.justice.gov.il/En/Units/FBPS/DNFBPDuties/Pages/List-of-Terrorist-Organizations-and-Individuals.aspx.

http://www.mchs.gov.ru/operationalpage/Operativnaja_informacija/item/5216330/.

http://www.mfa.gov.il/MFA/ForeignPolicy/Terrorism/Palestinian/Pages/Victims%20of%20Palestinian%20Violence%20and%20Terrorism%20sinc.aspx.

https://nationalpost.com/news/malaysia-airlines-mh17-black-boxes-reportedly-recovered-russia-denies-it-will-take-them-from-rebels.

http://papers.rumsfeld.com/.

https://www.prosecutionservice.nl/topics/mh17-plane-crash/criminal-investigation-jit-mh17.

https://www.prosecutionservice.nl/topics/mh17-plane-crash/prosecution-and-trial/status-investigation-and-position-on-progress-trial---part-2.

https://rm.coe.int/CoERMPublicCommonSearchServices/DisplayDCTMContent?documentId=090000168008371b.

https://www.state.gov/j/ct/rls/other/des/123085.htm.

http://theglobalcoalition.org/en/home/.

http://theglobalcoalition.org/en/partners/.

https://www.un.org/counterterrorism/ctitf/un-global-counter-terrorism-strategy.

https://www.un.org/counterterrorism/international-legal-instruments.

https://www.un.org/sc/ctc/resources/databases/recommended-international-practices-codes-and-standards/united-nations-security-council-resolution-1373-2001/.

https://visasam.ru/emigration/vybor/strany-bez-ekstradicii-v-rossiyu.html.

http://wordnetweb.princeton.edu/perl/webwn.

Index

Ius, Lex et Res Publica

Studies in Law, Philosophy and Political Cultures

Edited by

Anna Jaroń

Vol. 1 Anna Jaroń: Socio-Economic Constitutional Rights in Democratisation Processes. An Account of the Constitutional Dialogue Theory. 2012.

Vol. 2 Stanisław Filipowicz: Democracy – The Power of Illusion. 2013.

Vol. 3 Teresa Dukiet-Nagórska (ed.): The Postulates of Restorative Justice and the Continental Model of Criminal Law. As Illustrated by Polish Criminal Law 2014.

Vol. 4 Agnieszka Kupzok: Enforcement of Patents on Geographically Divisible Inventions. An Inquiry into the Standard of Substantive Patent Law Infringement in Cross-Border Constellations. 2015.

Vol. 5 Alicja Jagielska-Burduk / Wojciech Szafrański: Legal Issues in Cultural Heritage Management. A Polish Perspective. 2016.

Vol. 6 Maciej Mataczyński (ed.): The Takeover of Public Companies as a Mode of Exercising EU Treaty Freedoms. 2017.

Vol. 7 Maciej Barczewski (ed.): Value of Information. Intellectual Property, Privacy and Big Data. 2018.

Vol. 8 Pawel Smoleń, Marcin Burzec: Introduction to Polish Tax Law. 2018.

Vol. 9 Łukasz Pohl, Konrad Burdziak: Judicial Interpretation of the 1997 Criminal Code Provisions on Self-Defence. 2019.

Vol. 10 Adam Szot: Judicial Review of Administrative Discretion. The Influence of Court Decisions on Administrative Actions. 2019.

Vol. 11 Michał Peno / Konrad Burdziak (eds.): The Concept of Modern Law. Polish and Central European Tradition. 2019.

Vol. 12 Leszek Leszczyński / Bartosz Liżewski / Adam Szot (eds.): Potential of Precedent in the Statutory Legal Order. 2019.

Vol. 13 Łukasz Bolesta: In Search of a Model for the Legal Protection of a Whistleblower in the Workplace in Poland. A legal and comparative study. 2020.

Vol. 14 Paweł Chmielnicki / Adam Sulikowski (eds.): New Perspectives on Legislation. A Comparative Approach. 2020.

Vol. 15 Marcin Burzec / Beata Kucia-Guściora / Paweł Smoleń: Agricultural Activity in Poland: A Fiscal and Legal Study. 2020.

Vol. 16 Magdalena Półtorak / Ilona Topa (eds.): Women, Children and (Other) Vulnerable Groups. Standards of Protection and Challenges for International Law. 2021.

Vol. 17 Josef Albert Fox: Die polnische Verfassung vom 3. Mai 1791. Hintergründe der Entstehung und der Außerkraftsetzung. Stellung Polens im Zeitalter der Aufklärung. 2021.

Vol. 18 Barbara Janusz-Pohl (ed.): Juvenile Justice Systems: Poland-Brazil-Portugal. 2021.

Vol. 19 Leszek Leszczyński: General Reference Clauses in the Judicial Process. Context of Legislative Intentions Interpretative Discretion. 2021.

Vol. 20 Francisco J. Campos Zamora: Das Problem der Begründung richterlicher Entscheidungen. Eine Analyse auf der Grundlage der Theorie der juristischen Argumentation. 2021.

Ius, Lex et Res Publica
Studies in Law, Philosophy and Political Cultures

Edited by
Barbara Janusz-Pohl and Anna Jaroń

Vol. 21 Aneta Skorupa-Wulczyńska: Language Rights of the Citizen of the European Union. 2022.

Vol. 22 Mateusz Osiecki: International Legal Aspects of Aerial Terrorism. Methods of Law Enforcement in Aviation. 2022.

www.peterlang.com

www.ingramcontent.com/pod-product-compliance
Ingram Content Group UK Ltd.
Pitfield, Milton Keynes, MK11 3LW, UK
UKHW041824031026
15587UKWH00002B/553

9 783631 875391